10/10

D0521434

Read & Think
ENGLISH

Read & Think
ENGLISH

Los editores de la revista *Think English!*

Mc Graw Hill

New York Chicago San Francisco Lisbon London Madrid Mexico City
Milan New Delhi San Juan Seoul Singapore Sydney Toronto

2 3 4 5 6 7 8 9 10 11 12 13 14 15 16 17   FGR/FGR   0 9 8 (0-07-149914-8)
1 2 3 4 5 6 7 8 9 10 11 12 13 14 15 16 17   FGR/FGR   0 9 8 (0-07-160362-X)

ISBN 978-0-07-149914-9 (book alone)
MHID   0-07-149914-8 (book alone)

ISBN 978-0-07-160362-1 (book for set)
MHID   0-07-160362-X (book for set)

ISBN 978-0-07-149916-3 (book and CD set)
MHID   0-07-149916-4 (book and CD set)

McGraw-Hill books are available at special quantity discounts to use as premiums and
sales promotions or for use in corporate training programs. To contact a representative,
please visit the Contact Us pages at www.mhprofessional.com.

This book is printed on acid-free paper.

Contents

Culture

Travel

Tradition

Celebration

People

Business

Empowerment

History

Geography

Gastronomy

Introducción

Read & Think English representa un enfoque innovador y fácilmente accesible al aprendizaje de una lengua extranjera. Se trata de un método dinámico de inmersión al lenguaje, diseñado para usar en casa y aumentar su dominio del inglés a través del estudio de la vida y cultura de los Estados Unidos.

Hemos creado *Read & Think English* con el siguiente propósito: hacer más fácil el perfeccionamiento y la fluidez de su inglés, y aumentar su conocimiento sobre la vida y cultura norteamericanas para así incrementar sus oportunidades de éxito en los Estados Unidos.

Nuestro sistema de aprendizaje ha sido diseñado para hacer uso de sus conocimientos previos del inglés y ampliarlos, presentando el vocabulario y las frases en contextos relevantes y estimulantes, que además ponen énfasis en las cuatro aptitudes del lenguaje: la lectura, la escritura, el lenguaje hablado y la comprensión del idioma.

Read & Think English hace del inglés una lengua viva! Lea sobre la historia de los Estados Unidos y descubra las personas que contribuyeron a su formación. Explore las tradiciones y peculiares costumbres que se asocian con este país. Y, recuerde que, mientras Ud. disfruta con los fascinantes artículos, está aprendiendo inglés.

Profesores y estudiantes de todas las edades usan *Read & Think English* para aumentar el dominio de su inglés de una manera natural y eficaz. Tanto si el programa se usa como complemento en el salón de clase o como guía privada de estudio, los resultados son los mismos: Ud. desarrollará y mejorará sus conocimientos de vocabulario y gramática.

La información provista en cada capítulo facilita la mejor comprensión de la vida en los Estados Unidos y esto, a su vez, fomenta un mayor interés y éxito en el aprendizaje del inglés. Cada artículo va acompañado de un glosario bilingüe, de manera que se puede leer y aprender sin pararse a buscar palabras en el diccionario o en un manual de conversación.

Read & Think English se ajusta a diferentes niveles de aptitud, desde el elemental hasta el avanzado:

Elemental: Se recomienda que el nivel de conocimiento de inglés del estudiante sea equivalente al de la escuela secundaria o al del primer semestre de universidad. Tanto si su experiencia previa con el inglés ha sido a través de estudios escolares o bien personales, *Read & Think English* le permitirá sumergirse en la lengua y la cultura y también aumentará su comprensión sobre la estructura de la oración y el uso de los verbos.

Intermedio: Como estudiante de nivel intermedio, Ud. aprenderá más vocabulario y frases nuevas y notará un aumento en su fluidez y su capacidad de comprensión.

Avanzado: El estudiante avanzado continuará adquiriendo información valiosa y relevante, ya que el aprendizaje de una lengua es un esfuerzo para toda la vida.

Read & Think English es un método eficaz, divertido y asequible, sin importar cual es su nivel actual de conocimientos.

Experimente Ud. el entusiasmo y la satisfacción que vienen de aprender un nuevo idioma y descubrir una nueva cultura. Lea, hable, disfrute… Piense en Inglés.

Instrucciones para el éxito

El programa *Read & Think English* está dividido en capítulos que guían al estudiante a través de la vida en los Estados Unidos. Al final de cada capítulo hay una sección llamada "Compruebe su comprensión." Esta sección fomenta el desarrollo de la comprensión de lectura y favorece la comprensión del inglés escrito.

No es necesario leer *Read & Think English* de principio a fin, ni tampoco en un orden determinado. Se puede leer por capítulos o escoger un capítulo o artículo que sea de especial interés para el lector. Se pueden completar las preguntas de las pruebas artículo por artículo, o bien por capítulos. Esta flexibilidad le permite al usuario avanzar a su propio ritmo, leyendo y releyendo el material según su necesidad. Los artículos, que son de gran interés, hacen que el estudio sea más agradable y la lectura más estimulante.

> En primer lugar, lea el artículo para tener una idea general del tema. No se preocupe si al principio no comprende todo el vocabulario.

> Una vez que comprenda de qué se trata el artículo, léalo de nuevo fijándose en el vocabulario que no conoce. Ponga especial atención al contexto donde se usa dicho vocabulario.

> Lea el artículo en voz alta.

> Si tiene acceso a un sistema de grabación, haga práctica grabando los artículos o pídale a alguien que habla español que se los grabe. Luego, escuche las grabaciones y observe cómo su comprensión auditiva va mejorando con el tiempo.

¡Repita, Repita, Repita! Esto es especialmente importante cuando se trata de memorizar partes y formas de las palabras que son importantes. La repetición activa es, algunas veces, la única manera de recordar detalles difíciles de retener en la memoria. Estas frecuentes repeticiones orales ayudan a fijar las formas en su "oído interno." Esta dimensión auditiva le ayudará a recordar las palabras más adelante. Con *Read & Think English*, Ud. tiene la oportunidad de repetir diferentes procesos de aprendizaje tantas veces como quiera y tan a menudo como lo considere necesario. Lea, escuche y hable una y otra vez: esto le será de gran ayuda para alcanzar su meta de dominar la lengua inglesa.

Glosario bilingüe a la medida

Al lado de cada artículo se encuentra un glosario bilingüe correspondiente fácilmente accesible. Entonces, como ya no es necesario interrumpir la lectura para usar un diccionario, la comprensión y la adquisición de vocabulario se producen de una manera mucho más cómoda y rápida.

Cada artículo contiene gramática nueva y también vocabulario y frases nuevas, así como repeticiones de vocabulario y frases previamente estudiados. Las repeticiones a lo largo de los artículos sirven para aumentar la comprensión de la lectura y facilitar la memorización. Los artículos están escritos desde distintas perspectivas, y, aunque la mayoría de ellos están escritos en la tercera persona, hay algunos escritos en la primera también. Este cambio de persona gramatical ayuda al lector a reconocer la conjugación de los diferentes tiempos de los verbos.

Muchos profesores de inglés recomiendan "crear una imagen mental" de las palabras extranjeras o asociarlas con objetos y situaciones familiares para aumentar la memorización de las mismas. Sin embargo, con *Read & Think English*, no necesitará "crear" ninguna imagen. Las imágenes se crean automáticamente en su imaginación con el desarrollo de la historia. Lea sin prisas y, al leer, imagínese la historia tal y como está escrita y vaya absorbiendo el vocabulario nuevo. Si una palabra o frase es especialmente difícil, trate de asociarla con una imagen que ella representa en la historia, mientras la pronuncia en voz alta.

Los verbos están escritos en el glosario, primero en la forma conjugada con que aparecen en la historia y después en el infinitivo. Por ejemplo: **looking for/to look for:** buscando /buscar

Compruebe su comprensión

Las preguntas de las pruebas que hay al final de cada capítulo están diseñadas para que Ud. siga desarrollando sus destrezas de comprensión de la lectura y para asegurar su éxito en el estudio del inglés. Además, Ud. aprenderá a usar el contexto para determinar significados. Cuando se entiende el contexto en general, muchas veces se puede "adivinar" el significado de palabras desconocidas basándose en el contexto de una oración, un párrafo o un artículo. Las respuestas se encuentran al final del

Información Sobre la Autora

Los artículos contenidos en este libro fueron escritos, coordinados y recopilados bajo la dirección de Kelly Garboden, Fundadora y Editora de la editorial Second Language Publishing (SLP). SLP es una editorial educativa que publica las revistas *Think Spanish Magazine* y *Think English Magazine*. SLP se especializa en la elaboración de productos interesantes e informativos dedicados al aprendizaje de idiomas. Dichos productos tienen como objetivo superar las barreras de comunicación y fomentar el aprendizaje del idioma y la integración cultural. Para más información sobre Second Language Publishing y *Think English Magazine* visite la siguiente dirección web: www.thinkenglishmagazine.com

Un Agradecimiento Especial Para:

Jean Garboden, Miguel Romá, Lucía Terra and LuciaTerra.com, Karen Young, Mesia Quatro and LatPro.com, Jessica Harrison, Ian Chaplin and Cleo Chaplin

Read & Think
ENGLISH

I like to see a man proud of the place in which he lives.
I like to see a man live so that his place will be proud of him.

Abraham Lincoln

Culture

The American Dream

The American Dream is **often associated** with immigration. For years, the dream of **prosperity** and **freedom** has **driven** immigrants to the United States. America is **viewed** as the **land of opportunity** and immigrants from all over the world **have settled** in the U.S. with dreams of a **fresh start** and a **new life**.

By the 1900's, the **promise** of the American Dream **had begun to attract** large numbers of immigrants **looking for** work in large cities. With hard work and determination immigrants **hoped to escape** the **class boundaries** of their home countries.

The Industrial Revolution **helped shape** the American Dream by **creating thousands** of jobs. The **development** of **big business**, the Transcontinental Railroad, and the increase in oil production improved the American **standard of living**. "Rags to riches" stories of business **tycoons** led to the belief that if you had intelligence, and a **willingness** to work hard, you would have a successful life.

When people **think** of the American Dream they think of a successful and satisfying life. The term usually **implies financial security** and **material comfort**, but can also mean living a fulfilling life.

James Truslow Adams **coined the term** "American Dream" in his book *The Epic of America*. However, Truslow's coinage of the phrase had a **broader meaning**.

The American Dream is *"that dream of a **land** in which life should be better and richer and fuller for everyone, with opportunity for each **according** to **ability** or achievement. It is not a dream of motor cars and high **wages merely**, but a dream of social order in which each man and each woman shall **be able to attain** to the **fullest stature** of which they are **innately capable**, and be **recognized** by others for what they are, regardless of the fortuitous circumstances of **birth** or **position**."*

How do you **achieve** the American Dream? That **answer depends** upon your personal definition of the term. **Luckily** for us, **living** in America—the land of opportunity, there are many dreams **to choose from**!

A Melting Pot

The **term** melting pot is **strongly associated with** the United States. The United States is a melting pot of **people** from different cultures and **races**. **Throughout** the country **you will notice differences** in the **way** people **live**, **eat** and **even talk**.

While American English is **generally standard**, American **speech** can **differ according to** what part of the **country** you are in.

Certain **traits** and **personalities** are **connected** with certain regions. Westerners are **known as** the **least** traditional of Americans, and the **most tolerant** of **change** and differences. Midwesterners are known for being **honest, straightforward** people of traditional **values**.

The southwest has had the least influence by European immigrants. Much of its culture **has been defined** by native Americans and by the Spanish.

Southerners are **probably** the most **distinctive** of all American groups, with more **relaxed attitudes** and traditional ways than their **neighbors** to the north. They are known for their **hospitality**.

The Northeast is well known for its culture with excellent theaters and **museums**. It is also **regarded** for its educational system with some of the most **highly rated** and **respected** universities in the country. This region is also known for its large **mix** of **ethnic groups**.

Every time we speak, we **say volumes** about where we are from; the **neutral tones** of the Midwest, the **rapid speech** of New York City, the **long drawl** that **characterizes** the South. If you say a **certain word** or **phrase**, people will **most likely** be able to **guess** where you are from.

term: término
strongly: fuertemente
associated with: asociados con
people: personas
races: razas
throughout: por todos
you will notice: tú notarás
differences: diferencias
way: forma
live/to live: vive/vivir
eat/to eat: come/comer
even: incluso
talk/to talk: habla/hablar
while: aunque
generally: generalmente
standard: estándar
speech: habla
differ: diferir
according to: dependiendo de
country: país
traits: rasgos
personalities: personalidades
connected/to connect: conectadas/conectar
known as: conocidos como
least: menos
most tolerant: más tolerantes
change: cambio
honest: honesta
straightforward: directa
values: valores
has been defined/to define: ha sido definida/definir
probably: probablemente
distinctive: distintivo, característico
relaxed attitudes: actitudes relajadas
neighbors: vecinos
hospitality: hospitalidad
museums: museos
regarded: respetado, estimado
highly rated: altamente valoradas
respected: respetadas
mix: mezcla
ethnic groups: grupos étnicos
every time: cada vez
say/to say: decimos/decir
volumes: mucho
neutral tones: tonos neutrales
rapid speech: habla rápida
long drawl: largo acento arrastrado
characterizes/to characterize: caracteriza/caracterizar
certain: cierta
word: palabra
phrase: frase
most likely: seguramente
guess: adivinar

The American Cowboy

The **central character** of America's **colorful ranching** heritage is the cowboy. The American cowboy **has played** an important part in American culture and history. The cowboy influence **is embedded** in **stories**, **songs**, **legends**, movies, art and fashion.

Although the cowboy is **generally considered** an American **icon,** the traditional cowboy actually **comes from** a Hispanic tradition, which originated in Central Mexico, known as "charro."

At the end of the **Civil War**, many **soldiers** had no home, and no place to go. They started **drifting** to the West. To many, this term **means guns**, **cattle**, horses and **gunfights**. It was a **rugged country** with few **amenities** and a lot of **danger.** The Western territories were **appealing** to the adventurous, and they were **open and untamed**. Many of these men only **owned** what they could **carry** on **horseback**. **Ranchers hired** these **hard-working** men as **ranch hands**. The ranch hands **tended to the herd** and did work around the ranch. **When the time came** to sell the beef, the ranch hands would **round up** the herd from the **open prairie** and **drive** the cattle to **market.**

Popular stories about the cowboys **depicted** them as **rustlers** or professional gunfighters. **While** this is true **in some cases**, the average American cowboy was **often lonely**, lived in **harsh conditions**, and was frequently **exposed** to danger. **Despite this**, the cowboys always kept their sense of humor and **joked** about everything. They did not make much money and enjoyed the **simple way of life.**

Tough as nails, but **generous** and **hospitable**, these were the true *Wild West* American cowboys. The cowboy was the **embodiment** of **rugged independence**. Some names you might be familiar with are Butch Cassidy and The Sundance Kid, Buffalo Bill, Billy the Kid, Wyatt Earp and Doc Holiday.

Many of these cowboys became legends in **real life** and **later** legends of the **silver screen**. They rode horses. They **sang** songs. Their horses **did tricks** and their guns were **shiny**. They became American heroes.

MODERN **WORKING** COWBOYS

Being a cowboy is certainly not **a thing of the past**. Throughout the U.S., you will find cowboys working on ranches and **farms**. The **exact** number of working cowboys is **unknown**. Cowboys are **responsible** for **feeding** the **livestock**, **branding** cattle and horses, and **tending to injuries**. They also **move** the livestock to different **pasture locations**, or **herd** them into corrals. In addition, cowboys **repair fences**, **maintain** ranch equipment, and **perform** other **odd jobs** around the ranch.

And **last, but not least**: the **cowgirl**! The history of women in the west is **not as well documented** as that of men. However, in recent years **companies have dedicated** time and money to **researching** the cowgirl tradition. The **National Cowgirl Museum and Hall of Fame** has made great efforts **to document** the history of cowgirls.

tough as nails: duros como clavos *(una expresión)*
generous: generosos
hospitable: hospitalarios
embodiment: personificación
rugged independence: fuerte independencia
real life: vida real
later: más tarde
silver screen: pantalla
sang/to sing: cantaban/cantar
did tricks: hacían trucos
shiny: brillantes
working: que trabajan
being: ser
a thing of the past: una cosa del pasado
farms: granjas
exact: exacto
unknown: desconocido
responsible: responsables
feeding: alimentar
livestock: ganado
branding/to brand: marcar/marcar
tending to: ocuparse de
injuries: heridas, lesiones
move: mudarse
pasture locations: ubicación de pasto
herd/to herd: guarda/guardar, reunir o llevar en manada
repair/to repair: reparan/reparar, arreglar
fences: cercas
maintain/to maintain: mantienen/ mantener
perform/to perform: realizan/realizar
odd jobs: tareas sueltas
last, but not least: último, pero no menos importante
cowgirl: vaquera
not as well documented: no tan bien documentada
companies: compañías, empresas
have dedicated/to dedicate: han dedicado/dedicar
researching/to research: investigar/ investigar
National Cowgirl Museum and Hall of Fame: Museo Nacional y Sala de Fama de la Vaquera
to document: para documentar

American Jazz

is considered: está considerado
significant: importante, relevante
to emerge/to emerge: que ha surgido/ surgir
widely known: ampliamente conocido
birthplace: lugar de nacimiento
make/to make: hacer/hacer
listener: oyente
feel/to feel: se sienta/sentir
happy: alegre
sad: triste
mellow: sosegado
energetic: energizado
sound/to sound: sonar/sonar
loud: fuerte
soft: suave
performers: intérpretes
improvise/to improvise: improvisan/ improvisar
create/to create: crean/crear
has its roots: tiene sus raíces
century: siglo
to develop: a desarrollar
gospel music: música evangelico
sad songs: canciones tristes
slavery: esclavitud
the first true: la primera verdadera
happened/to happen: ocurrió/ocurrir, tener lugar
during: durante
came out of/to come out of: se originó en/originarse en
to gain popularity: adquirió popularidad
became/to become: se hizo *(famoso)*/ hacerse *(famoso)*
trumpet: trompeta
unusual: poco corriente
call/to call: llaman/llamar
Golden Age: Edad de Oro
as time passed: con el tiempo
danced/to dance: bailaba/bailar
led/to lead: dirigió/dirigir
swing bands: bandas de swing
presented/to present: presentó/ presentar
playing together: tocando juntos
first time: primera vez

Jazz **is considered** the most **significant**, influential and innovative music **to emerge** from the United States. New Orleans, Louisiana, is **widely known** as the **birthplace** of jazz.

Jazz can **make** the **listener feel happy** or **sad**, **mellow** or **energetic**. Jazz can **sound loud** or **soft**. **Performers** of jazz **improvise** and **create** music as they play.

Jazz **has its roots** in the nineteenth **century**. In the late 1880's, African-Americans began **to develop** new forms of music. They created blues music from the **gospel music** and **sad songs** of their years in **slavery**. From the blues came **the first true** jazz music. This **happened during** the early 1900's in Louisiana. Classic, traditional or Dixieland jazz **came out of** the music originating in New Orleans.

During the 1920's, jazz continued **to gain popularity**. Louis Armstrong **became** famous for his performances on the **trumpet** and for his **unusual** voice. Louis Armstrong became one of the most influential and loved U.S. jazz musicians. Historians **call** the 1920's the **Golden Age** of American Jazz.

As time passed, a jazz form called "swing" became very popular in America. People **danced** to swing music until after World War II. Benny Goodman **led** one of America's most successful **swing bands**. People called Goodman "The King of Swing." Goodman also **presented** black and white jazz musicians **playing together** for the **first time**.

After World War II, swing jazz became **less** popular. Americans **began to listen** to different **sounds**. One was bebop. **Young** musicians had created bepop in the 1940's and it **gained** popularity **slowly** over the years. The music seemed **harshly different** to the **ears** of the public. Bebop appeared to sound **racing**, **nervous**, and often **fragmented**. **Nevertheless**, bebop was an exciting and beautiful **revolution** in the art of jazz.

In the 1950's, cool jazz became popular. Cool jazz instruments sound **softer** than bebop and the rhythm is **more even.**

With cool jazz came many **new** listeners. People went to jazz **clubs** and **bought** jazz **recordings**. The introduction of the **long-playing record** also **helped** the music become more popular.

In the 1960's a new kind of music, rock and roll, grew very popular in the United States. People **throughout** the world **listened to** the rock music of Elvis Presley and the Beatles. This new music **cut into** the popularity of jazz.

In the 1980's, trumpet player Wynton Marsalis helped **lead a return** to more traditional jazz. This **mainstream** jazz **borrows** sounds from swing, bebop and cool jazz. Marsalis is one of the **most well known** and **praised** jazz musicians.

Today, jazz musicians play **all types** of music. Jazz can sound like swing or bebop. It can sound like rock and roll. It can sound like American Western music. It can sound like the music of several nations and ethnic groups. Or, it can sound traditional. With **so many options to choose from**, people of all **ages** and **all walks of life** can **find enjoyment** and an **appreciation** for American jazz.

less: menos
began to listen: empezaron a escuchar
sounds: sonidos
young: jóvenes
gained/to gain: ganó/ganar
slowly: lentamente
harshly different: marcadamente diferente
ears: oídos
racing: rápida, relativa a las carreras
nervous: nerviosa
fragmented: fragmentada
nevertheless: sin embargo, no obstante
revolution: revolución
sound/to sound: suenan/sonar
softer: más suave
more even: más parejo
new: nuevos
clubs: clubes
bought/to buy: compraba/comprar
recordings: grabaciones
long-playing record: disco long-play
helped/to help: ayudó/ayudar
throughout: a través de, por todo
listened to/to listen to: escuchaban/escuchar
cut into/to cut into: quitó una parte/quitar, interrumpir
lead a return: dirigir una vuelta
mainstream: corriente dominante
borrows/to borrow: toma prestados/tomar prestado
most well known: bien conocido
praised: alabados
today: hoy en día
all types: todo tipos
so many options: tantas opciones
to choose from/to choose: de las cuales elegir/elegir
ages: edades
all walks of life: de toda condición
find/to find: encontrar/encontrar
enjoyment: diversión
appreciation: aprecio

beginnings: comienzos
can be traced back to: se remontan a
bar room singers: cantantes en bares
gospel choirs: coros de gospel (*música religiosa*)
early: temprano, primero
have their roots: tienen sus raíces
started/to start: empezaron/empezar
at first: al principio
were recorded/to record: eran grabados/grabar
only: solo, solamente
performed/to perform: interpretados/ interpretar
live: en vivo
passed down/to pass down: pasaron/ pasar, transmitir
oral tradition: tradición oral
storytelling: contar cuentos o historias
produced/to produce: produjo/ producir
leading: punteros
came out/to come out: surgieron/ surgir, salir
known as: conocido como
museums: musios
are located: están ubicados
because of: debido a
served as/to serve as: servía como/ servir como
vehicle: vehículo
to convey: transmitir
daily: cotidiana
early forms: formas tempranas
which allowed: el cual permitía
laborers: trabajadores
field: campo
to keep in contact: mantenerse en contacto
dancing: baile
combined/to combine: combinaron/ combinar
with a new type: con un nuevo tipo
marked a new era: marcó una nueva era
eventually: finalmente
would contribute to/to contribute to: contribuiría a/contribuir a
you can/can: tú puedes/poder
around: alrededor
legendary: legendarios

Singing the Blues

America's **beginnings** in music **can be traced back to** "the blues." **Bar room singers** in the south, **gospel choirs**, rock and roll, pop styles and **early** jazz all **have their roots** in blues music.

The blues **started** in Mississippi after the Civil War. **At first** blues **were recorded only** by memory, and **performed** only **live** and in person. The blues **passed down** from generation to generation through an **oral tradition** much like **storytelling**.

Mississippi **produced** many **leading** blues musicians, including Charley Patton, Robert Johnson, Howlin' Wolf, Muddy Waters and B.B. King. These musicians **came out** of the area **known as** the Mississippi Delta. Three blues **museums are located** in the Mississippi Delta—the Delta Blues Museum in Clarksdale, the Blues & Legends Hall of Fame Museum in Robinsonville and the Highway 61 Blues Museum located in Leland.

Because of the early African-American experience and slavery, "singing the blues" **served as** functional music offering African-Americans a **vehicle to convey** their **daily** experiences. **Early forms** of the blues include the "field holler," **which allowed laborers** in the **fields to keep in contact** with each other, while the "ring shout" was used for **dancing**.

The blues **combined** the styles of the past **with a new type** of song. The popularity of the blues **marked a new era** for music. The result was the creation of a style of music that **would eventually contribute** to the development of jazz.

You can experience the blues live at festivals all **around** the U.S. For a complete listing of **legendary** rhythm and blues festivals visit: www. bluesfestivals.com

Native American Culture

The America **discovered by** the **first** Europeans was not an **empty wilderness**. Approximately 2 – 18 million people **lived** in **what is now called** the United States. These people, Native American Indians, were the first people to live here. The name "Indian" was first **applied** by Christopher Columbus. Columbus **mistakenly thought** America was part of the Indies, in Asia.

Indian customs and culture were extremely diverse due to the **expanse** of the land and the many different **environments** they **had adapted to**. Most tribes **combined gathering**, **hunting**, and the **cultivation** of corn and other products for their food supplies. The women **cared for** the children, and were **in charge of farming** and the distribution of food. The men hunted and **participated in** war. Indian culture in North America was **tied closely** to the land. Nature was part of their religious **beliefs**.

Initially, the Europeans **were welcomed enthusiastically** by the Native Americans. Conflicts soon **arose**. The **value systems** were different for each group. The natives were **in tune** to the **rhythms** and **spirit** of **nature**. Nature to the Europeans was a **commodity**: a **beaver colony** was a number of **pelts**, a **forest** was **timber** for **building**. The Europeans **expected to** own land and **claimed** it. The Indians, **on the other hand**, were considered by the Europeans as **nomadic** with no interest in land **ownership**.

It was the Europeans' materialistic **view** of the land that the Indians **found repellent**. The conflicts and wars continued until the end of the 19th **century**. On June 2, 1924, Congress **granted citizenship** to all Native Americans born in the U.S. The right to vote **was governed** by state law. In some states, Native American Indians **were prohibited** from voting until 1948.

Many Native Americans are politically and socially active, **holding fast** to the **ancient** values of their ancestors. **Prayers** for peace, respect for the environment, and love for all things living is a **legacy** that **remains** today.

discovered by: descubierta por
first: primero
empty wilderness: desierto vacío
lived/to live: vivían/vivir
what is now called: lo que ahora se llama
applied: aplicado
mistakenly: equivocadamente
thought/to think: pensó/pensar
expanse: extensión
environments: ambientes, entornos
had adapted to/to adapt to: se habían adaptado/adaptarse a
combined/to combine: combinaban/combinar
gathering: recolección
hunting: caza
cultivation: cultivo
cared for/to care for: cuidaban de/cuidar de
in charge of: a cargo de
farming: agricultura
participated in: participaban en, tomaban parte en
tied closely: estrechamente vinculada
beliefs: creencias
were welcomed: fueron acogidos
enthusiastically: con entusiasmo
arose/to arise: surgieron/surgir
value systems: sistemas de valores
in tune: en armonía
rhythms: ritmos
spirit: espíritu
nature: naturaleza
commodity: bien de consumo
beaver colony: colonia de castores
pelts: pieles
forest: bosque, selva
timber: madera
building: construir
expected to: esperaban
claimed/to claim: reclamaron/reclamar
on the other hand: por otro lado
nomadic: nómada
ownership: propiedad
coupled with: junto con
view: visión, perspectiva
found/to find: encontraron/encontrar
repellent: repelente, repulsivo
century: siglo
granted citizenship: concedió la ciudadanía
was governed/to govern: estaba gobernado/gobernar, estar dirigido
were prohibited/to prohibit: se les prohibía/prohibir
holding fast: apegándose fuertemente
ancient: antiguos
prayers: oraciones
legacy: legado
remains/to remain: permanece/permanecer

African Heritage

Unlike other immigrants, **many** Africans **came** to North America **against their will**. They **were caught up** in a brutal system of human exploitation—the transatlantic **slave trade**.

African Americans **waged** a **centuries-long** battle for dignity, **freedom**, and for **full involvement** in American **society.** Their participation **transformed** the United States, and **shaped the world we live in today**. Our customs have been influenced or **remade** by the efforts of African American **workers**, artists, **activists**, **organizers**, and **thinkers**.

More than 35 million Americans **claim** African **ancestry**. The number of African immigrants to the U.S. **increases every year**.

Explorers and Colonists

When Africans first came to the Americas, they came of their own **free will**. They arrived at the same time in history as the first Europeans. During the sixteenth **century**, African adventurers participated in the **Age of Exploration**. In the early 1500s, Africans explored Ecuador, Mexico, and Peru. The African explorer Estevanico helped the Coronado expedition **open up** what is now the **Southwestern** United States.

During the 300 years of the transatlantic slave trade, approximately 20 million Africans **were transported** to the Americas as slaves. Of these, more than 400,000 were sent to the 13 **British colonies** and, **later**, the United States. We may never know a **precise** number, but **current estimates report** that more than 1 million Africans **died** on the **journey**.

Today, Africans are coming to America **again**.

From Togo, Ghana, Ethiopia, Mali, Nigeria—Africans are again **making their way** to American **shores to start** new lives.

---

unlike: a diferencia de
many: muchos
came/to come: vinieron/venir
against their will: contra su voluntad
were caught up: quedaron atrapados
slave trade: tráfico de esclavos
waged/to wage: libraron/librar
  (una batalla)
centuries-long: que duró siglos
freedom: libertad
full involvement: participación
  absoluta
society: sociedad
transformed/to transform:
  transformó/transformar
shaped/to shape: dio forma/dar forma
the world we live in today: el mundo
  en el cual vivimos
remade: rehechas
workers: trabajadores
activists: activistas
organizers: organizadores
thinkers: pensadores
more than: más de
claim/to claim: declaran/declarar,
  reivindicar, reclamar
ancestry: ascendencia
increases/to increase: aumenta/
  aumentar
every year: cada año
explorers: exploradores
colonists: colonizadores
free will: libre voluntad
century: siglo
Age of Exploration: época de
  exploraciones
open up/to open up: abrir/abrir
Southwestern: suroeste
during: durante
were transported/to transport: fueron
  transportados/transportar
British colonies: colonias británicas
later: luego, más tarde
precise: preciso, exacto
current estimates: cálculos
  aproximados
report/to report: informan/informar
died/to die: murieron/morir
journey: viaje
today: hoy
again: otra vez
making their way: encontrando su
  camino
shores: costas
to start: empezar

More than 500,000 Africans came to the United States in the 1990's **alone**. This is more African immigrants **than had come** in all the 150 years **before**.

Today, Africans are immigrating to a **country profoundly shaped** by the long African experience in the United States. America is a country where people of African ancestry now **hold positions** of power, prestige, and influence, even as the nation **continues** to **grapple** with the **aftermath** of segregation and **inequality**. The United States is a country that has seen three of its most prominent African American citizens awarded the Nobel Peace Prize; the diplomat Ralph Bunche, the **civil rights leader** Martin Luther King Jr., and the novelist Toni Morrison.

Perhaps most important, America is a country that continues to be **enriched** by and **to recognize** its African heritage.

Martin Luther King, Jr., was the **most famous leader** of the **American civil rights movement**, a political activist, a Baptist **minister**, and was one of America's greatest orators.

In 1964, King became the youngest man awarded the **Nobel Peace Prize** for his work as a **peacemaker**, promoting **nonviolence** and equal treatment for different races.

On April 4, 1968, King **was assassinated** in Memphis, Tennessee. In 1977, he **was posthumously awarded** the Presidential **Medal of Freedom** by Jimmy Carter.

In 1986, *Martin Luther King Day* was established as a United States **holiday.** Martin Luther King is **one of only** three persons to receive this **distinction** (including Abraham Lincoln and George Washington), and of these persons the only one not a U.S. president, **indicating** his extraordinary position in American history.

In 2004, King was posthumously awarded the **Congressional Gold Medal**. King **often called for** personal responsibility in **fostering world peace**. King's most influential and well-known public address is the "I Have A Dream" **speech**, **delivered** on the **steps** of the Lincoln Memorial in Washington, D.C. in 1963.

myths: mitos
legends: leyendas
songs: canciones
written: escrito
perhaps: quizás
documented: documentado
journals: diarios
recounting: contando, refiriendo
topics: temas
were prompted by: se inspiraban en
discussing: discutiendo
religious foundations: bases religiosas
increasing desire to produce: deseo
  creciente de producir
emerged/to emerge: emergieron/
  emerger
key: claves
shocking: impresionante, escandaloso
work: trabajo, obra
he claimed/to claim: él afirmó/afirmar
to do away with: suprimir, eliminar
reach/to reach: alcanzar/alcanzar
spiritual state: estado espiritual
studying/to study: estudiando/
  estudiar
responding to/to respond to:
  respondiendo a/responder a
nonconformist: inconformista
wooded: arbolado
pond: estanque
urges/to urge: urge/urgir
organized society: sociedad organizada
first: primer
major: importante
away from: lejos de
masterpieces: obras maestras
literary style: estilo literario
highly evocative: altamente sugerente
irreverently funny: divertido de forma
  irreverente
changed the way: cambió la forma
set the scene: preparó la escena
working-class people: gente de clase
  trabajadora
struggle: lucha, pelea
to lead: dirigir, llevar (una vida)
masterpiece: obra maestra
tells/to tell: cuenta/contar
entering/to enter: entrando/entrar
will find/to find: encontrarán/
  encontrar
will include/to include: incluirán/
  incluir
stunningly: sorprendentemente
will chronicle/to chronicle:
  registrarán/registrar

Early American Literature

Early American literature began with the **myths**, **legends**, and **songs** of Indian cultures. There was no **written** literature during this time. **Perhaps** the first **documented** written literature is historical literature in **journals recounting** the exploration of early settlers of the United States.

Topics of early American writings **were prompted by** discussions of religion. John Winthrop wrote a journal **discussing** the **religious foundations** of the Massachusetts Bay Colony. The War of 1812 prompted an **increasing desire to produce** unique American work. From this **emerged** a number of **key** literary figures, including Edgar Allan Poe, Washington Irving, and James Fennimore Cooper.

In 1836, Ralph Waldo Emerson published a **shocking** nonfiction **work** called *Nature*. In it, **he claimed** it was possible **to do away with** organized religion and **reach** a **spiritual state** by **studying** and **responding to** the natural world.

Emerson's friend was Henry David Thoreau. Thoreau was a **nonconformist**. After living alone for two years in a cabin by a **wooded pond**, Thoreau wrote *Walden*, a memoir that **urges** resistance to **organized society**.

Mark Twain was the **first major** American writer to be born **away from** the East Coast—in the state of Missouri. His **masterpieces** were the memoir *Life on the Mississippi* and the novel *Adventures of Huckleberry Finn*. Twain's **literary style** was direct, **highly evocative**, and **irreverently funny**. Mark Twain's literature **changed the way** Americans write.

John Steinbeck was born in Salinas, California, which **set the scene** for many of his stories. Steinbeck wrote about poor, **working-class people** and their **struggle to lead** a decent life. *The Grapes of Wrath*, considered his **masterpiece,** is a novel that **tells** the story of a family's journey to California.

At universities across the United States, students **entering** a class in American literature **will find** that their studies **will include** books that are **stunningly** diverse. Future American writers will write of a new experience. New American literature **will chronicle** the experiences of different ethnic groups and immigrants that make up the United States.

Artistic Expression

The **artistic expression** of Americans is **as diverse as** the people who live in America. Two **famous** American artists **who believed** that art **belonged to** the **people** are **featured** in this article; Norman Rockwell, whose work **represented** life in America; and Andy Warhol, who **sparked a revolution** in art during the 1960's.

NORMAN ROCKWELL *(February 3, 1894–November 8, 1978)*
Rockwell is most famous for the **cover illustrations** he created for *The Saturday Evening Post* **magazine**.

In 1943, **during** the Second World War, Rockwell painted the *Four Freedoms* series. The work **was inspired by** a speech by Franklin D. Roosevelt, who **had declared** that there were four **principles** for **universal rights**: Freedom from Want, **Freedom of Speech**, Freedom to **Worship**, and Freedom from **Fear**. Rockwell considered "Freedom of Speech" to be **the best** of the four.

Norman Rockwell was very **prolific**, and **produced** over 4000 original **works**, most of which have been either **destroyed** by **fire** or are in permanent collections. Original magazines in **mint condition** that **contain** his work are **rare** and are **worth** thousands of dollars.

ANDY WARHOL *(August 6, 1928–February 22, 1987)*
Warhol was an American artist **associated with** the definition of **Pop Art**. Warhol was a painter, a **commercial illustrator**, an **avant-garde filmmaker**, music industry **producer**, **writer** and celebrity.

Warhol studied commercial art at Carnegie Mellon University in Pittsburgh. He showed an early **artistic talent**. He moved to New York City in 1949 and **began** a **career** in advertising and magazine illustration.

During the 1960s Warhol began to make paintings of famous American products such as Campbell's Soup Cans and Coca-Cola, as well as paintings of **celebrities** like Marilyn Monroe. Warhol sparked a revolution in art—his work **quickly** became very controversial, and popular. Warhol became **one of the most famous** American artists of the day.

artistic expression: expresión artística
as diverse as: tan diversa como
famous: famosos
who believed: quienes creyeron
belonged to/to belong to: pertenecía a/ pertenecer a
people: gente
featured/to feature: caracterizados/ caracterizar
represented/to represent: representaba/representar
sparked a revolution: provocó una revolución
cover illustrations: ilustraciones de portada
magazine: revista
during: durante
was inspired by/to inspire: fue inspirado por/inspirar
had declared/to declare: había declarado/declarar
principles: principios
universal rights: derechos universales
freedom of speech: libertad de expresión
worship: adoración, *(libertad de)* creencia
fear: miedo, aprensión
the best: el mejor
prolific: prolífico
produced/to produce: produjo/ producir
works: obras
destroyed/to destroy: destruidas/ destruir
fire: fuego
mint condition: en perfecto estado
contain/to contain: contienen/ contener
rare: raras, poco comunes
worth/to be worth: valen/valer
associated with: asociado con
Pop Art: arte pop, *(popular)*
commercial illustrator: ilustrador comercial
avant-garde filmmaker: cineasta vanguardista
producer: productor
writer: escritor
artistic talent: talento artístico
began/to begin: empezó/empezar
career: carrera
celebrities: celebridades
quickly: rápidamente
one of the most famous: uno de los más famosos

The Birthplace of Broadway

New York City is the **birthplace of** Broadway, which began in the early 1900s. **Characterized by simplicity** and **charm**, Broadway soon became the **cultural center** of New York. The theatre district **fascinated** large groups of **middle-class people in search of** music, excitement, and romance. The **best seats in the house** cost only $2.00.

The **relationship** between **audience** and actors was **lively** and **high-spirited**. Audiences became **caught up in** the plays, talking to the actors, **hissing** and **booing**, or **clapping** and **cheering.**

To escape the reality of World War II, many used Broadway plays as an entertaining **getaway. However,** the Broadway community became especially active in **assisting** the **war effort.** The play *Yip, Yip, Yaphank* at the Century Theatre helped **raise money** for war **relief.**

After World War II ended, Times Square **was filled** with **crowds** of **enthusiastic citizens** carrying **flags** and celebrating. **Since that day,** Times Square has continued as a **gathering place** for the people of New York City.

Broadway **reached its prime** during the 1920s. **Fresh ideas** and **hope** filled the theatre. Lawrence Langner, **organizer** of the Theatre Guild, helped Broadway become a **dazzling** performing arts center that **influenced** the theatre of the world.

After the **stock-market crash** of 1929 and the Great Depression, Broadway **plunged.** The number of productions **declined** and **put** many theatre people **out of work.** Ironically, this became a creative period. Established writers organized the Playwrights Company, and continued **to write** interesting **plays** that were concerned with the **state of affairs** in America.

Many off Broadway theatres now **included** dramas of social protest, using the slogan "Theatre as a **Weapon.**" Many **playwrights** used the theatres to make **social commentary.**

Broadway began **to compete with** television and movies during the 1940s. Most theatres on Broadway **were being turned into** film houses. Movies **were beginning to take over** the **entertainment business**. Also **by this time**, television was becoming a **competitor**. Television was providing the public with **free** entertainment.

In the 1950's Broadway had become **less of** an industry **and more of a loose array of** individuals. This period in America was one of increasing intolerance and political persecution, but Broadway **was not afraid** to **express nonconformist opinions**. Broadway **did not fear** the government. Although Broadway theatre **had lost some of its range**, it still **retained** its liveliness and joyfulness. In a country that now required **conventionality**, Broadway held onto a sense of **freedom of speech** and action. These were the ideals on which the nation **was founded.**

Many memorable **musicals emerged** in 1950-1970. Some of these included *West Side Story, My Fair Lady, The Sound of Music, Fiddler on the Roof, Man of La Mancha,* and *Hair.*

Modern day Broadway is **alive and well** and Broadway theatre is considered the most prestigious form of professional theatre in the United States, as well as the most well known to the general public.

Seeing a Broadway **show** is a **popular tourist activity** in New York. Some **ticket booths sell same-day tickets** for many Broadway shows at **half price**. This service helps sell **seats** that would **otherwise go empty**, and makes seeing a show in New York more affordable. Many theatres also offer special student **rates, same-day "rush" tickets,** or **standing-room tickets** to help **ensure** that their theatres are **full.**

Theatres all across America **produce** Off-Broadway and original plays, musicals and dance productions. American Theatre offers a diverse **range** of entertainment. With many **themes** to **choose** from you are **certain to find** a show that **interests you**.

to compete with: competir con
were being turned into: estaban siendo convertidos en
were beginning to/to begin to: estaban empezando a /empezar a
to take over: asumir cargo de
entertainment business: negocios de entretenimiento
by this time: para este momento
competitor: competidor
free: gratis
less of…and more of: menos… y más
a loose array of: una serie de sueltos
was not afraid: no temía
express nonconformist opinions: expresar opiniones inconformistas
did not fear/to fear: no temía/temer
had lost/to lose: había perdido/ perder
some of its range: parte de su alcance
retained/to retain: retenía/retener
conventionality: adherencia a lo convencional
freedom of speech: libertad de expresión
was founded/to found: fue fundada/ fundar
musicals: obras musicales
emerged/to emerge: surgieron/surgir
modern day: actual
alive and well: vivito y coleando *(literalmente: vivo y bien)*
seeing: ver
show: espectáculo
popular tourist activity: popular actividad turística
ticket booths: taquilla, ventanilla de venta de entradas
sell/to sell: venden/vender
same-day tickets: entradas para el mismo día
half price: mitad de precio
seats: asientos, localidades
otherwise: de otra forma
go empty: quedar vacíos
rates: tarifas
same day "rush" tickets: entradas "urgentes" para el mismo día
standing-room tickets: entradas populares, "de parado"
ensure: asegurar
full: llenos
produce/to produce: producen/producir
range: gama
themes to choose from: temas de los cuales elegir
certain to find: seguro encontrará
interests you: te interese

ask/to ask: preguntas/preguntar
cultural values: valores culturales
you might receive blank stares: puede
 que recibas miradas sin expresión
no response: ninguna respuesta
society: sociedad
diverse: diversa
likely: probable
answers: respuestas
has been enriched/to enrich: ha sido
 enriquecida/enriquecer
belief systems: sistemas de creencias
a few select: algunos pocos y selectos
core: núcleo
nearly: casi
would agree upon: estarían de
 acuerdo en
individual freedom: libertad individual
whether you call it: ya sea si lo llamas
cornerstone: piedra angular
destiny: destino
influenced/to influence: influyó/
 influir, influenciar
government: gobierno
was established/to establish: fue
 establecido/establecer
guaranteed: garantizados
large corporations: grandes
 corporaciones
majority of: la mayoría de
businesses: negocios
owned: pertenecientes
dream: sueño
own boss: propio patrón
being: ser
most appealing ways to improve:
 formas más atrayentes de mejorar
is regarded/to regard: está considerada/
 considerar
key to opportunity: clave para la
 oportunidad
including: incluyendo
approach: enfoque
classroom: salón de clase
internships: pasantías
considered: consideradas
lifelong: durante toda la vida
continuing education programs:
 programas de educación continua
belief: creencia
be all that you can be: sé todo lo que
 puedas ser
emanates/to emanate: emana/emanar
heritage: herencia
early settlers: primeros colonos
to improve themselves: mejorarse a
 ellos mismos
to develop: desarrollar
talents: talentos
neighbors: vecinos

Cultural Values

If you **ask** Americans what the **cultural values** in the U.S. are, **you might receive blank stares** and little or **no response**. In a **society** as **diverse** as the United States, there is **likely** to be a multitude of **answers.** American culture **has been enriched** by the values and **belief systems** of almost every part of the world. **A few select** values are at the **core** of the American value system.

INDIVIDUAL FREEDOM — One value that **nearly** every American **would agree upon** is **individual freedom**. **Whether you call it** individual freedom, or independence, it is the **cornerstone** of American values.

The concept of an individual having control over his/her own **destiny influenced** the type of **government** that **was established** here. Individual rights are **guaranteed** in the United States Constitution.

While our economic system may be dominated by **large corporations**, the **majority of** American **businesses** are small, and many are **owned** by an individual or a family. It is part of the "American **dream**" to "be your **own boss**." **Being** an entrepreneur is one of the **most appealing ways to improve** one's economic future.

CHOICE IN EDUCATION
Education **is regarded** as the **key to opportunity, including** financial security. Americans take a pragmatic **approach** to learning. What one learns outside the **classroom** through **internship** and extra-curricular activities is often **considered** as important as what is learned in the classroom. **Lifelong** learning is valued which is why you will find many adult and **continuing education programs**.

The **belief** that Americans should "**be all that you can be**" **emanates** from our Protestant **heritage**. Since the majority of the **early settlers** were Protestant, they believed that they had a responsibility **to improve themselves**, to be the best they could be, **to develop** their **talents**, and to help their **neighbors**.

THE FAMILY — The **main purpose** of the American family is to bring about the **happiness** of each individual family member. The traditional family values **include love** and respect for **parents, as well as** for all members of the family.

The **emphasis** on the individual and his/her right to happiness can be **confusing**. It **allows** children **to disagree**, even **argue** with their parents. While in most other cultures such **action** would be a **sign** of **disrespect**, that is not the case in the United States. It is considered a part of **developing** one's independence.

PRIVACY — **Privacy** is important to Americans. The **notion** of individual privacy may make it **difficult** to make friends. Because Americans respect one's privacy, they **may not go beyond** a **friendly** "hello."

The **rugged** individualism valued by most Americans **stems from** our **frontier heritage**. Early settlers had to be **self-sufficient**, which **forced** them to be **inventive**. Their **success** gave them **optimism** about the future, a belief that problems could be **solved**. This positive spirit **enables** Americans **to take risks** in areas where others might only dream. This **results in** tremendous **advances** in technology, **health** and science.

In addition to such basic American values as individual freedom, self-reliance, equality of opportunity, **hard work**, **material wealth**, and **competition**, we see a **trend toward** conservation. There is an emphasis on **recycling** and **preserving** the **environment**. Also there is a greater sensitivity to cooperation on a **global scale**.

No matter what changes the next **century** brings or whether you **agree** with American values, the opportunity **to live** in the United States is a wonderful and new experience.

El artículo anterior fue escrito por Thomas E. Grouling, Ph.D. El profesor Grouling es Director Asistente del Departamento de Programas y Servicios Internacionales de la Universidad Drake. Trabaja como consejero de estudiantes y académicos extranjeros, así como director del Programa de Inglés Intensivo. El professor Grouling ha trabajado con estudiantes internacionales y minorías étnicas por aproximadamente 40 años y dicta un seminario anual en Estudios Americanos en la Universidad Drake.

main purpose: propósito principal
happiness: felicidad
include/to include: incluyen/incluir
love: amor
parents: padres
as well as: así como
emphasis: énfasis
confusing: confuso
allows/to allow: permite/permitir
to disagree: estar en desacuerdo
argue/to argue: discutir/discutir
action: acción
sign: señal
disrespect: falta de respeto
developing: desarrollar
privacy: intimidad
notion: noción
difficult: difícil
may not go beyond: pueden no ir más allá
friendly: amigable
rugged: determinado
stems from/to stem from: deriva de/derivar de
frontier heritage: herencia de frontera
self-sufficient: autosuficientes
forced/to force: forzó/forzar
inventive: inventivos
success: éxito
optimism: optimismo
solved/to solve: resueltos/resolver
enables/to enable: permite/permitir
to take risks: tomar riesgos
results in: resulta en
advances: adelantos
health: salud
in addition to: además de
hard work: trabajo duro
material wealth: riqueza material
competition: competición
trend toward: tendencia hacia
recycling: reciclar
preserving: preservar
environment: medio ambiente
global scale: escala global
no matter what: no importa que
changes: cambios
century: siglo
agree/to agree: estás de acuerdo/estar de acuerdo
to live: vivir

Test Your Comprehension

The American Dream, page 4

1. ¿Con qué se asocia generalmente el sueño americano?

2. ¿De qué manera determinó la revolución industrial el sueño americano?

3. Además de seguridad económica y comodidad material, ¿qué otra cosa significa el sueño americano?

A Melting Pot, page 5

1. ¿Qué es el "melting pot" (crisol de culturas)?

2. ¿Qué región de los Estados Unidos es considerada más tolerante con los cambios y las diferencias?

3. ¿Qué grupo étnico influyó más en el suroeste de los Estados Unidos?

The American Cowboy, page 6

1. ¿Cuál es el origen del vaquero estadounidense?

2. ¿Qué hacen los vaqueros modernos hoy en día en los Estados Unidos?

3. ¿Dónde puedes aprender sobre la tradición de las vaqueros?

American Jazz, page 8

1. ¿Cuál es el lugar de nacimiento del jazz?

2. ¿Qué grupo étnico es la raíz del jazz?

Examina tu comprensión

Early American Literature, page 14

1. ¿Quién fue el primer escritor estadounidense de notoriedad que nació fuera de la costa este?

2. ¿Qué escritor escribió sobre las personas de clase trabajadora y su lucha?

Artistic Expression, page 15

1. Norman Rockwell pintó The Four Freedoms (Las cuatro libertades). ¿Cuáles eran las cuatro libertades?

2. ¿Andy Warhol fue famoso por qué tipo de arte?

The Birthplace of Broadway, page 16

1. ¿En que ciudad estadounidense empezó Broadway?

2. La gente iba al teatro para escapar de la realidad de la guerra, pero ¿qué esfuerzo apoyó Broadway?

Cultural Values, page 18

1. ¿Cuál es el valor con el que casi todo estadounidense estaría de acuerdo?

2. ¿Qué valor es considerado la clave de la oportunidad, incluyendo la seguridad económica?

Though we travel the world over to find the beautiful,
we must carry it with us or we find it not.

Ralph Waldo Emerson

Travel

Camping Trips

several: varias
options: opciones
camping: acampar
throughout: por todo
different types: diferentes tipos
to choose: elegir
depends/to depend: depende/
 depender
interests: intereses
level: nivel
include/to include: incluyen/
 incluir
car camping: acampar con carro
full-facility campgrounds:
 campamentos con todos los servicios
backcountry: campo
limited facilities: servicios
 limitados
wilderness: tierras vírgenes,
 naturaleza
must carry out: debes llevarte
carry in: traes, entras
accept/to accept: aceptan/aceptar
official site: sitio oficial
prefer/to prefer: prefieres/preferir
things: cosas
to consider: considerar
questions: preguntas
to ask: preguntar
making/to make: estés haciendo/
 hacer
available: disponibles
such as: tal como
water: agua
power: electricidad
hookups: conexiones
showers: duchas
picnic tables: mesas para picnic
grills: barbacoas
maximum number: número
 máximo
vehicles: vehículos
permitted: permitidos
consecutive: consecutivos
length: largo, extensión
stay: estadía
regarding pets: en relación a
 mascotas
whatever: cualquiera
help preserve: ayuda a mantener
beauty: belleza
outdoors: aire libre, naturaleza
generations to come: generaciones
 venideras
responsibly: con responsabilidad

There are **several** opportunities and **options** for **camping throughout** the United States and several **different types** of camping **to choose** from. The type of camping you choose **depends** on your **interests** and your **level** of experience. The different options **include car camping** at **full-facility campgrounds**, **backcountry** camping with **limited facilities**, and **wilderness** camping with no facilities at all and you **must carry out** everything you **carry in**.

Many of the U.S. national parks with campgrounds that **accept** reservations are part of the National Park Reservation Service. The **official site** for the National Park Service where you can make reservations is: www.reservations.nps.gov

If you **prefer** backcountry camping, the website www.recreation.gov offers complete information and reservations.

If you are going camping at a campground, here are some **things to consider** and **questions to ask** when **making** reservations:

- What facilities are **available**, **such as water** and **power hookups**, bathrooms, **showers**, **picnic tables**, and **grills**.

- What is the **maximum number** of people and **vehicles permitted** per campsite?

- Is there a limit on the number of days or **consecutive** days you can camp at a park? Are there other restrictions on **length** of **stay**?

- What are the restrictions **regarding pets** in the campground?

Whatever type of camping you choose, please **help preserve** the **beauty** of the great **outdoors** for yourself and **generations to come** by camping **responsibly**.

Rafting the Grand Canyon

When most people **think** of the Grand Canyon they think of **peering over** the **rim** and **admiring** the **beauty** from **up above**.

But **what about** being in the canyon and **looking up**? The Grand Canyon is one of the seven **natural wonders** of the world and a **trip down** the Colorado **River allows** you to **experience** the beauty and **ruggedness** from the **heart** of the canyon. Over the **course** of 250 miles the river **runs through unruly rapids**, making for a **wilder ride** than you're **likely to find** on **dry land**.

A river trip down the Grand Canyon **ranges from navigating** through **world-class** rapids to **swimming** in the **side** canyons and **hiking** through **remote areas** not **seen** by most **travelers**. On this **once-in-a-lifetime** adventure you will experience astounding views of **hidden waterfalls** and you will **discover ancient Indian ruins.**

The **diversity** of Grand Canyon's **scenery** is **matched** by the **surprising** diversity of its **plant** and animal life. There are 287 species of **birds** in the Grand Canyon, 88 species of **mammals**, 26 species of **fish**, and 58 species of **reptiles** and **amphibians**.

A **guide** for your rafting trip is highly recommended and **required** in some parts of the river. There are several **tour companies** that **book weekend** or **weeklong** trips. Some tours **provide special interest** trips including history, **geology** and **photography** tours.

Down by the Boardwalk

beaches: playas	

The boardwalks of American **beaches** are major tourist attractions. The first boardwalks **were built** in New Jersey in the **late** 1800's. They were originally **designed** as **walkways** so **beachgoers** could **stroll along** the **shore** without **tracking sand** into the **hotel lobbies**. Today's boardwalks **have something** for everyone; **arcades, carnival rides, clothing boutiques, gourmet candy shops**, restaurants and **nightclubs**. From **sunup** to **sundown**, boardwalks are **packed** with people of all ages, **making the most of** their **summertime fun.**

The boardwalk is a **true** American beach tradition. We **celebrate** the boardwalk with a list of the best America has **to offer**.

Atlantic City is the **largest** of New Jersey's boardwalks and it is where it all **started** in 1870. Atlantic City **has become** more famous for its casinos in **recent years**, but the boardwalk is **still** packed in the summer with locals and tourists **alike**. A **family-friendly** boardwalk can be **found** in Ocean City. This popular **promenade runs beside** beautiful **wide** sand beaches. The boardwalk has a Victorian **feel, reminiscent** of the **seaside resorts** that **once populated** the mid-Atlantic coast. At all of the New Jersey coast towns you **will find fresh** saltwater taffy being made at **family-owned shops**. Saltwater taffy is **another** beachside tradition that started in New Jersey.

Glossary

beaches: playas
were built/to build: fueron construidos/construir
late: fines de
designed: diseñados
walkways: calzadas, pasarelas, veredas
beachgoers: personas que van a la playa
stroll: dar un paseo
along: a lo largo de
shore: costa
tracking: dejar huellas
sand: arena
hotel lobbies: vestíbulos de los hoteles
have something: tienen algo
arcades: galerías
carnival rides: atracciones en parques de diversiones
clothing boutiques: tiendas de ropa
gourmet candy shops: tiendas de dulces gourmet
nightclubs: clubes nocturnos
sunup: salida del sol
sundown: puesta del sol
packed: llenas, repletas
making the most of: aprovechando al máximo
summertime: tiempo de verano
fun: diversión
true: verdadera
celebrate/to celebrate: celebramos/celebrar
to offer: ofrecer
largest: más grande
started/to start: empezó/empezar
has become/to become: se ha convertido/convertirse
recent years: años recientes
still: todavía
alike: igualmente
family-friendly: para la familia
found/to find: encontrarse/encontrar
promenade: paseo marítimo
runs/to run: corre/correr
beside: al lado de
wide: anchas
feel: ambiente, sensación
reminiscent: que recuerda a
seaside resorts: lugar de vacaciones en la playa o costa
once: una vez
populated/to populate: poblaron/poblar
will find/to find: encontrarás/encontrar
fresh: fresco/a
family-owned shops: tiendas pertenecientes a familias
another: otra

The west coast is not **as well known** for its boardwalks but Santa Cruz, California has a seaside **amusement park** that is one of the best in the nation. It is California's **oldest** amusement park and the **only** major seaside amusement park on the Pacific Coast. Here you will find a **wonderful blend** of **old** and **new** carnival rides. The Looff Carousel and the Giant Dipper **roller coaster** are National Historic Landmarks.

Virginia Beach's famous **oceanfront** boardwalk has been **named** by many the most **beautiful** boardwalk in the **country**. Its popular **three-mile** walkway has **recently** been **updated**. There is also a **bike path** that runs **alongside** the boardwalk making it popular for bikes, skateboards and rollerblades. **Concerts** are a big **attraction** here at one of the three oceanfront **stages**.

Myrtle Beach, South Carolina was **nearly empty** of boardwalk attractions **twenty years ago. Since that time** an **enormous growth** of shops, amusement parks, **theaters** and restaurants has **transformed** the boardwalk at Myrtle Beach into a major tourist center. **In addition to** the usual boardwalk **fare**, Myrtle Beach also **boasts** an **aquarium** and an IMAX theater. A wonderful new **addition** to Myrtle Beach is a **glass butterfly pavilion**.

Ocean City Maryland **is home to** a famous boardwalk that **buzzes** with activity. You will find **activities** and **events** that **appeal** to all ages. Ten miles of white-sand beaches and three miles of world-famous Boardwalk make Ocean City **picture-perfect**. From the **tiny train** that **chugs** along the three-mile promenade to the **antique** carousel that **dates back to** 1902, Ocean City has **kept** its **sense** of a **bygone era** while **keeping** its attractions fresh.

as well known: tan conocida
amusement park: parque de diversiones
oldest: más viejo
only: único
wonderful blend: maravillosa mezcla
old: viejo
new: nuevo
roller coaster: montaña rusa
oceanfront: frente al mar
named: nombrado, llamado
beautiful: hermoso
country: país
three-mile: de tres millas
recently: recientemente
updated: renovada
bike path: sendero para bicicletas
alongside: al lado de
concerts: conciertos
attraction: atracción
stages: escenarios
nearly: casi
empty: vacío, desprovisto
twenty years ago: veinte años atrás
since that time: desde esos tiempos
enormous growth: crecimiento enorme
theaters: teatros
transformed/to transform: transformado/transformar
in addition to: además de
fare: comida
boasts/to boast: se jacta/jactarse
aquarium: acuario
addition: adición
glass butterfly pavilion: pabellón de vidrio para mariposas
is home to: alberga
buzzes/to buzz: zumba/zumbar
activities: actividades
events: espectáculos
appeal/to appeal: atraen/atraer, interesar
picture-perfect: perfecto como en una foto, "de película"
tiny train: tren diminuto
chugs/to chug: resopla/resoplar *(tren)*
antique: antiguo
dates back to: se remonta a
kept/to keep: mantenido/mantener
sense: sentido
bygone era: época pasada
keeping/to keep: mantiene/mantener

islands: islas	

islands: islas
have long been considered: han sido consideradas desde hace tiempo
treasure: tesoro
gorgeous sandy beaches: magníficas playas de arena
spectacular sunsets: puestas de sol espectaculares
breathtaking beauty: belleza que quita el aliento
surprise: sorpresa
spots: puntos, sitios
packed full: repleta
diversity: diversidad
find/to find: encontrar
depending: dependiendo
also: también
see: ver
miles: millas
barren lava flow: corriente de lava estéril
museums: museos
skiing: esquí
snow-peaked mountain: montaña con el pico nevado
often: a menudo
landing spot: sitio de aterrizaje
largest city: mayor ciudad
probably best known: probablement mejor conocida
hums/to hum: zumba/zumbar
activity: actividad
outdoor activities: actividades al aire libre
well worth your time: bien vale la pena tu tiempo
to visit: visitar
world-famous surf: oleaje famoso a nivel mundial
relaxed: relajada
friendly: amigable
spread across: dispersas a través
bicycling: andar en bicicleta
volcano: volcán
shopping: ir de compras
snorkeling: hacer esnórquel
lovely cove: cala encantadora
tropical rain forest: selva tropical lluviosa

Treasure Islands

The **islands** of Hawaii **have long been considered** the **treasure** of the United States. **Gorgeous sandy beaches**, **spectacular sunsets** and **breathtaking beauty**, it is no **surprise** that Hawaii is one of the most popular vacation **spots** in the U.S.

Oahu, Maui, Kauai and The Big Island are the four most popular islands. Each island is **packed full** of beauty and **diversity**. You will **find** perfect beaches on each island, but **depending** on your destination, you may **also see miles** of **barren lava flow**, **museums** and even **skiing** on a **snow-peaked mountain**!

OAHU

Oahu is **often** the **landing spot** for most visitors and home to the **largest city** in the state, Honolulu. Oahu is **probably best known** for the city and beaches of Waikiki. Waikiki **hums** with **activity**. Here you  can do more than just experience the **outdoor activities** of the islands. It is **well worth your time to visit** Pearl Harbor and the Polynesian Cultural Center. And you must visit the North Shore of Oahu for **world-famous surf**.

MAUI

Relaxed and **friendly**, Maui is home to some of the most beautiful resorts and gorgeous sandy beaches in the world. Activities are **spread across** the entire island and you can easily find something different to do every day. **Bicycling** down a **volcano**, **shopping** in historic Lahaina Town, world-class golf, **snorkeling** in a **lovely cove** or camping in a **tropical rain forest**; the Island of Maui has a lot to offer for all ages.

KAUAI

Known also as the **garden isle**, Kauai is **considered by many** to be the most beautiful of the islands. Poipu Beach **is consistently voted** one of the prettiest beaches in the world. **Lush** tropical rain forests **compete** for your attention with **dramatic canyons** and **coastline**. You won't find a **great deal** of **night life** here, but your time will be best **spent hiking**, **exploring** and kayaking during the day. Kauai is one of the **wettest** spots on Earth, with an **annual average rainfall** of 460 inches. The high annual rainfall has **eroded deep valleys** in the central mountain, **carving out** canyons and **creating** the many **scenic waterfalls**.

THE BIG ISLAND

Larger than all the other islands **combined**, The Big Island of Hawaii is a **remarkable contrast** of geography and **climates**. Tropical forests with beautiful waterfalls on one side, **stark** lava beds on the other. The **landscape** is **dominated** by mountains, particularly the **twin peaks** of Mauna Kea and Mauna Loa. Mauna Kea is the only **place** in Hawaii where you can **strap on skis** and **hit the slopes**.

If you can't **make up your mind** about which Island to visit you can **take** an **island-hopping cruise**. Norwegian Cruise Line has seven-day **itineraries** visiting Oahu, Maui, Kauai and the Big Island.

By **land** or **sea**, Hawaii is a great place for your **next** vacation!

known also as: también conocida como

garden isle: isla jardín

considered by many: considerada por muchos

is consistently voted: es votada consistentemente

lush: exuberante

compete/to compete: compiten/ competir

dramatic canyons: dramáticos cañones

coastline: litoral, costa

great deal: mucha

night life: vida nocturna

spent: usado, pasado *(tiempo)*

hiking: desenderismo

exploring: explorar

wettest: más húmedos

annual average rainfall: precipitación anual promedio

eroded/to erode: erosionó/erosionar

deep valleys: valles profundos

carving out/to carve out: excavando/ excavar, labrar, forjar

creating/to create: creando/crear

scenic waterfalls: cascadas pintorescas

larger: más grande

combined: en conjunto

remarkable contrast: contraste notable

climates: climas

stark: inhóspitas

landscape: paisaje

dominated/to dominate: dominado/ dominar

twin peaks: picos gemelos

place: lugar

strap on skis: ponerse esquíes

hit the slopes: esquiar *(literalmente: tirarse por las laderas)*

make up your mind: decidirse

take: tomar

island-hopping cruise: crucero que va de isla en isla

itineraries: itinerarios

land: tierra

sea: mar

next: próxima

The First National Park

The National Parks in the United States **offer more than** just **outdoor recreation**—they offer a **chance to learn** about our nation's diverse history, geography, and culture.

The **first** official national park of the United States was California's Yosemite National Park. **Inspired** by the **beauty** of Yosemite and **worried** about the possible exploitation of Yosemite's **natural wonders**, conservationists **appealed** to Senator John Conness to help **protect** the park. On June 30, 1864, President Abraham Lincoln **signed** a bill **granting** Yosemite Valley and the Mariposa Grove of Giant Sequoias to the State of California as an **inalienable public trust**. This was the first **time** in history that a federal government had **set aside scenic lands** to protect them and **to allow** for their **enjoyment** by all people. This idea was the **spark** that made Yosemite the first official national park in 1890.

Yosemite National Park is best **known** for its **waterfalls**, but within its nearly 1,200 **square miles** you will **find** an **abundance** of **wildlife, spectacular scenery** and **vast wilderness to explore**.

The best time **to see** waterfalls is during **spring**, when most of the **snowmelt occurs**. Yosemite Falls is one of the world's **tallest** and is made up of three **separate** falls: Upper Yosemite Fall (1,430 feet), the middle cascades (675 feet), and Lower Yosemite Fall (320 feet). Another popular waterfall, Bridal Veil, **flows** all year and you can **walk** to the base in just a few minutes.

Ancient giant sequoias can be **found** in the Mariposa **Grove**. The Mariposa Grove is the largest group of giant sequoias in Yosemite. The General Sherman, a Giant Sequoia, is **generally considered** to be the largest tree in the world. This tree is **located** in Sequoia National Park, just south of Yosemite.

Two famous **rock formations** in Yellowstone are Half Dome and El Capitan. Half Dome is **perhaps** the most **recognized symbol** of Yosemite. **Rising** nearly 5,000 feet **above** the Valley floor, some people **attempt** the **treacherous hike** or **rock climb** to the **top**. Experienced rock climbers enjoy El Capitan. It rises more than 3,000 feet above the Valley floor and is the largest **monolith** of **granite** in the world.

Yosemite National Park is home to **hundreds** of American **black bears**. These bears are very **curious** and have an amazing **sense of smell**. Most bears that **rely** on natural **food sources** are **active** during the day. However, when **hungry**, they **quietly sneak around** and **grab unattended** food at night. **Precautions** and information on bear **safety** can be found at **nature centers** in the park.

You don't need reservations **to visit** Yosemite National Park, but reservations **to stay overnight** in the park are **mandatory**. **Lodging** options in Yosemite National Park **range from** simple **cabins** to **deluxe rooms** at The Ahwahnee Hotel. Camping is the most popular way **to spend the night** in Yosemite National Park. There are 13 campgrounds located throughout the park and reservations are **necessary** for **most** locations. Information and reservations for Yosemite, **as well as** every national park in the United States, can be **found** online at: www.nps.gov.

rock formations: formaciones rocosas
perhaps: quizás
recognized: reconocido
symbol: símbolo
rising: elevándose
above: sobre, arriba
attempt/to attempt: intentan/intentar
treacherous hike: excursión traicionera
rock climb: trepada por las rocas
top: cima
monolith: monolito
granite: granito
hundreds: cientos
black bears: osos negros
curious: curiosos
sense of smell: sentido del olfato
rely/to rely: dependen/ depender
food sources: fuentes de comida o alimento
active: activos
hungry: hambrientos
quietly sneak around: acercarse sigilosamente
grab/to grab: agarran/agarrar
unattended: desatendida
precautions: precauciones
safety: seguridad
nature centers: centros con información sobre la naturaleza
you don't need: no necisita
to visit: visitar
to stay overnight: quedarse por la noche
mandatory: obligatorios
lodging: alojamiento
range from: van desde
cabins: cabañas
deluxe rooms: habitaciones de lujo
to spend te night: pasar la noche
necessary: necesarias
most: la mayoría de
as well as: así como
found/to find: encontrados/ encontrar

most: la mayoría
think/to think: piensan/pensar
visiting: visitar
lifetime: vida
hard to arrange: difícil de organizar o coordinar
arrangements: arreglos
through: a través de
requires/to require: requiere/requerir
extensive: extenso, de gran alcance, a fondo
planning: planeamiento
ahead of time: por adelantado
of course: por supuesto
worth: valer
effort: esfuerzo
successful: exitoso (*si obtienes los resultados esperados*)
besides: además de
packed full: repleta
places: lugares
to visit: visitar
taking: tomar
self-guided tour: visita auto-guiada
learning/to learn: se aprende/aprender
government: gobierno
prominent landmark: punto de referencia prominente
stands/to stand: se eleva/elevarse
tall: alto, altura
landing: rellano
views: vistas
unique feature: rasgo único
carved memorial stones: lápidas talladas
line/to line: bordean/bordear
pay tribute: rinden homenaje
achievements: logros
honors/to honor: honra/honrar
symbolizes/to symbolize: simboliza/simbolizar
belief: creencia
should be free: deberían ser libres
contains/to contain: contiene/contener
statue: estatua
houses/to house: aloja/alojar
stone tables: mesas de piedra
engraved: grabadas
building: edificio
based on: basado en
classic style: estilo clásico
introduced/to introduce: introdujo/introducir
walls: paredes
describe/to describe: describen/describir
beliefs: creencias
freedom: libertad

A Walking Tour of D.C.

When **most** people **think** of a trip to Washington, D.C. they think of **visiting** the White House. A trip to the White House is an experience of a **lifetime**; however it can be **hard to arrange**. You must have a group of ten or more people and make your **arrangements through** your member of Congress. This **requires extensive planning** well **ahead of time**. It is, **of course**, **worth** the **effort** if you are **successful**.

Besides the White House, Washington, D.C. is **packed full** of interesting, historical and educational **places to visit**. **Taking** a **self-guided tour** of the national monuments is a great way to explore the city while **learning** about the history, **government** and people of the United States.

THE WASHINGTON MONUMENT

The most **prominent landmark** in Washington, D.C. is the Washington Monument. It **stands** 555 feet **tall**. An elevator takes visitors to the 500-foot **landing** for magnificent **views** of the city. A **unique feature** of the Washington Monument is the 193 **carved memorial stones** that **line** the interior of the monument. These stones **pay tribute** to the **achievements** of George Washington.

THE LINCOLN MEMORIAL

The Lincoln Memorial **honors** Abraham Lincoln, the 16th President of the United States. The memorial **symbolizes** Lincoln's **belief** that all people **should be free**. The chamber inside the memorial **contains** a **statue** of Lincoln. The chamber also **houses** two **stone tables**; one **engraved** with Lincoln's Second Inaugural Address, and the other with the Gettysburg Address.

THE JEFFERSON MEMORIAL

The Jefferson Memorial honors Thomas Jefferson, author of the Declaration of Independence, first Secretary of State, and third President. The structure of the **building** is **based on** the **classic style** of architecture Jefferson **introduced** into this country. In the center of the memorial is a statue of Jefferson. On the **walls** are four inscriptions. They **describe** his **belief** in **freedom** and education.

VIETNAM VETERANS MEMORIAL

The Vietnam Veterans Memorial honors the men and women who **served** in the Vietnam War. The memorial **consists** of three parts: the Wall of **names**, the Three **Servicemen** Statue and **Flagpole**, and the Vietnam Women's Memorial. The Memorial Wall **contains** the names of the 58,220 men and women who were **killed** and **remain missing** from the war.

KOREAN WAR VETERANS MEMORIAL

The Korean War Veterans Memorial is a **reminder** of the Korean War and the sacrifices and **hardships** of those who **fought** in this war. This memorial consists of a **platoon** of **stainless steel** soldiers. Engraved on a **nearby** wall are the total **casualties** of **both** the United States and the United Nations' **troops** along with the words "FREEDOM IS NOT FREE".

NATIONAL WORLD WAR II MEMORIAL

The National World War II Memorial is a National memorial to Americans who served and **died** in World War II. The **design** of the National World War II Memorial **incorporates** many **symbolic elements** representing **unity**, **sacrifice**, **victory** and freedom.

UNITED STATES MARINE CORPS MEMORIAL

The Marine Corps War Memorial is a symbol of America's **gratitude** to the U.S. Marines who died in **combat**. The statue **portrays** one of the most famous **events** of World War II: the U.S. victory of Iwo Jima.

THE TOMB OF THE UNKNOWNS

The **Tomb** of the **Unknown Soldier** is **located** at Arlington National Cemetery. It was **constructed to mark** the **grave** of an **unidentified** American soldier from World War I. Three **Greek figures** are engraved into the **marble** and represent **Peace**, Victory, and Valor. **On the back** of the Tomb is the **following inscription**: **HERE RESTS** IN HONORED **GLORY** AN AMERICAN SOLDIER **KNOWN** BUT TO **GOD**.

Unique Accommodations

ready: dispuesto/a
something: algo
next: próxima
skip/to skip: saltéate/saltearse
spend/to spend: pasa/pasar
lighthouse: faro
romantic towers: torres románticas
provide/to provide: proveen/proveer
unique: únicas
accommodations: alojamiento
country: país
allow/to allow: permiten/permitir
guests: huéspedes
to perform: hacer, llevar a cabo
keeper's duties: obligaciones del guardar
raising/to raise: levantar *(izar)*
flag: bandera
recording/to record: tomar nota de
odd jobs: trabajos esporádicos
maintain: mantener
scenery: paisaje
surroundings: alrededores
range from: va de
upscale: exclusivo
gourmet meals: comidas gourmet
rugged: rústico
bunk beds: literas
tiny: minúscula
entire: entero
yourself: ti mismo
restored: restaurado
open: abiertos
daily: diariamente
departs/to depart: parte/partir
own: propia
rent: alquilar
second-floor: segundo piso
agree to do: aceptan hacer
hour's worth: equivalente a una hora
record-keeping: tomar notas
chores: tareas
landmark: punto de referencia
red-brick: ladrillo rojo
built/to build: construido/construir
overnight: por la noche, de un día para el otro
public tours: visitas públicas guiadas
operational: en funcionamiento
enjoy: disfrutar
swimming: nadar
picnicking: hacer excursiones
bird watching: observar aves
reached/to reach: alcanzada/alcanzar
boat: bote
nature trail: ruta ecológica
village: pueblo

Ready for **something** different? On your **next** vacation **skip** the hotel and **spend** the night in a **lighthouse**! These **romantic towers provide** some of the most **unique accommodations** in the **country**. Some lighthouses **allow guests to perform** various **keeper's duties** such as **raising** the **flag**, **recording** the weather, and other **odd jobs** to help **maintain** the property. All lighthouses provide spectacular **scenery**, historic **surroundings**, and an extraordinary opportunity. The lighthouses **range from upscale** bed and breakfasts with **gourmet meals** to more **rugged** accommodations with **bunk beds** and no electricity.

The lighthouse on **tiny** Rose Island, in Rhode Island's Narragansett Bay, is one of the few authentic lighthouses in America that allows you to have the **entire** lighthouse to **yourself** and become keeper for a week. The island and **restored** lighthouse are **open** from 10 a.m. to 4 p.m. **daily**. But when the last ferry **departs**, the island becomes your **own**. Up to four adults can **rent** the **second-floor** apartment if they **agree to do** an **hour's worth** of daily **record-keeping** and **chores**.

A **landmark** on the Hudson River, the Saugerties Lighthouse, is a **red-brick** lighthouse **built** in 1869. The lighthouse offers **overnight** bed and breakfast accommodations, **public tours** and special events. The **operational** light-tower offers a panoramic view of the Hudson River. On this small island you can **enjoy swimming**, **picnicking** and **bird-watching**. The Lighthouse can be **reached** by **boat** or the half-mile **nature trail** at the end of Lighthouse Drive in the **village** of Saugerties, New York.

The East Brother Light Station is located **less** than an hour from San Francisco but **once** you **arrive**, **city life feels** a **world away**. The Light Station operates as a four-room bed and breakfast and is **accessible only** by boat. **Gourmet dinners** are **served** with **wine** and breakfasts **have been made popular** by the Lighthouse French Toast Soufflé. The day can be **spent hiking** the island, bird and **whale** watching or **learning** about the history of the lighthouse.

Travel **back in time** with a stay at the Isle Au Haut Lighthouse in Maine. This authentic Keeper's House is **without telephones** and electricity. Guests **use kerosene lanterns** for **light** and **woodstoves** for **heat.** To reach this 1907 lighthouse, take a 40-minute boat ride to the **remote** island of Isle au Haut. **Bikes** are **provided** to guests for **transportation around** the island. There are six **bedrooms furnished** with **antiques**, island **crafts** and **coastal memorabilia**.

Charity Island Lighthouse in Au Gres, Michigan, offers overnight lodging in the **spring** and **fall**. It is operational as a bed and breakfast with four bedrooms. **Upon arrival** guests **receive** a 30-minute **presentation** on the history of the island and the lighthouse. The island **consists** of **almost three hundred acres** of **forest** and is home to a **multitude** of **wildlife** including **songbirds**, **bald eagles**, **raccoons**, and **foxes**. The island is **preserved** as a wildlife **sanctuary** and is considered a bird-watcher's **paradise**.

less: menos
once: una vez
arrive/to arrive: llegas/llegar
city life: vida urbana
feels/to feel: se siente/sentirse
world away: un mundo de distancia
accessible only: accesible solamente
gourmet dinners: cenas gourmet
served/to serve: servidas/servir
wine: vino
have been made popular: han sido popularizadas
spent/to spend: pasado/pasar
hiking/to hike: caminando/caminar
whale: ballena
learning/to learn: aprendiendo/aprender
back in time: atrás en el tiempo
without telephones: sin teléfonos
use/to use: usan/usar
kerosene lanterns: faroles a queroseno
light: luz
woodstoves: estufas a leña
heat: calor
remote: remota
bikes: bicicletas
provided/to provide: provistas/proveer, proporcionar
transportation: transporte
around: alrededor
bedrooms: dormitorio
furnished: amueblados
antiques: antigüedades
crafts: artesanías
coastal memorabilia: recuerdos de la costa
spring: primavera
fall: otoño
upon arrival: a la llegada
receive/to receive: reciben/recibir
presentation: presentación
consists/to consist: consiste/consistir
almost: casi
three hundred acres: trescientos acres
forest: bosque
multitude: multitud
wildlife: vida silvestre
songbirds: pájaros cantores
bald eagles: águilas calvas
raccoons: mapaches
foxes: zorros
preserved: preservada
sanctuary: santuario
paradise: paraíso

Made in the USA

All over the United States, in **cities big and small**, you **will find factories** that **give tours** to the public. Why **visit** a factory? Factory tours are **educational** and **entertaining**. The **behind-the-scenes** view of how **everyday things** are **made** can be interesting to **both** kids and adults. If you are **taking** a **road trip**, **stopping** to visit a factory can make a nice **break**. If you are visiting a new city it can **provide valuable insight** into what makes that city special. At the **end** of the tour, the tour **guide** will often **hand out free samples** of their products. **In addition**, factory tours are generally free to the public, **resulting in** an **affordable activity** for you and your family.

There are more tours than we could **list** in one article. A **great place to plan** your factory tour is at Factory Tours: www.factorytoursusa.com

Jelly Belly Factory (www.jellybelly.com) **Put on** a **white paper hat**, **follow friendly** tour guides through the **sweet-smelling** factory and **watch** how Jelly Bellies are made. With the interesting **flavors** that **range from buttered popcorn** to jalapeño, the Jelly Belly tour is a **unique candy** experience.

U.S. Department of the Treasury (www.moneyfactory.com) Do you want to see how money is **made**? Here you can watch **bills** go from **large reams** of **blank paper** into **intricately inked currency**. There are two **locations**—one in Washington, D.C., and the other in Fort Worth, Texas.

Ben and Jerry's (www.benjerry.com) This **favorite ice cream brand** is one of the most popular tours in the United States. Samples are **tasted** in their FlavoRoom and tours starting at 9am give you the perfect excuse **to eat** ice cream for **breakfast**.

Gibson Guitar Factory (www.gibsonmemphis.com) At this factory in Memphis, Tennessee, you will watch the **guitar-making process.** For over 100 years, the company has been **assembling quality** American guitars **by hand**.

---

all over: todo alrededor de
cities: ciudades
big and small: grandes y pequeñas
will find/to find: encontrarás/encontrar
factories: fábricas
give/to give: dan/dar
tours: visitas guiadas
visit: visitar
educational: educativas
entertaining: entretenidas
behind-the-scenes: trastienda
everyday things: cosas de todos los días
made/to make: hechas/hacer
both: ambos
taking/to take: tomando/tomar, hacer
road trip: viaje por carretera
stopping: parar
break: descanso
provide: proveer
valuable insight: valiosa perspectiva nueva
end: final
guide: guía
hand out/to hand out: reparte/repartir
free samples: muestras gratis
in addition: además
resulting in: lo que resulta en
affordable activity: actividad asequible
list: listar
great place: gran sitio
to plan: para planear
put on/to put on: ponte/ponerse
white paper hat: sombrero de papel blanco
follow/to follow: sigue/seguir
friendly: amigables
sweet-smelling: perfumado, fragrante, de olor agradable
watch/to watch: mira/mirar
flavors: sabores
range from: se extiende desde
buttered popcorn: palomitas de maíz con mantequilla
unique: única
candy: dulce
made/to make: hecha/hacer
bills: billetes
large reams: grandes resmas
blank paper: papel en blanco
intricately inked currency: papel moneda intrincadamente entintado
locations: ubicaciones, lugares
favorite ice cream brand: marca de helado favorita
tasted/to taste: probadas/probar
to eat: para comer
breakfast: desayuno
guitar-making process: proceso de hacer guitarras
assembling/to assemble: armando/armar
quality: calidad
by hand: a mano

Home on the Range

Have you **ever wanted to live** like a **cowboy**? **Well**, you can **spend** a **weekend** as a cowboy at one of the many "dude ranches" **located across** the United States.

The dude ranch, **also known as** a **guest ranch**, is a ranch that is **open** for **visitors**. They **allow** visitors **to experience** ranch activities **first-hand** on weekend or weeklong vacations. **Daily** activities usually **include horseback riding lessons, trail rides**, picnics, **hiking**, **cookouts**, and rodeos. They **often host nightly** entertainment around a **campfire**.

Working ranches are another option for a more authentic experience. As the name **implies**, they are real working ranches that are in the **business** of **raising cattle** or horses and/or **farming**. They usually offer more rustic **accommodations** for **a smaller** number of guests and **less organized** activities. Daily activities include horseback riding and **sightseeing**, but you also have the opportunity to work with real cowboys in their daily ranch work.

Most dude ranches are **located out west** in the "**big sky country**" **states** such as Montana, Idaho, Colorado and Wyoming. Part of the **joy** of visiting a Dude Ranch is the spectacular **scenery** that you get to experience. The majestic mountains, green **rolling hills**, beautiful **rivers and lakes** are a **delight to view** and an **adventure to explore**. Exploring the **countryside** on horseback **allows** you to see things at a **slower pace** and the chance to see more wildlife such as **eagles**, buffalo, **deer** and even **wild bears**.

Before you **pick** a dude ranch to visit, go to websites such as www.ranchweb.com and www.duderanches.com to **read reviews** from other travelers. And, before you go, **make sure** you are prepared to **dress the part**—**don't forget to pack** your cowboy hat!

ever wanted: alguna vez quisiste
to live: vivir
cowboy: vaquero
well: bueno
spend: pasar
weekend: fin de semana
located: ubicados
across: a través de, a lo largo de
also known as: también conocido como
guest ranch: hacienda hostería
open: abierta
visitors: visitantes
allow/to allow: permiten/permitir
to experience: experimentar
first-hand: primera mano
daily: diarias
include/to include: incluyen/incluir
horseback riding lessons: clases de equitacion
trail rides: cabalgar en senderos
hiking: caminatas, excursiones a pie
cook-outs: parrilladas
often: a menudo
host/to host: presentan/presentar
nightly: todas las noches
campfire: fogata
working: en funcionamiento
implies/to imply: implica/implicar
business: negocio
raising cattle: criar ganado
farming: cultivar
accommodations: alojamiento
a fewer: menos, unos pocos
less organized: menos organizadas
sightseeing: hacer turismo
located out west: ubicados en el oeste
"big sky country" states: estados con tierras de grandes cielos
joy: alegría
scenery: paisaje
rolling hills: onduladas colinas
rivers and lakes: ríos y lagos
delight to view: delicia de ver
adventure: aventura
to explore: explorar
countryside: campo
allows/to allow: permite/permitir
slower pace: ritmo más lento
eagles: águilas
deer: ciervo
wild bears: osos salvajes
before: antes
pick: elegir
read: leer
reviews: críticas, reseñas
make sure/to make sure: asegúrate/asegurarse
dress the part: vestirte adecuadamente
don't forget/to forget: no te olvides/olvidarse
to pack: llevar

San Juan Orcas

Some of the **best whale watching** on the continent **is found** in the San Juan Islands off the coast of Washington.

The Puget Sound **is home to** 400 islands and home to 90 orcas. The **protected waters** and miles of **coastline** are ideal for **camping** and **kayaking**, and seeing pods of orcas and other **wildlife**.

Orcas, also **called** "killer whales," are the **largest** members of the **dolphin family**. Orcas are beautiful whales with **striking** black and white **markings**. Orcas **feed** almost exclusively on **fish**, with chinook salmon being their favorite **meal**. **During certain times** of the year you are **guaranteed** a whale sighting in this area.

The whales are **predictably seen** from **spring** until **autumn**, when they **follow** the **migrating** salmon through **shore** waters. July, August and September are the **warmest** and **driest** months and the best time to see orcas, porpoises and also gray whales.

There are many whale watching **tours** that **will take** you **aboard** one of their "whale-friendly" **vessels**. You may see the whales **swimming, breaching, chasing** fish—or **all of the above**! Orcas **communicate** with each other on a **regular basis**. Some boats have an **underwater** microphone so you can **listen** to their "conversations." This **adds** another **magical dimension** to the experience.

For an **even closer view** you can kayak with orcas in the San Juan Islands. On **multi-day** trips, you will **paddle** four to five hours a day**, stopping** to watch wildlife or **hike around** the islands. As you **explore**, the **guides** will **point out** wildlife and **explain** the ecology of the area.

The best place to see orcas from **land** is Lime Kiln Point State Park in Friday Harbor. This park is also called "Whale Watch Park." **While** you are there, don't **miss** the Whale Watch **Museum**.

Go to Jail!

Alcatraz, which is also known as 'the Rock', is the famous American **prison located** on Alcatraz Island, in San Francisco Bay. A **trip** to the island **offers** a **close-up look** at a **historic** and **notorious** federal prison. More than a million visitors a year **climb** the **steep hill** from the **ferry dock to view crumbling cell blocks**, and the **former living quarters** of prisoners and **guards**.

Before **being used as** a prison it was home to the **first** and **oldest operating lighthouse** (1854) and the first US **Fort** on the West Coast (1859).

This **military fortress** that had **protected** San Francisco Bay since California's Gold Rush days was a federal prison between 1934 and 1963. The bay's **icy water** and **strong currents** made "The Rock" **escape-proof**. **However**, it is **reported** that five prisoners tried to escape and are **officially listed** as **missing** and **presumed drowned**.

Between 1969 and 1971 the island was **taken over** by Native Americans. **Today**, the **entire** island is **preserved** as part of the National Park **System** and is a **venue** for tourists rather than criminals. A few former prisoners and guards can be **heard** on the prison's **audio tour** of the famous Cell House.

The **refreshing ferryboat ride**, with **stunning views** of San Francisco Bay, **adds** a special **beginning** and **end** to this popular **tour**.

also known as: también conocida como
prison: cárcel
located: ubicada
trip: viaje
offers/to offer: ofrece/ofrecer
close-up look: mirada de cerca
historic: histórica
notorious: notoria
climb/to climb: trepan/trepar
steep hill: colina empinada
ferry dock: muelle del ferry
to view: para mirar, para ver
crumbling cell blocks: bloques de celdas que se desmoronan
former living quarters: antiguas habitaciones
guards: guardias
being used as: ser usado como
first: primer
oldest: más viejo
operating lighthouse: faro en funcionamiento
fort: fuerte
military fortress: fortaleza militar
protected/to protect: protegía/ proteger
icy water: agua helada
strong currents: fuertes corrientes
escape-proof: a prueba de fugas
however: aunque
reported/to report: informado/ informar
officially: oficialmente
listed/to list: listados/listar
missing: desaparecidos
presumed: dados por
drowned: ahogados
taken over/to take over: tomada/ tomar, apoderarse de
today: hoy
entire: entera
preserved/to preserve: conservada/ conservar
system: sistema
venue: lugar de reunión
heard/to hear: oídos/oír
audio tour: visita guiada con audio
refreshing: refrescante
ferryboat ride: paseo en ferry
stunning views: vistas impresionantes
adds/to add: agrega/agregar
beginning: comienzo
end: final
tour: visita guiada

Test Your Comprehension

Camping Trips, page 24

1. ¿Cuáles son los tres tipos de campamento disponibles en los parques nacionales?

2. Si usted está planeando un viaje de campamento, ¿qué debería hacer primero?

3. Cuando deja un campamento estadounidense, ¿qué debe recordar para las generaciones futuras?

Rafting the Grand Canyon, page 25

1. ¿Qué río corre por el Gran Cañon?

2. ¿Cuáles son algunos de los viajes de interés especial que se ofrecen en el Gran Cañón?

Down by the Boardwalk, page 26

1. ¿Cuándo y dónde fueron construidos los primeros paseos marítimos entarimados?

2. ¿Cuál es el paseo marítimo más grande?

3. ¿Cuál es la nueva adición al Camino Marítimo de la Playa Myrtle de Carolina del Sur?

Treasure Islands, page 28

1. ¿Qué isla de Hawaii tiene la ciudad más grande?

2. ¿Qué isla, también conocida como la isla jardín, es considerada por muchos como la más bella?

3. La gran isla de Hawaii tiene diversos paisajes. ¿A qué se parece?

Examina tu comprensión

America's First National Park, page 30

1. ¿Qué parque fue el primer parque nacional de los Estados Unidos?

2. ¿Quién firmó el proyecto de ley poniendo a este parque nacional en fideicomiso público?

3. ¿Qué dos famosas formaciones rocosas están en este parque nacional?

Walking Tour of D.C, page 32

1. ¿Qué tan alto es el Monumento a Washington?

2. El monumento conmemorativo de Lincoln tiene dos mesas de piedras grabadas ¿con qué?

2. El diseño del monumento conmemorativo de la Segunda Guerra Mundial incorpora 4 elementos simbólicos ¿representando lo qué?

Made in the USA, page 36

1. ¿Cuáles son algunos de los sabores de dulces que encontrarás en una visita guiada de la fabrica Jelly Belly?

2. ¿A dónde irías para ver hacer dinero?

San Juan Orcas, page 38

1. ¿Frente a la costa de qué estadi están ubicadas las islas San Juan?

2. ¿Cuándo emigran las ballenas y pueden ser vistas?

3. ¿Cuál es la mejor manera de ver a las orcas de cerca?

A love for tradition has never weakened a nation,
indeed it has strengthened nations in their hour of peril.

Sir Winston Churchill

Tradition

Choices in Education

People in the United States have a **choice** between **free tax-funded public schools** or **tuition-based private schools**.

All public school systems are **required to provide** an education **free of charge** to everyone of school age. All schools, public and private, are **monitored** by the Department of Education. Educational standards and **standardized testing** decisions are **made** by state governments.

People are required **to attend** school until the age of 16–18. If a child is not attending school the parents could be in **trouble with the law**.

Education is **divided** into three **levels**: **elementary**, **junior high**, and **senior high**. **Grade** levels **vary** from area to area.

Elementary school, also known as **grade school**, is a school of the **first** six grades. The **basic subjects** of math, English and **science** are **taught.**

Junior high school is grades 5–8 **depending upon** the school structure. The basic subjects are **expanded on**. A **foreign language** is often **added**.

High school **runs** from grades 9–12. Each grade number also has a name: freshman, sophomore, junior and senior. There are a minimum number of courses students are **required to complete to receive** a high school diploma. Starting in ninth grade, grades **become** very important because they are part of a student's **official transcript**. In the last two years of high school students take standardized tests **to apply** for college. The SAT and ACT are the most common standardized tests

Post-secondary education in the United States is known as college or university. It **consists of** four years, or more, of study. Students apply to receive admission into college. Admissions **criteria** involve the grades **earned** in high school, **GPA**, and standardized test **scores**. After **finishing** a four-year degree students may continue to a more advanced degree such as a **master's degree**.

As a whole, the population of the United States is **becoming** more educated. Post-secondary education is **valued** very **highly** by American society and is one of the main determinants of class and **status**.

Prom and Homecoming

"Prom" is the **name** for a **special dance held** at the **end** of the **high school academic year**.

Traditionally the prom is a **special night** for the **junior and senior classes**. **Younger guests** may go to the prom only if their **date** is a junior or a senior. Prom is a memorable and important night for most high school students. **Some feel** that it is the most romantic **night** of their lives and the **highlight** of their senior year!

Shopping for the prom **dress** can be an event of its own. **Formal wear** is **worn** by both girls and boys. Sometimes there is a prom **theme** and the **couples** dress **according** to the theme.

The prom **festivities** generally **include dinner** and a dance. The prom is often held at the school; however, some schools **rent ballrooms** or hotels or more **unusual venues** such as a **cruise boat** to **host** prom night. A prom **king** and **queen** are **announced** and **crowned** during the night. Traditionally the prom queen and king are **chosen** by their **fellow students**. **Campaigns** are held in the **weeks before** the prom and students **cast votes** for who they want to be king and queen. The king and queen are crowned and dance together **to celebrate** their election.

Homecoming is another annual academic tradition that happens in high school and colleges. Homecoming is **largely associated** with football. People, **towns**, high schools and colleges **come together**, usually in late September or October, **to welcome** back **alumni**. The activities consist of a football game played on the school's football field, activities for students and alumni, a **parade** featuring the school's **marching band**, and the coronation of a homecoming queen and king, similar to the prom queen and king.

name: nombre
special dance: baile especial
held/to hold: se celebra/celebrar
end: final
high school: secundaria, liceo
academic year: año académico
special night: noche especial
junior and senior classes: *los dos últimos años en el sistema escolar estadounidense*
younger guests: invitados más jóvenes
date: cita
some: algunos
feel/to feel: sienten/sentir
night: noche
highlight: lo más destacado
shopping: ir de compras
dress: vestido
formal wear: traje de etiqueta
worn/to wear: usada/ usar, llevar *(ropa)*
theme: tema
couples: parejas
according: de acuerdo
festivities: festividades
include/to include: incluyen/ incluir
dinner: cena
rent/to rent: alquilan/alquilar
ballrooms: salones de baile
unusual venues: locales poco comunes
cruise boat: barco de crucero
host: ofrecer
king: rey
queen: reina
announced: anunciados
crowned: coronados
chosen/to choose: elegidos/elegir
fellow students: compañeros de estudios
campaigns: campañas
weeks: semanas
before: antes
cast votes: emitir votos
to celebrate: celebrar
largely associated: en gran parte asociado
towns: pueblos
come together: se reúnen
to welcome: dar la bienvenida
alumni: ex-alumnos
parade: desfile
marching band: banda marcial

begin/to begin: empiezan/empezar
parties: fiestas
sizes: tamaños
held/to hold: celebran/celebrar
across: a través de
gather/to gather: se reúnen/reunirse
watch/to watch: miran/mirar
part of: parte de
midnight hour: hora de medianoche
approaches/to approach: se avecina/
    avecinarse, acercarse
time zone: huso horario
able to watch: posibilidad de ver
televised: transmitida por televisión
nationally: a nivel nacional
before: antes de
brightly lit ball: pelota muy
    iluminada
begins to drop: empieza a caer
slowly: lentamente
pole: poste
perched: colocado
count down: contar de forma regresiva
seconds: segundos
reaches/to reach: alcanza/alcanzar
bottom: fondo
hug/to hug: se abraza/abrazarse
kiss/to kiss: se besa/besarse
cheers: ovaciones
heard/to hear: oyen/oír
another: otra
to sing: cantar
song: canción
stroke: campanada, aquí: al dar
    (la medianoche)
played/to play: se toca/tocar
    (una canción)
to welcome in: para recibir
literally: literalmente
means/to mean: significa/
    significar
households: hogares, familias
to spend: pasar
afternoon: tarde
watching/to watch: mirando/mirar
parade: desfile
game: juego

Traditions for the New Year

New Year's celebrations **begin** on December 31, New Year's Eve. New Year's **parties** of all **sizes** are **held across** the United States. Friends and family **gather** at home and **watch** television as **part of** the festivities. As the **midnight hour approaches** your own **time zone** you are **able to watch** New Year's celebrated all across the world.

Times Square in the heart of New York City hosts a very popular New Year's celebration and is **televised nationally**. At one minute **before** midnight, a **brightly lit ball begins to drop slowly** from a **pole perched** on one of the buildings. People begin to **count down** the **seconds** as the ball drops. When it **reaches** the **bottom**, it is the New Year. People **hug** and **kiss**, confetti falls, and **cheers** of "Happy New Year!" are **heard** everywhere.

Another New Year's tradition is **to sing** the **song** "Auld Lang Syne" at the **stroke** of midnight. This song is **played** in English-speaking countries **to welcome in** the new year. "Auld Lang Syne" **literally means** "old long ago," or "the good old days."

New Year's Day

On January 1, it is a tradition in many **households** for families and friends **to spend** the **afternoon watching** the Rose Bowl. The Tournament of Roses **parade** and the Rose Bowl football **game** are on many television sets across America.

The parade first **started** in 1890 and is held in Pasadena, California. In 1902, the parade committee **decided to add** a football game to the day's celebrations. By 1920 the **crowds outgrew** the football stands. The tournament's president **envisioned** a grand stadium and **put** his vision into action. He **built** a **new stadium** and **named** it the Rose Bowl.

Today the Tournament of Roses Parade is **more than** five miles **long** with **thousands** of people **participating, marching** in bands or **dance troops** and on **floats**. **City officials ride** in the cars **pulling** the floats and **waving** at the crowd. A celebrity is **chosen** to be the official **master** of ceremonies. The **queen** of the tournament rides on a special float **made from more than** 250,000 **flowers**.

New Year's resolutions are made on New Year's Day. Americans **write down** their resolutions and **promise to keep** them for the year **to come**. New Year's resolutions usually **include** things like **getting healthy** or **losing weight** and generally **encompass** something that **involves bettering** your **life**.

Regardless of the way the New Year is celebrated, the sentiments are the **same**. With a new year, people **hope for** a **fresh start**. They **wish** each other **good luck** and **best wishes** for the upcoming year.

started/to start: empezó/empezar
decided/to decide: decidió/decidir
to add: agregar
crowds: muchedumbre, público
outgrew/to outgrow: desbordaba/ desbordar
envisioned/to envision: se imaginó/ imaginarse
put/to put: puso/poner
built/to build: construyó/construir
new: nuevo
stadium: estadio
named/to name: llamó/llamar
more than: más de
long: de largo
thousands: miles
participating/to participate: participando/participar
marching/to march: marchando/ marchar
dance troops: grupos de danza
floats: carrozas
city officials: funcionarios de la ciudad, funcionarios municipales
ride/to ride: van/ir (en auto)
pulling/to pull: tirando de/tirar de
waving/to wave: saludando/saludar
chosen/to choose: elegida/elegir
master: maestro/a
queen: reina
made from more than: hecho de más de
flowers: flores
write down/to write down: escriben/escribir, anotar
promise/to promise: prometen/prometer
to keep: cumplir (promesa)
to come: que viene
include/to include: incluyen/incluir
getting healthy: ponerse saludable
losing weight: perder peso
encompass/to encompass: abarca/ abarcar
involves/to involve: implique/implicar
bettering: mejorar
life: vida
regardless: sin importar
same: mismos
hope for/to hope for: espera/esperar
fresh start: nuevo comienzo
wish/to wish: desean/desear
good luck: buena suerte
best wishes: mejores deseos

Going to the Chapel

Wedding traditions in the United States are **some of** the **most flexible** in the **world**. **Due to** the many religions and **ethnic backgrounds**, the wedding ceremonies and traditions can **vary widely**.

Weddings in the United States can be very elaborate, especially when it is the **bride's first** wedding. Traditionally the bride **wears** a white wedding **dress** and **veil**. It is **considered bad luck** for the **groom to see** the bride in her wedding gown **before** the wedding.

It is traditional for the bride to have a bridal shower and the groom to have a bachelor party before the wedding. During the bridal shower the bride-to-be will **receive gifts**, usually gifts **to be used** on her **honeymoon**. A bachelor party is held for the groom in the **weeks** before the wedding and is **intended** as a "final celebration" as a **single man**!

Wedding ceremonies may be religious or civil. The ceremony may **include vows written** by the bride and the groom. The vows **speak of** their **love** and promises to each other. The **newlyweds kiss** at the end of the ceremony to **seal their union.**

After the ceremony the wedding is **celebrated** at a reception. The newlyweds have their first **dance** together as **husband** and **wife**. **Toasts** are **given** by family and friends, **wishing** the **couple happiness**. The bride and the groom make the first **cut** in the **cake** together, symbolizing their **shared future**. **It is thought** of as good luck for the bride **to throw** her wedding bouquet **backwards over her shoulder** towards the **single female guests**. The one who **catches it** is **supposed to be** the next one married.

Couples who **do not wish** to have an elaborate wedding ceremony may **choose to elope**. An elopement **involves much less** preparation and is becoming more common, especially for **second** weddings. The couple is **quickly** married at the **justice of the peace**. They **may or may not invite** a small number of friends and/or family.

---

wedding: boda, casamiento
some of: algunas de
most flexible: más flexibles
world: mundo
due to: debido a
ethnic backgrounds: orígenes étnicos
vary widely: varían ampliamente
bride's: de la novia
first: primer
wears/to wear: lleva/llevar, usar
dress: vestido
veil: velo
considered: considerado
bad luck: mala suerte
groom: novio
to see: ver
before: antes
receive: recibir
gifts: regalos
to be used: para ser usados
honeymoon: luna de miel
weeks: semanas
intended: planeado, pretendido, previsto
single man: hombre soltero
include: incluir
vows: votos
written: escritos
speak of: hablan de
love: amor
newlyweds: recién casados
kiss: beso
seal/to seal: sella/sellar
their union: su unión
after: después
celebrated/to celebrate: celebra/celebrarse
dance: baile
husband: marido, esposo
wife: mujer, esposa
toasts: brindis
given/to give: hacer *(brindis)*
wishing/to wish: deseando/desear
couple: pareja
happiness: felicidad
cut: corte
cake: torta
shared future: futuro compartido
it is thought: se piensa
to throw: tirar, lanzar
backwards over her shoulder: para atrás sobre su hombro
single female guests: invitadas solteras
catches it/to catch: lo atrapa/atrapar
supposed to be: supone que es
do not wish: no desean
choose: optar por
to elope: fugarse para casarse
involves/to involve: implica/implicar
much less: mucha menos
second: segundas
quickly: rápidamente
justice of the peace: juez de paz
may or may not invite: pueden invitar o no

April Fools!

April Fool's Day is a **lighthearted holiday** that **takes place** on April 1st. It is a **time** for **playful pranks** and **practical jokes**. The history of April Fool's Day is not well **documented** or **clearly known**. There does not **seem** to be a first April Fool's Day that can be **declared** on the calendar. The **closest date** that can be **identified** as the start of this tradition was in the **late** 1500s, in France.

Today, on April 1, Americans **play tricks** on friends and **strangers alike**. Pranks **performed** on April Fool's Day **range from** simple jokes, **such as** saying, "Your **shoe's untied**!," **to** more elaborate pranks, such as **setting a roommate's alarm clock back an hour**, making them late. **School children** might **tell** a **classmate** that school has been **canceled**. Whatever the prank, the trickster **ends** the joke by **yelling**, "April Fool!"

April Fool's Day is not a **serious** holiday. Schools are not **closed**, **gifts** are not given and no one gets the day **off from work**. It's **considered** a **fun** holiday. It is also a holiday in which you must **remain** alert; you **never know** when you might be the **next** April Fool!

KNOCK-KNOCK!   Knock-Knock jokes are **well-known jokes** in the United States and a favorite "**call and answer**" **game** among **children**. They are the **best-known format** of the **pun**. **In addition** to being **silly** and fun, they are also **helpful** in children **advancing** their **language skills**. The **standard** format has five **lines**. The person **telling** the joke says "Knock, knock." The other person **answers accordingly**, and hopefully, **laughs**!

Knock, knock!	*Who's there?*
Cow go.	*Cow go who?*
Cow go moo!	

Knock, knock!	*Who's there?*
Olive	*Olive who?*
Olive you!	*(I love you!)*

lighthearted: alegre, poco seria
holiday: día festivo, fiesta
takes place: tiene lugar
time: tiempo, momento
playful: juguetonas, traviesas
pranks: bromas
practical jokes: bromas
documented: documentada
clearly: claramente
known: sabida
seem/to seem: parece/paracer
declared: declarado
closest date: fecha más cercana
identified/to identify: identificada/ identificar
late: tarde *(aquí: finales de)*
today: hoy, hoy día
play tricks: gastar bromas
strangers: extraños
alike: tanto a... como a...
performed/to perform: practicadas/ practicar *(bromas)*
range from...to: van desde...hasta
such as: tal(es) como
shoe's untied: zapato está desatado
setting...back an hour: atrasar... una hora
roommate's: del compañero de habitación
alarm clock: despertador
school children: colegiales, escolares
tell/to tell: decirle/decir
classmate: compañero de clase
canceled/to cancel: cancelada/cancelar
ends/to end: termina/terminar
yelling/to yell: gritando/gritar
serious: serio
closed/to close: cerradas/cerrar
gifts: regalos
off from work: *(día)* libre en el trabajo
considered/to consider: considera/ considerar
fun: divertidos
remain: permanecer
never: nunca
know/to know: sabes/saber
next: próximo
well-known jokes: chistes conocidos
call and answer game: juego de llamar y contestar
children: niños
best-known format: formato más conocido
pun: juego de palabras
in addition: además
silly: tontos
helpful: útiles
advancing: avanzar *(aquí: mejorar)*
language skills: aptitudes lingüísticas
standard: estándar, normal
lines: líneas
telling/to tell: que cuenta/contar
answers/to answer: contesta/contestar
accordingly: como corresponde
laughs/to laugh: se ríe/reírse

An American Christmas

The United States is **consistently referred** to as a "melting pot"—a nation of cultures and traditions **blended together**. Christmas celebrations in the U.S. are **another indication** of this melting pot. Americans **sing** Christmas carols from **England** and **decorate trees**, a tradition that came from **Germany**. Santa Claus, in a **red suit**, originated in Scandinavia. His **arrival** through the **chimney to fill stockings** is a tradition that started in the **Netherlands**. His **sleigh pulled** by **reindeer** began in Switzerland. American Christmas traditions and customs **range** from religious symbols to the **legend** of Santa Claus. The origins and history are Christian and pagan.

Regions of the United States **set aside** their **own** Christmas traditions.

- In Colorado, a **star** is **placed** on a mountain **symbolizing** the star of Bethlehem.

- In Washington, D.C., the president **presses** a button and **magically lights up** an **enormous outdoor** tree.

- In Boston, carol singing **festivities** are more famous than anywhere else in the United States.

- In Arizona, **they follow** the Mexican tradition, *Las Posadas.*

American families **gather together** for a special Christmas **meal** that **consists** of **stuffed turkey, mashed potatoes** and **gravy,** and **pumpkin pie**. The majority of Americans celebrate Christmas by **exchanging gifts** with family and friends. Children generally **believe** in Santa **until** the age of 10. They are told that Santa has a **naughty** and a **nice** list. He **checks** the list before Christmas and if you are on the naughty list you might not get any **presents** and your stocking might be **filled** with **coal**!

---

consistently: consistentemente
referred: *(se lo)* conoce
blended together: mezcladas juntas
another indication: otro indicio
sing/to sing: cantan/cantar
England: Inglaterra
decorate trees: decoran árboles
Germany: Alemania
red suit: traje rojo
arrival: llegada
chimney: chimenea
to fill: para llenar
stockings: medias, calcetines
Netherlands: los Países Bajos
sleigh: trineo
pulled/to pull: tirado/tirar
reindeer: renos
range/to range: varían/variar
legend: leyenda
set aside/to set aside: apartan/apartar
own: propias
star: estrella
placed/to place: colocada/colocar
symbolizing: simbolizando
presses/to press: aprieta/apretar
magically: mágicamente
lights up/to light up: ilumina/iluminar
enormous: enorme
outdoor: al aire libre
festivities: festividades
they follow: ellos siguen
gather together: se juntan, se reúnen
meal: comida
consists/to consist: consiste/consistir
stuffed turkey: pavo relleno
mashed potatoes: puré de papas
gravy: jugo de la carne asada
pumpkin pie: tarta de calabaza
exchanging gifts: intercambiando regalos
believe/to believe: creen/creer
until: hasta
naughty: travieso
nice: bueno
checks/to check: revisa/revisar
presents: regalos
filled/to fill: llenado/llenar
coal: carbón

Every family has different traditions during the holiday season. Some traditions are **passed on** from generation to generation. The **following** list **highlights** some traditions that are representative of American families **celebrating** Christmas.

- A Christmas Carol is a **song** or **hymn sung** during the Christmas season. Christmas Carolers can be **heard** at parties, **malls** and Christmas festivals.

- Americans **send** Christmas **cards** to their friends and family during the holiday season. Some families **include letters reviewing** the **past year** and a family photo.

- The Christmas **shopping** season officially **begins** the day **after** Thanksgiving. A Christmas shopping trip is made extra special by the Christmas decorations in all of the **stores**.

- Eggnog is a very popular holiday **drink**. It is **made** with **milk**, cream, **sugar**, **beaten eggs** and generally **flavored** with **rum** or brandy.

- **For children and grownups alike**, Christmas **cookies** may be the best Christmas tradition of all.

- Each Christmas season, stockings can be **found** throughout American homes. Children **awake** on Christmas **morning** to find their stockings full of **treats**.

- The brilliant colors and **cheer** of Christmas **lights** are a **sight to behold**. In some **neighborhoods** all of the houses **participate** in decorating their homes and **allow** people to take a **driving tour to enjoy** the lights.

Whatever your region or tradition, Christmas is one of the most celebrated and enjoyed holidays in the nation. The most important thing **to remember** during the holiday season is to make **cherished memories** with your **loved ones**. Celebrate **deep-rooted** traditions and **continue to create** new holiday traditions **to share** with your family and friends.

every: toda, cada
passed on/to pass on: transmitidas/transmitir
following: siguiente
highlights/to highlight: destaca/destacar
celebrating: celebrando
song: canción
hymn: himno
sung/to sing: cantado/cantar
heard/to hear: oídos/oír
malls: centros comerciales
send/to send: envían/enviar
cards: tarjetas
include/to include: incluyen/incluir
letters: cartas
reviewing/to review: repasando/repasar
past year: año pasado
shopping: compras
begins/to begin: empieza/empezar
after: después
stores: tiendas
drink: bebida
made: hecha
milk: leche
sugar: azúcar
beaten eggs: huevos batidos
flavored: sazonado
rum: ron
for...and...alike: tanto para... como para
children: niños
grownups: adultos
cookies: galletitas
found/to find: encontrados/encontrar
awake/to awake: se despiertan/despertarse
morning: mañana
treats: regalos
cheer: animación
lights: luces
sight to behold: vista para contemplar
neighborhoods: barrios
participate/to participate: participan/participar
allow/to allow: permiten/permitir
driving tour: paseo en coche
to enjoy: para disfrutar
whatever: cualquiera
to remember: a recordar
cherished memories: recuerdos preciados
loved ones: seres amados
deep-rooted: fuertemente enraizadas
continue/to continue: continúa/continar
to create: creando
to share: para compartir

Giving Thanks

Thanksgiving is **a time** for **giving thanks** and **sharing**. **Family members** and friends **gather together** on this day **to enjoy** a feast and **give thanks** for the many **good things** they have. In the **spirit** of sharing, **homeless shelters offer free meals** to homeless people in their communities. Thanksgiving **falls on** the fourth Thursday of November, a different **date every year**.

Almost every culture in the world **has held** celebrations of thanks for an **abundant harvest**. The American Thanksgiving holiday **began** almost 400 years **ago**. It **started** in the **early days** of the American colonies.

In 1620, a **boat sailed across** the Atlantic Ocean **to settle in** the New World. These people were **called** Pilgrims. The Pilgrims settled in what is now the state of Massachusetts. Their first **winter** was difficult. They arrived **too late** in the **season to grow** new **crops**. They had **limited food** and almost **half** of their people **died** from **disease**. When **spring arrived** the Indians **taught them** how to grow **corn**. Corn was a new food for the colonists. The Indians **showed them** other crops to grow and taught them about the **unfamiliar soil**. They showed them how and where **to hunt** and **fish**.

In the **fall** of 1621, crops of corn, **beans** and **pumpkins** were harvested. The colonists were **thankful for** the **help** from the Indians and the abundance of food. They **planned** a feast and **invited** the local Indian **chief** and several Indians. The Indians **brought deer to roast** with the **turkeys** that had been **prepared** by the colonists. The pilgrims had **learned** how **to cook** cranberries and different kinds of **squash** from the Indians and these **dishes** were also **served**.

For **years to come**, the pilgrims **continued** to celebrate the fall harvest with a feast. After the United States became an independent country, Congress **recommended** that the whole nation **set aside** one day a year for thanksgiving. George Washington **suggested** the date November 26 as Thanksgiving Day. In 1863, at the **end** of a **long civil war**, Abraham Lincoln **asked** all Americans to set aside the last Thursday in November as a day of thanksgiving.

On **dinner tables** throughout the United States, the same foods eaten at the first thanksgiving are the traditional foods **still** served today.   Turkey, corn and pumpkins are symbols that represent Thanksgiving. You will **find** many of these symbols on holiday decorations and **greeting cards**. Cranberry **sauce**, or cranberry **jelly**, was on the first Thanksgiving table and is still served today.

For millions of Americans, Thanksgiving Day traditions are **closely connected to** football. From football games in the **backyard** to **watching** the **yearly** games of the Detroit Lions and Dallas Cowboys, football is **linked with** the **holiday season**.

America's Thanksgiving Day **Parade** is also an important tradition. It was **first held** in 1924 in Detroit, Michigan. The parade **began** as a small event. Its popularity **grew** with each **passing year** and so did its **size**. In 1952 the parade **received national coverage** on TV and is to this day a very popular televised event.

The most popular parade is the Macy's Thanksgiving Day Parade. The three-hour event is held in New York City starting at 9:00 A.M. on Thanksgiving Day and is televised nationwide.

Important **features** of Thanksgiving parades are **enormous floats**, **scenes** from Broadway **plays** or TV **shows**, **gigantic balloons** of **cartoon characters**, and **marching bands**. The parade **ends** with Santa Claus's **image passing by** the **crowds**. The Thanksgiving Day parade tradition is **meant** to celebrate Thanksgiving and American traditions and **call forth** the next holiday, Christmas.

America's Favorite Sport

Football is an important part of American life. Since 1916, when the Rose Bowl game **became** a famous **annual event**, football **has developed** a national **following** of **dedicated fans**. **Visitors** to the United States can **watch** a game to **see for themselves** the **spirit** and enthusiasm Americans **feel** for this **sport**. Football is the most popular **spectator** sport in the United States. The Gallup Poll has **reported** football to be America's favorite sport every year since 1972.

Professional football developed in small **towns** of Pennsylvania and the Midwest. The National Football League (NFL), **founded** in Canton, Ohio, is the largest professional American football **league** and **consists** of thirty-two American teams.

The Super Bowl is the **biggest event** in the football season. On Super Bowl Sunday people of all ages **gather** for large parties in celebration of the big game. There is a **noticeable lack of traffic** on the **roads** as almost everyone is at home **watching** the game on TV. Traditional **food** at Super Bowl parties consists of **beer**, pizza, barbecue, and **chips and dip**. Super Bowl Sunday is the **second-largest** U.S. food **consumption** day, **following** Thanksgiving.

Tailgate parties are another tradition **associated** with football. **Some consider** the tailgate party **as much or more fun** than the actual game. Tailgating is a **pre-game** party that **takes place** in the **parking lot** or stadium where the game is held. The food is **served** and the party is held on and around the **open** tailgate of a vehicle. People still **participate even if** their vehicles do not have tailgates. Tailgate parties **range from** full **kitchens** set up in **motor homes to pick-up trucks** with **hibachi grills** to **lawn chairs** set around a **cooler** full of beer.

The **halftime show** is a very popular and important **element** of an American football game. During the **interval between** the second and third **quarters**, 20 minutes of **entertainment** is **presented** on the football field. A halftime show can consist of performances by **cheerleaders**, **dance teams**, **marching bands**, or an assortment of other performances. At high school and most college games, the bands of the two **competing** teams perform at halftime. For the Super Bowl game, an elaborate show involving famous musicians, dancers, **fireworks** and **special effects** is customary. The halftime show for the Super Bowl is a **highlight** of the event and can **cost** millions to create.

Football and cheerleading **go hand in hand**. Cheerleading **first started** at Princeton University in the 1880s. **Surprisingly**, cheerleading started as an **all-male** activity as a way **to encourage school spirit** at football games. Females started **to participate** in cheerleading in the 1920s. Today 97% of cheerleaders are female. In the 1960s, NFL teams began **to organize** professional cheerleading teams. The Dallas Cowboys Cheerleaders **gained** the **spotlight** with their **revealing outfits** and **sophisticated** dance **moves** first **seen** at the 1976 Super Bowl. This **caused** the **image** of cheerleaders to permanently **change**, as many other teams began **to copy** them. The Dallas Cowboys Cheerleaders are one of the most famous cheerleading teams in the world.

Marching bands are part of every football game. At college football games they play the college **fight song**s. College fight songs are songs **written** specifically for that college team. In professional and **amateur** sports, fight songs are a popular way for fans **to cheer** for their team. Fight songs are a **time-honored** tradition. In **singing** a fight song, fans **feel** like they are **part of** the team.

The **true spirit** of a football game **can only be felt** by **attending** a **live** game. **Whether** it's a high school, college or professional game, you will feel part of this American tradition and part of America's favorite sport —football!

The National Pastime

beloved: amadas
since: desde
called/to call: llamado/llamar
national pastime: pasatiempo nacional
appeals/to appeal: atrae/atraer
wide age range: amplia gama de edades
learning: aprendiendo
to catch: atrapar
ball: pelota
lifelong fans: aficionados de toda la vida
strong: fuertes
ties: lazos
unite/to unite: unen/unir
developed/to develop: desarrollado/desarrollar
eating: comer
peanuts: maní
Cracker Jacks: *palomitas de maíz y maní recubierto en caramelo*
chants: cánticos, consignas
cheers: vítoreos, ovaciones
stadium: estadio
bring/to bring: traen/traer
gloves: guantes
hope/to hope: esperan/esperar
catch: atrapar
foul balls: pelotas extraviadas
wear/to wear: visten/vestir
team jerseys: jerseys del equipo
pride: orgullo
player: jugador
away from: lejos de
continue/to continue: continúan/continuar
trading: intercambiando
baseball cards: tarjetas de béisbol
collecting: coleccionando
autographs: autógrafos
joining: uniéndose a
fan clubs: clubes de fans
broken up/to break up: dividida/dividir, separar
leagues: ligas
season: temporada
played: jugadas
advance/to advance: avanzan/avanzar
begins/to begin: empieza/empezar
first: primera
next round: siguiente ronda
playoffs: eliminatorias
declared/to declare: declarado/declarar
chance: oportunidad
to become: de convertirse
grand finale: gran final
common social ground: tema social de interés común
strangers: extraños, desconocidos
love: amor
turns/to turn: vuelve/volver
friends: amigos
rich: rica
legends: leyendas

Baseball is one of America's most **beloved** traditions. **Since** 1856, The United States has **called** baseball its "**national pastime**."

Baseball **appeals** to a **wide age range**—from children just **learning** how **to catch** a **ball** to **lifelong fans** of the game. **Strong ties unite** Americans and baseball. Rituals and customs have **developed** from America's personal connection to the game, from **eating** hot dogs, **peanuts**, and **Cracker Jacks** to **chants** and **cheers** in the **stadium**.

At the ballpark, many **bring** their own **gloves** and **hope** to **catch foul balls**. Some fans **wear team jerseys** with **pride** for their favorite **player**. **Away from** the stadium, the traditions **continue** by **trading baseball cards**, **collecting autographs**, and **joining fan clubs**.

American major league baseball is **broken up** into two **leagues**, the American League and the National League. The baseball **season** is 162 games, **played** from April through September. The best teams in these 162 games **advance** to the post-season. The post-season **begins** the **first** week in October with the division championship series. The first team to win three games advances to the **next round** of the **playoffs**. The first team in each league to win four games is **declared** league champion, and advances to the World Series for the **chance to become** world champion. Called the Fall Classic, the World Series is the **grand finale** of the sport's postseason and takes place in October. The first World Series was held between Boston of the American League and Pittsburgh of the National League in 1903.

Baseball is more than just a game. It is part of American culture and a **common social ground** between **strangers**. At baseball games all across the nation the **love** for this sport **turns** strangers into **friends**. Baseball is an American tradition **rich** in **legends** and history.

Famous Names in Baseball

Babe Ruth is **regarded** by many historians and fans as the greatest baseball player of **all time**. He was the first player **to hit** 60 **home runs** in a season and the only player to hit 3 home runs **twice** in a World Series game.

Hank Aaron played from 1954 to 1976. He is **best known** for **breaking** Babe Ruth's **long-standing** record of 714 home runs in a **career** with his own record of 755. He is regarded by many as the greatest **hitter** of all time. He is the first player **to reach** 3,000 hits and 500 home runs and the **only** player to hit at least 30 home runs in 15 seasons.

In 1998 Mark McGuire and Sammy Sosa **battled it out** for **most** home runs in a season with McGuire **winning** with 69 to Sosa's 66.

In 2001 Barry Bonds hit the most home runs in one season with 73 home runs. On August 7, 2007, Bonds hit his 756th home run, breaking the record held for 33 years by Hank Aaron.

Baseball **Lingo**

Another tradition **associated** with baseball is the **language** of baseball. Paul Dickson **says** in his introduction to *The New Dickson Baseball Dictionary*, "The influence of baseball on American English is **stunning** and **strong**. **No other sport has contributed** so richly to American English as baseball."

Listed below are some American idioms that **derived** from baseball lingo. They have **dual meanings**, phrases **used** in and out of the game.

1. curveball — A **surprise**. "She really **threw** me a curveball." *The curveball is a **pitch** in baseball **designed to fool** the **batter**.*
2. **drop** the **ball** — To **fail** in one's responsibilities, make an error, or **miss** an opportunity.
3. **play** ball — To **get going**, or **to start**. *Before every baseball game, the **umpire shouts** "play ball" to start the game.*
4. **cover** one's bases; cover all the bases — **Ensure safety**. *In baseball, a player covers a base by **standing close** to it.*

The American Flag

many: muchos
symbolizes/to symbolize: simboliza/simbolizar
freedom: libertad
pride: orgullo
country: país
public: público
government: gobierno
take/to take: toman/tomar
seriously: seriamente, con seriedad
laws: leyes
regulations: reglamentos
amended/to amend: enmendadas/enmendar
documented/to document: documentadas/documentar
rules: reglas
customs: costumbres
etiquette: etiqueta
set forth/to set forth: expuestas/exponer
pertaining to: referente a
display: exposición
included: incluidas
cover: cubrir
ceilings: techos
folded: doblada
write: escribir
ships: barcos
lower: bajar
slightly: ligeramente
greeting/to greet: saludan/saludar
each other: el uno al otro
otherwise: de otra forma
customary: costumbre
fly: izar
daily: diariamente
meant/to mean: significa/significar
demonstrate: demostrar
loyalty: lealtad
honors/to honor: honra/honrar
served/to serve: sirvieron/servir
wars: guerras
died/to die: murieron/morir
also called: también llamada
pieces: piezas
fabric: tela
needed/to need: necesitan/necesitar
to complete: para completar
alternating: alternadas
stripes: rayas
stars: estrellas
background: fondo
represent/to represent: representan/representar
states of the Union: estados de la Unión
seamstress: costurera
credited/to credit: atribuye/atribuir
sewed/to sew: cosió/coser

For **many** Americans the American flag **symbolizes freedom** and **pride** in their **country**. The American **public** and the American **government** **take** the flag very **seriously**.

National flag **laws** and **regulations** were **amended** and **documented** in 1976. **Rules**, **customs** and **etiquette** were **set forth pertaining to** the **display** and use of the flag. **Included** in the regulations are such rules as the national flag cannot **cover** a monument or any **ceilings**. It must not be **folded** while being displayed. No one should **write** on an American flag. **Ships** can **lower** their flags **slightly** in **greeting each other**, but **otherwise** should not be lowered for any other object or person.

It is **customary** to **fly** the flag on national holidays, and many people fly the flag **daily** from their homes. Flying the flag is **meant** to **demonstrate** patriotism and **loyalty** to the United States. The flag flown on Memorial Day and Veterans Day **honors** the men and women who **served** in **wars** and in honor of those who **died** during war.

Also called "Stars and Stripes," or "Old Glory," the American flag is one of the most complicated flags in the world. Sixty four **pieces** of **fabric** are **needed to complete** its construction. The flag has 13 red and white **alternating stripes** and 50 **stars** on a blue **background**. The stripes **represent** the original 13 **states of the Union**. The 50 stars represent each of the 50 states. Betsy Ross, who was a **seamstress**, is **credited** as the American woman who **sewed** the first American flag.

In 1949, President Harry S. Truman **proclaimed** June 14 as Flag Day. Flag Day celebrates the adoption of the flag of the United States. The President **announces** the commemoration **each year**, and **encourages** all Americans to display the flag. Individual states **determine** how they will observe the day. Pennsylvania is the **only** state that declares Flag Day a **public holiday**.

The Pledge of Allegiance is an **oath of allegiance** to the United States as **represented** by its national flag. It is regularly **recited** at public events, and public school children across the nation recite The Pledge of Allegiance **in front of** the flag every **morning.**

The Pledge of Allegiance was **written** by author and **Baptist minister** Francis Bellamy. It **appeared** in the popular children's **magazine** *Youth's Companion* in 1892. The **owners** of *Youth's Companion* were **selling** flags to schools, and asked Bellamy to write something for their **advertising campaign**. The Pledge was **published** in the September 8th issue. A few **changes** were made to the pledge **over** the years. The current Pledge of Allegiance reads: I pledge allegiance to the flag of the United States of America, and to the republic for which it stands, one nation under God, indivisible, with liberty and justice for all.

During the War of 1812 lawyer Francis Scott Key was **transporting** a prisoner **abroad** a **ship** when he **saw** an American flag flying in Baltimore **Harbor**. The flag **inspired** him to write a **poem**. This poem is "The Star Spangled Banner," the national **anthem** of the United States. The **actual** flag that inspired the song now **hangs** in the Museum of American History in Washington, D.C. "The Star-Spangled Banner" was **officially made** the national anthem by Congress in 1931.

The "Star-Spangled Banner" is sung at large public **gatherings** and at **sporting events**. When the song is **performed** in public, it is customary for American citizens **to stand** and **face** the flag while **placing** their **right hand over** their **heart**. This **formality** also **applies** to the Pledge of Allegiance. Men are encouraged **to remove** their **hats** during the performance.

Trick or Treat

In the **evening** of October 31, if you **take a walk down** a **neighborhood street you might see pirates**, **ghosts**, **princesses** and **witches**! But **don't be alarmed**, these "ghosts" are **costumed children knocking** on their neighbors' doors. When the door **opens** the children **hold out a bag** and **yell**, "Trick or Treat." They are **hoping** their **bags** will be full of **candy** by the **end** of the night. Halloween is a **popular holiday** in the United States for **young and old alike**.

Halloween parties or **masquerade** parties for adults are common. At children's parties traditional **games** are **played**. One of the most popular games is "bobbing for apples." One child **at a time** has to get apples from a **tub of water without using hands**. They do this by **sinking** their **face** into the water and **attempting to bite** the apple. **Typical homemade** Halloween **treats include dried pumpkin seeds**, caramel apples and **popcorn balls**.

Halloween **started** as a celebration connected with ghosts and **evil spirits**. Witches **flying on broomsticks**, **black cats**, ghosts, goblins and skeletons have **since evolved** as symbols of Halloween. Black and orange are the traditional Halloween colors. In the weeks before October 31, Americans **decorate windows** of houses and schools with **silhouettes** of the various Halloween symbols. Pumpkins are another main symbol of Halloween. **Carving** pumpkins into "jack-o-lanterns" is a Halloween custom that came from Ireland. Today jack-o'-lanterns in the windows of a house on Halloween night **let** children **know** that there are **goodies waiting** if they knock and say "Trick or Treat!"

Remembrance and Honor

Memorial Day, **originally** called Decoration Day, is **observed** on the **last** Monday in May. Memorial Day is a day of **remembrance** for those who were **killed** in **war defending** the United States.

Waterloo, N.Y. was **officially declared** the **birthplace** of Memorial Day. However it's **difficult to confirm** the exact origins of the day. Most people **agree** that it is not important where or when it **first started**. What is important is that Memorial Day was **established**. Memorial Day is about **coming together** to honor those who **gave** their lives for their country. The day is **celebrated** with **parades**, memorial **speeches** and ceremonies, and the decoration of **graves** with **flowers** and **flags**. On Memorial Day, the President or Vice President gives a speech and **lays** a **wreath** on the Tomb of the Unknown Soldier at Arlington Cemetery in Washington, D.C.

Veterans Day was originally called Armistice Day. It is observed **either** on November 11th **or** on the fourth Monday of October. Veterans Day **honors** the men and women who **served** during wars with the U.S. **armed forces**. On November 11, 1918, a **treaty** was **signed bringing** World War I **to an end**. November 11, 1919 was **set aside** as Armistice Day in the United States, to remember the sacrifices that men and women made during World War I. In 1954 the holiday was **changed** to Veterans Day and **declared** a National holiday.

Americans still **give thanks** for **peace** on Veterans Day. There are ceremonies and speeches and, in some towns, parades. Throughout the day, many Americans **observe** a moment of silence, remembering those who **fought** for peace.

American Veterans have established **support groups** such as the American Legion and Veterans of Foreign Wars. These groups **sell paper poppies** made by **disabled** veterans to **raise funds** for their **charitable activities.** The **poppy** is a **bright** red flower that became a symbol of World War I after a **bloody battle took place** in a **field** of poppies in Belgium.

originally: originalmente
observed: observa *(aquí: conmemora)*
last: último
remembrance: recuerdo
killed/to kill: muertos/matar
war: guerra
defending/to defend: defendiendo/ defender
officially: oficialmente
declared/to declare: declarado/declarar
birthplace: lugar de nacimiento
difficult to confirm: difícil de confirmar
agree/to agree: están de acuerdo/estar de acuerdo
first started: empezó por primera vez
established/to establish: establecido/ establecer
coming together: reunirse
gave/to give: dieron/dar
celebrated/to celebrate: celebra/ celebrar
parades: desfiles
speeches: discursos
graves: tumbas
flowers: flores
flags: banderas
lays/to lay: coloca/colocar, poner
wreath: corona *(de flores)*
either ... or ...: ya sea ... o
honors/to honor: honra/honrar
served/to serve: sirvieron/servir
armed forces: fuerzas armadas
treaty: tratado
signed/to sign: firmado/firmar
bringing...to an end: poniendo fin a
set aside/to set aside: reservado/reservar
changed/to change: cambiado/ cambiar
declared/to declare: declarado/declarar
give thanks: dan gracias, agradecen
peace: paz
observe/to observe: observan/observar *(aquí: guardan)*
fought/to fight: pelearon/pelear
support groups: grupos de apoyo
sell/to sell: venden/vender
paper poppies: amapolas de papel
disabled: discapacitados
raise funds: juntar fondos
charitable activities: actividades benéficas
poppy: amapola
bright: brillante
bloody: sangrienta
battle: batalla
took place/to take place: tuvo lugar/ tener lugar
field: campo

Test Your Comprehension

Choices in Education, page 44

1. ¿Hasta qué edad debe asistir a la escuela la gente en los Estados Unidos?

2. Los Estados Unidos proveen educación gratis en los tres primeros niveles escolares. ¿Cuáles son esos niveles?

3. La educación terciaria se conoce como "college" o universidad. ¿De cuántos años consiste?

Traditions for the New Year, page 46

1. ¿Cuándo comienzan las celebraciones de Año Nuevo?

2. ¿Qué ciudad recibe el Año Nuevo con una pelota iluminada descendiendo mientras la multitud cuenta en forma regresiva?

3. ¿Qué partido de fútbol americano se mira en el día de Año Nuevo en los Estados Unidos?

April Fools!, page 49

1. ¿Qué día de abril es el "Día de los Inocentes"?

2. Según lo que sabemos, ¿en qué país comenzó esta tradición?

3. ¿Qué pasa en el "Día de los Inocentes"?

An American Christmas, page 50

1. Menciona algunos de los países europeos que trajeron la celebración de Navidad a los Estados Unidos.

2. ¿Cuál es una bebida festiva popular?

Examina tu comprensión

Giving Thanks, page 52

1. ¿Cuándo se observa el Día de Acción de Gracias en los Estados Unidos?

2. ¿Quiénes fueron invitados al primer Día de Acción de Gracias en 1621?

America's Favorite Sport, page 54

1. El fútbol americano se convirtió en una parte importante de la vida estadounidense en 1916 cuando un famoso evento anual se desarrolló. ¿Cuál fue el evento?

2. ¿Dónde se fundó la Liga Nacional de Fútbol Americano?

3. ¿Cuáles son las animadoras más famosas?

The National Pastime, page 56

1. ¿Qué rituales y costumbres se han desarrollado a partir de la conexión de Estados Unidos con el béisbol?

2. ¿Qué gran jugador de béisbol fue el primero en conseguir 60 jonrones en una temporada?

The American Flag, page 58

1. ¿Qué simboliza la bandera estadounidense?

2. ¿Quién escribió el "Juramento de Lealtad"?

Remembrance and Honor, page 61

1. ¿Cómo se llamaba el Día de los Caídos originalmente?

2. ¿Por qué se celebra el Día de los Caídos?

The more you praise and celebrate your life,
the more there is in life to celebrate.

Oprah Winfrey

Celebration

Luck of the Irish

Irish vocabulary list:

Irish: irlandés
brought/to bring: trajeron/traer
celebrating: celebrar
first: primera
took place/to take place: tuvo lugar/ tener lugar
during: durante
organized/to organize: organizó/ organizar
first: primer
parade: desfile
today: hoy, hoy en día
ethnicities: etnicidades
wear/to wear: llevan/llevar *(puesto)*
green-colored clothing: ropas de color verde
pin/to pin: sujetan/sujetar, prender con alfileres
shamrock: trébol
shirt: camisa
caught/to catch: descubiertos/ descubrir, atrapar
pinched/to pinch: pellizcados/pellizcar
include/to incluye: incluyen/incluir
enjoying: disfrutar
folk music: música folclórica
food: comida
consuming: consumir
quantities: cantidades
beer: cerveza
dyed green: teñida de verde
has become/to become: se ha convertido/convertirse
largest: más grande
world: mundo
unique: única
coloring: teñir
river: río
started/to start: empezó/empezar
pounds: libras
added/to add: agregadas/agregar
stayed/to stay: permaneció/ permanecer
week: semana
still: aún
continues/to continue: continúa/ continuar
heritage: patrimonio
wonderful way: maravillosa manera
to honor: de honrar
rich: rica

Irish immigrants **brought** the tradition of **celebrating** Saint Patrick's Day to the United States. The **first** U.S. celebration of Saint Patrick's Day **took place** in 1737 in Boston, Massachusetts. **During** this first celebration The Irish Society of Boston **organized** the **first** Saint Patrick's Day **Parade** on March 17.

Today, Americans of all **ethnicities** celebrate Saint Patrick's Day on March 17. Many people **wear green-colored clothing** or **pin** a **shamrock** to their **shirt**. Traditionally, those who are **caught** not wearing green on Saint Patrick's Day are **pinched**. The most common traditions on Saint Patrick's Day **include enjoying** Irish **folk music** and **food,** and **consuming** large **quantities** of Irish **beer**, often **dyed green**.

Parades are a big part of the Saint Patrick's Day celebration. The New York parade **has become** the **largest** Saint Patrick's Day parade in the **world**.

The city of Chicago has a very **unique** Saint Patrick's Day tradition of **coloring** the **river** water green. This tradition **started** in 1962 when 100 **pounds** of green vegetable dye were **added** to the river, and the river water **stayed** green for a **week**. The tradition **still continues** today!

Irish-American **heritage** has become an important part of American culture. Saint Patrick's Day celebrations in the United States are a **wonderful way** for people **to honor** Irish heritage and celebrate its **rich** culture and traditions.

Groundhog Day

Groundhog Day, February 2nd, is a **whimsical holiday** in the United States. It is the day that the groundhog **comes out** of his **hole** after a **long winter sleep to look for** his **shadow**.

If he **sees** his shadow, he **regards it** as an **omen** of six more **weeks** of **bad weather** and **returns** to his hole.

If the day is **cloudy** and he doesn't see his shadow, he takes it as a **sign** of **spring** and **stays above ground**.

The **first** official Groundhog Day was **announced** on February 2, 1886 in Punxsutawney, Pennsylvania, with a **proclamation** by the **newspaper's editor**, Clymer Freas: "Today is Groundhog Day and **up to the time** of **going to press** the **beast has not seen** its shadow."

The **legendary** first Groundhog Day celebration was made the **following year** by a group of **spirited** groundhog **hunters** who **called themselves** "The Punxsutawney Groundhog Club." Clymer, a member of the club, used his editorial **clout to name the one and only** official **weather predicting** groundhog, Phil, the Punxsutawney groundhog.

Today a trip to the Punxutawney Groundhog Day celebration is a **weekend** of **action-packed** events **including trivia contests**, **dances**, Groundhog Day **weddings**, music, **food**, **fun** and **games**. **If you happen** to be celebrating a **birthday** on February 2nd, then you are **invited to join** others who **share** the special day with Phil the groundhog and **receive** a **free souvenir**.

groundhog: marmota
whimsical holiday: día de fiesta caprichoso
comes out/to come out: sale/salir
hole: agujero
long winter sleep: largo sueño invernal
to look for: para buscar
shadow: sombra
sees/to see: ve/ver
regards it: a considera
omen: presagio
weeks: semanas
bad weather: mal tiempo
returns/to return: vuelve/volver
cloudy: nuboso
sign: singo
spring: primavera
stays/to stay: se queda/quedarse
above: sobre
ground: suelo, tierra, superficie
first: primer
announced/to announce: anunciado/ anunciar
proclamation: proclamación
newspaper's editor: director del periódico
up to the time: hasta el momento
going to press: del cierre de la edición
beast: bestia
has not seen: no ha visto
legendary: legendaria
following year: año siguiente
spirited: enérgicos
hunters: cazadores
called themselves: se llamaban a ellos mismos
clout: influencia
to name: para nombrar
the one and only: el único, el irrepetible
weather predicting: que predice el tiempo
weekend: fin de semana
action-packed: lleno de acción
including: incluyendo
trivia contests: competencias de preguntas y respuestas
dances: bailes
weddings: casamientos
food: comida
fun: diversión
games: juegos
if you happen: si por casualidad tú
birthday: cumpleaños
invited/to invite: invitado/invitar
to join: a unirte
share/to share comparten/compartir
receive: recibir
free souvenir: recuerdo gratis

Powwows

A powwow is a **gathering** of North America's **indigenous people**. The word powwow is **derived from** a **term** which **referred to** a gathering of **medicine men** and **spiritual leaders**. The powwow is North America's **oldest** public festival. Native Americans have celebrated with seasonal ceremonies of **feasting**, **dancing**, **singing** and **drumming**. Originally powwows were **planned** around **seasonal changes**, but as non-Native people **interacted** with the Native, customs were **altered**.

Typically, a powwow consists of people **meeting** to dance, sing and socialize. Native American and non-Native American **alike** are **invited to attend**. A powwow always **begins** with the **grand entry** of the **eagle feather standard**. All **spectators remove** their **hats** and **stand** as a **sign of respect**. The standard is **followed by** the tribal **chiefs** and the **esteemed village elders**, then by a procession of all of the dancers until the entire arena is **filled with** Indian dancers **adorned** in **colorful** and elaborate **costumes**.

The annual Denver Powwow in March begins the season of pow-wows. In 1990, it **attracted** thirty-thousand people, **half of whom** were not Native Americans. In the Denver Coliseum different tribes sing songs that have been **passed down** for **thousands of years**. They are **accompanied by** the **beat** of a large drum, played by five to ten drummers. Dancers of different tribes **show** their **skills**. Dancers with **fancy shawls look like** delicate **flying birds** as they **raise** their **cloth-covered arms to the beat of** the drums. **Grass dancers** wear costumes of **brightly-colored yarn**.

Native American culture **comes alive** at the Gathering of Nations powwow in Albuquerque, New Mexico. Over 3,000 Native American dancers and singers representing more than 500 tribes from Canada and the United States **gather together** in April at North America's **biggest** powwow. The Indian Traders **Market** is also part of the celebration and **offers** a very special **shopping** experience and exhibition of Native American **artifacts**. Over 800 artists, **crafters**, and **traders** place their **wares** on **display** and **for sale**.

One of the **longest-running contest** powwows in the country is held each year in North Dakota. The United Tribes International Powwow typically **attracts** 800 dancers, more than two dozen drum groups, and over 15,000 spectators. Held annually since 1969, the **four-day** event is a large **outdoor** powwow that takes place at the **end** of the **summer season**.

Powwows **mean** different **things** to different people. They are **still religious** or **war** celebrations, but **themes** and **goals** have **changed with the times**. Now **instead of giving thanks** to their **gods** for a war victory, Indians **honor** those of their tribes who have **served in** the American **armed forces**. **Young people return** from the bigger cities **to learn** traditional dances and songs **in order to keep** their heritage **alive**. People who are not Native Americans are **encouraged to participate** in the activities. **One thing** is **obvious** at every powwow: they are **true** community events. The tribal elders are always **held in high esteem** and the children are **cherished**. Family, tribe and **friendship** are **extolled**. Everyone is welcomed in a **spirit** of **peace** and **friendship**.

comes alive/to come alive: se anima/animarse
gather together: se reúnen
biggest: más grande
market: mercado
offers/to offer: ofrece/ofrecer
shopping: de compras
artifacts: artefactos
crafters: artesanos
traders: comerciantes
wares: mercancías
display: en exhibición
for sale: para la venta
longest-running: de más larga duración
contest: concurso
attracts/to attract: atrae/atraer
four-day: de cuatro días *(de duración)*
outdoor: al aire libre
end: final
summer season: temporada de verano
mean/to mean: significan/significar
things: cosas
still: todavía
religious: religiosas
war: bélicas
themes: temas
goals: objetivos
changed with the times: cambiado con los tiempos
instead of giving thanks: en vez de dar gracias
gods: dioses
honor/to honor: honran/honrar
served in/to serve in: servido en/servir en
armed forces: fuerzas armadas
young people: la gente joven
return/to return: vuelve/volver
to learn: para aprender
in order to keep... alive: para mantener... viva
encouraged to participate: se les anima a participar
one thing: una cosa
obvious: obvia
true: verdaderos
held in high esteem: mantenidos en alta estima
cherished/to cherish: amados/amar
friendship: amistad
extolled/to extol: ensalzados/ensalzar, alabar
spirit: espíritu
peace: paz
friendship: amistad

Seasonal Celebrations

In addition to the traditional holidays celebrated in the United States, **regional holidays** have **originated from** the **seasons**, geography and **climate** of the different parts of the **country.**

In the **northeastern states**, the **main** attractions are **festivals** that **welcome** the **arrival** of **autumn** and the **leaves changing colors**. As the leaves on the **trees** begin **to turn** red, orange and yellow people **come from all over** the U.S. to see the **spectacular** and colorful **foliage**. Warner, New Hampshire **holds** a Fall Foliage Festival which **offers** a **wood-chopping contest** and an **auction**. Vermont welcomes tourists who **drive** along the **scenic mountain roads to view** the impressive colors of the leaves.

The leaves turn color **later** in Bedford, Pennsylvania. In October the **townspeople** celebrate the fall foliage by **demonstrating ways** of **cooking** that have been **handed down** to them by their ancestors.

Winters are **long** and **cold** in many **midwestern** states, so winter festivals have become events for people **to get out of** the **house** and **socialize**. In St. Paul, Minnesota, the Winter Carnival **hosts ice skating shows**, ice **fishing** competitions and **snowmobile races.** In Houghton Lake, Michigan, a winter festival called Tip-Up-Town USA offers a contest for the **best sculpture carved in ice.**

In Washington, **spring** is **welcomed in** with a **Daffodil** Festival. A **parade** of **floats rides through town** made from these brilliant yellow flowers. Oregon **boasts** a **rose** festival in Portland, where bands play music in a parade of **flowers** and floats. Aspen, Colorado holds an annual summer Music Festival where musicians of classical and contemporary music **perform** and **teach classes**. Santa Barbara, California **pays tribute to** the **early settlers** who **came from** Spain by performing **historical plays during** the Old Spanish Days in August.

Spring in the southwest **finds** the townspeople of Okeene, Oklahoma **catching snakes** in the Rattlesnake Roundup. In Houston, Texans come to the Astrodome to see **cowboys ride horses** and **rope cattle** during the Livestock Show and Rodeo. Visitors **watch** the Hopi Indians **carry on** their strong tradition of **rain dancing**, a combination of dancing and **prayer to invoke rain** in a **hot**, **dry** August.

Alaska and Hawaii have climates different **from each other** and the rest of the country. Nome, Alaska has **daylight** almost **twenty-four hours a day** in June, so **midnight baseball games** and raft races are the main events in the Midnight Sun Festival. In Kodiak, a King Crab Festival is held in May during **crab harvesting season**. Hawaii is **warm year round,** and flower and **sun** festivals were held there **even before** it became a state.

These are a **small** representation of the **hundreds** of holidays and celebrations observed throughout the United States. Each state **has its own** individual history and people, and the **right** to celebrate its own tradition. **But one thing is certain**—all Americans **welcome you** to celebrate **with them**!

spring: primavera
welcomed in: bienvenida
daffodil: narciso
parade: desfile
floats: carrozas
rides through town: pasa a través del pueblo
boasts/to boast: ostenta/ostentar
rose: rosa
flowers: flores
perform/to perform: intepretan/ interpretar (*música*)
teach/to teach: enseñan/enseñar
classes: clases
pays tribute to: rinde tributo a
early settlers: primeros colonos
came from: vinieron desde
historical plays: obras de teatro históricas
during: durante
finds/to find: encuentra/encontrar
catching snakes: atrapando serpientes
cowboys: vaqueros
ride horses: montar a caballo
rope cattle: enlazar ganado (con una cuerda)
watch/to watch: ven/ver, mirar
carry on: mantienen, continúan
rain dancing: danza de la lluvia
prayer: rezo, plegaria
to invoke rain: para invocar a la lluvia
hot: caliente
dry: seco
from each other: uno del otro
daylight: luz diurna
twenty-four hours a day: veinticuatro horas al día
midnight baseball games: juegos de béisbol a la medianoche
raft races: carreras de balsas
crab harvesting season: temporada de recoger cangrejos
warm: cálido
year round: todo el año
sun: sol
even before: aun antes
small: pequeña
hundreds: cientos
has its own: tiene su propia
right: derecho
but one thing is certain: pero una cosa es cierta
welcome you: te dan la bienvenida
with them: con ellos

lobsters: langostas
potatoes: papas
regional food specialities:
  especialidades gastronómicas regionales
worth/to be worth: merecen/merecer
big and small: grandes y pequeños
towns: pueblos
hold/to hold: celebran/celebrar, tener
cooking competitions: concursos de
  cocina
all types: todo tipo
one thing in common: una cosa en
  común
enjoy/to enjoy disfruta/disfrutar
flavor: sabor
read about: leer sobre
craziest: más locas
tastiest: más sabrosas
avocados: aguacates
used to create: utilizados para crear
phenomenon: fenómeno
feeds/to feed: alimenta/alimentar
hungry: hambrienta
started: empezado
third-largest: tercero más grande
producer: productor
free...to enter: entrada gratis
competition: concurso
best: mejor
recipes: recetas
ice cream: helado
photography contest: concurso de
  fotografía
anything made with: cualquier cosa
  hecha con
goes: se acepta, es válido
heritage: patrimonio, herencia
local: local, de la localidad
chef: chef, cocinero
cooks/to cook: cocina/cocinar
help of: ayuda de
largest: más grande
measures/to measure: mide/medir
feet: pies
diameter: diámetro
stone-ground corn: maíz molido
  en piedra
gallons: galones
vegetable oil: aceite vegetal
red chili sauce: salsa de chile rojo
chopped onions: cebollas picadas
grated cheese: queso rallado
since: desde
polished off: se zamparon,
  despacharon, acabaron con
cold beer: cerveza fría
make ... complete: completa

Flavor of America

From Maine **lobsters** to the **potatoes** of Idaho, America's **regional food specialtie**s are always **worth** celebrating. **Big** and **small towns** across America **hold cooking competitions** and celebrations of **all types** with **one thing in common**—food! **Enjoy** the **flavor** of America as you **read about** a few of the **craziest** and **tastiest** food celebrations throughout the United States.

AVOCADO FESTIVAL

Over 2000 **avocados** are **used to create** this **phenomenon** that **feeds** a crowd of 12,000 **hungry** people. **Started** in 1987 because Santa Barbara County is the **third-largest** avocado **producer** in the country, the Avocado Festival is **free** for all **to enter.** There is a competition for the **best** guacamole and various other **recipes**, including avocado **ice cream!** There's also a **photography contest** and pop art show, where **anything made with** an avocado **goes**.

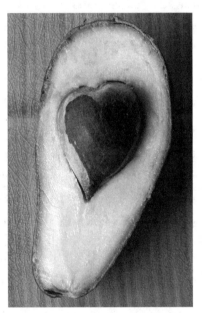

WHOLE ENCHILADA FIESTA

The city of Las Cruces, New Mexico celebrates its **heritage** every year when **local chef** Roberto Estrada **cooks** (with the **help of** eleven sous chefs) the world's **largest** enchilada. The enchilada **measures** over 30 **feet** in **diameter.** The ingredients are: 750 pounds of **stone-ground corn,** 175 **gallons** of **vegetable oil,** 75 gallons of **red chili sauce,** 50 pounds of **chopped onions,** and 175 pounds of **grated cheese.** Every year **since** 1980, over 70,000 hungry people have **polished off** the whole enchilada over the 3-day event. **Cold beer** and mariachi music **make** the event **complete.**

THE CRAWFISH CAPITAL OF THE WORLD

Celebrate **crawfish** in the crawfish capitol of the world: Bayou Teche, Louisana. Since 1959, the **first weekend** in May **brings** people, **crazy about** crawfish, **together to join** in the festivities. Enjoy crawfish **served any way** you can **imagine**: **boiled**, **fried**, etouffee, hot dogs, jambalaya, **pies**, bisque, gumbo, and the **list goes on**. **Make sure** you **stick around** for the crawfish **races** and the crawfish **eating contest**. The **winning crustacean** of the race is always **mounted** and **framed** for posterity. Other popular activities during this event include cooking contests, **fiddle** and **accordion** music, a dance contest, and the **crowning** of the Crawfish **Queen** and **King**.

NAPA VALLEY MUSTARD FESTIVAL

Napa Valley is a **wonderful place to visit** and **wine tasting feels like** a celebration any time of year! The months of February and March are an **especially lovely time** to visit **to partake in** the celebrations **surrounding** the Napa Valley **Mustard** Festival. **Fields, vineyards**, and **hillsides** vibrant with **wild** mustard **in bloom provide** a **breathtaking backdrop** during this event. **If** you have **never experienced** the Mustard Festival **you are in for a visual and culinary treat.**

SAY CHEESE!

Each year the town of Little Chute, Wisconsin celebrates the great Wisconsin Cheese Festival **to honor** one of their **largest exports**—cheese. The town **may be little** but its cheese production is **huge, producing two billion** pounds, or 25% of the **nation's** cheese per year.

The Great Wisconsin Cheese Festival is a three-day event the first weekend in June. The festival is a **family event** that **features** music, the Big Cheese parade, cheese tasting, a cheese **carving** demonstration, a cheese eating contest, **games** and entertainment.

Earth Day

In 1962 Gaylord Nelson, a United States **senator** from Wisconsin, became **concerned about** the **state** of the **environment**. Over the next eight years he **turned** his concerns into a **solution** and **called for** an environmental **teach-in**, or Earth Day, to be **held** on April 22, 1970. He **wrote letters** to all of the **colleges** and **newspapers urging** people **to join together** on this special day **to teach** everyone about the **things** that **needed changing** in our environment. Over 20 million people **participated** that year, and Earth Day is now **observed** each year on April 22.

Earth Day became very popular in the United States and **later around** the world. The first Earth Day had **participants** and **celebrants** in two **thousand** colleges and universities, ten thousand primary and secondary **schools**, and **hundreds** of communities across the United States. The **focus** of the first Earth Day was to *"**bring together** Americans **out into** the **spring sunshine** for **peaceful demonstrations** in favor of environmental **reform**."*

Earth Day is now celebrated in communities worldwide. Celebrations include educational **fairs** and **festivals** that **promote** environmental **awareness**. People **gather** together to **plant trees** and participate in **beach** and **river cleanups**.

Many important **laws were passed** by the Congress **thanks to continued efforts** of the 1970 Earth Day. These significant laws include the Clean Air Act, laws **to protect drinking water** and the ocean, and the **creation** of the United States Environmental Protection Agency.

The Earth Day Network **reports** that Earth Day is now the **largest secular holiday** in the world, celebrated by more than a **half billion** people every year.

Parents Appreciation Day

On the **second Sunday** in May, Americans of **all ages treat** their **mothers** to **something** special. It is the one day out of the year when children, **young and old**, **express how much** they **appreciate** their mothers.

Celebrating Mother's Day is a tradition that **came from England** and **became** an official **holiday** in the United States in 1915.

On Mother's Day **morning** some American children **follow** the tradition of **serving** their mothers **breakfast in bed**. Other children **will give** their mothers **gifts** which they **have made themselves** or **bought** in **stores**. Adults give their mothers **red carnations,** the official Mother's Day **flower**. If their mothers are **deceased** they may bring **white** carnations to their **grave sites**. This is the **busiest** day of the year for American restaurants. On her special day, family members **do not want** Mom **to cook dinner**.

The United States is one of the **few countrie**s in the world that has an official day on which **fathers** are **honored** by their children. On the third Sunday in June, fathers all across the United States are given presents, **treated** to dinner or **otherwise made to feel** special.

The origin of Father's Day is **not clear**. **Some say** that it began with a **church service** in West Virginia in 1908. Others say the first Father's Day ceremony was **held** in Vancouver, Washington.

In 1916, President Woodrow Wilson **approved** of this idea, but it was not until 1924 when President Calvin Coolidge made it a national event to "**establish** more **intimate** relations **between** fathers and their children and **to impress upon** fathers the **full measure** of their **obligations**." **Since then,** fathers have been honored and recognized by their families **throughout** the country on the **third** Sunday in June.

second Sunday: segundo domingo
all ages: todas las edades
treat/to treat: tratan/tratar, invitar
mothers: madres
something: algo
young and old: *(niños, hijos)* jovenes y mayores
express/to express: expresan/expresar
how much: cuánto
appreciate/to appreciate: aprecian/apreciar
came from England: vino de Inglaterra
became/to become: se convirtió/convertirse
holiday: día feriado, día festivo
morning: mañana
follow/to follow: siguen/seguir
serving: servir
breakfast in bed: desayuno en la cama
will give/to give: darán/dar
gifts: regalos
have made themselves: hicieron ellos mismos
bought/to buy: compraron/comprar
stores: tiendas, negocios
red carnations: claveles rojos
flower: flor
deceased: fallecidas
white: blancos
grave sites: tumbas
busiest: más ajetreado
do not want: no quieren
to cook dinner: cocine la cena
few countries: pocos países
fathers: padres
honored: honrados
treated/to treat: invitados/invitar
otherwise: de otra forma
made to feel: hacerlos sentir
not clear: no claro
some say: algunos dicen
church service: oficio religioso
held/to hold: celebrada/celebrar
approved/to approve: aprobó/aprobar
establish: establecer
intimate: íntimas
between: entre
to impress upon: para inculcar
full measure: completa medida
obligations: obligaciones
since then: desde entonces
throughout: a lo largo de
third: tercer

Season of Merriment

The **French expression** 'Mardi Gras' **literally translates to** 'Fat Tuesday'. It was called this **because of** the **feasting** that **took place** on this day. It is a celebration that is held **just before** the **beginning** of **Lent**.

By far the largest, most **lavish** Mardi Gras celebration in the U.S. is in New Orleans, Louisiana. Mardi Gras has been celebrated in New Orleans **since as early as** the 1700s. Festivities included **masked balls** and **bawdy street processions**, which by 1806 **had become so rowdy** that they were **forbidden**. In 1817 it became illegal **to wear** masks. These **laws** were **more or less ignored**. Both the festivities and masks became legal again by 1827, when New Orleans came under American control.

French **royals**, **feather-covered showgirls**, **painted clowns**, masked **lions**—**you can find** them all in the **streets** of New Orleans at Mardi Gras. By **dawn** on that most famous Tuesday, people have **claimed** the **best spots** on the streets **to watch** fabulous **floats**, outrageous **performers**, and **visiting celebrities** go by. Many **travel hundreds of miles to be a part of** the excitement.

Marching bands, some of them **founded** more than a **century** ago, also **take to the streets** with music and festive **dress**. They **open** the day by **spreading** jazz music through the city before more than 350 floats and 15,000 **costumed** people **take over** the **scene**. Crazy costumes and **wild make-up** are the **order of the day**.

KREWES: NEW ORLEANS ROYALTY

Mardi Gras **has long combined** wild street activities **open** to everyone with events **organized by private clubs known as** krewes. Today, thousands of people **belong to** about 60 krewes that **plan** the parades and balls of New Orleans' Mardi Gras. The **oldest** krewe, the Krewe of Comus, was founded in 1857 by men who **feared** the **outrageous antics** of Mardi Gras **would lead to** the holiday being **outlawed**. They **hoped** that **secret societie**s could **keep** the celebrations **alive**.

In 1872 the **Russian grand duke** Alexis Romanoff **visited** New Orleans at Mardi Gras. A group of **businessmen** organized the Krewe of Rex **to host** a parade for the occasion, and **appointed** a "**king for the day**" so that the grand duke could have a royal reception. **Naming** kings and queens at Mardi Gras balls **has been** a tradition of the krewes **ever since**. Today, the Rex parade is the **main event** on Mardi Gras. The King of Rex is the King of Carnival.

CATCHING BEADS

The millions of **colorful beaded necklaces thrown** from floats are the **most visible symbols** and **souvenirs** of Mardi Gras. **In addition,** millions of **cups** and **toy coins** known as "doubloons" are **decorated** with krewe **logos** and thrown to **parade-watchers**. Some "throws" are **especially prized** and people do outrageous **things to catch** the most **goodies**. Some **dress** their children in **eye-catching** costumes and **seat them** on **ladders** that **tower over** the **crowds**. Others **give up** on the costume **altogether**, finding that the tradition of **taking clothes off** can be the **quickest attention-getter**!

A Salute to Spring

People in the United States celebrate Easter **according to** their personal and **religious beliefs**. Christians **commemorate** Good Friday as the day that Jesus Christ **died** and Easter Sunday as the day that he was **resurrected**. Protestant **settlers brought** the custom of a **sunrise service**, a religious **gathering at dawn**, to the United States. All, **in some way or another,** are a **salute to spring, marking re-birth**.

On Easter Sunday **children wake up to find** that the **Easter Bunny** has **left them baskets** of **candy**. Children **hunt** for **eggs around** the **house** that they **decorated earlier** that **week. Neighborhoods** hold Easter egg hunts. The child who **finds** the most eggs **wins** a **prize**.

Traditionally, many celebrants **bought** new **clothes** for Easter which they **wore** to **church**. After church services, everyone went for a **walk** around the town. This **led to** the American custom of Easter **parades** all over the country.

In the **early** nineteenth **century**, Dolly Madison, the **wife** of the fourth American President, **organized** an **Easter egg roll** in Washington, D.C. She had been **told** that Egyptian children **used to roll** eggs **against** the **pyramids**, so she **invited** the children of Washington to roll **hard-boiled** eggs down the **lawn** of the new **Capitol building**! The event has **grown**, and today Easter Monday is the **only** day of the year when tourists **are allowed** on the White House **lawn**. The egg-rolling event is **open to** children **twelve years old** and **under**. Adults are allowed **only when accompanied** by children.

---

according to: de acuerdo a
religious beliefs: creencias religiosas
commemorate/to commemorate: conmemoran/conmemorar
died/to die: murió/morir
resurrected: resucitado
settlers: colonos
brought/to bring: trajeron/traer
sunrise service: oficio del amanecer
gathering at dawn: reunión al amanecer
in some way or another: de una forma u otra
salute to spring: saludo a la primavera
marking re-birth: marcando el renacimiento
children: niños
wake up: se despiertan
to find: para descubrir
Easter Bunny: conejo de Pascua
left them: les dejó
baskets: canastas
candy: dulces
hunt/to hunt: cazan/cazar
eggs: huevos
around: alrededor
house: casa
decorated/to decorate: decoraron/decorar
earlier: previamente
week: semana
neighborhoods: barrios
finds/to find: encuentra/encontrar
wins/to win: gana/ganar
prize: premio
bought/to buy: compraban/comprar
clothes: ropas, vestimentas
wore/to wear: llevaban/llevar, ponerse
church: iglesia
walk: caminata
led to/to lead to: llevó a/llevar a
parades: desfiles
early: comienzos
century: siglo
wife: esposa
organized/to organize: organizó/organizar
Easter egg roll: carrera de huevos de Pascua
told/to tell: dicho/decir
used to: tenían la costumbre de
roll: hacer rodar
against: contra
pyramids: pirámides
invited/to invite: invitó/invitar
hard-boiled: duros *(huevos)*
lawn: césped
Capitol building: efidicio del capitolio
grown/to grow: crecido/crecer
only: único
are allowed: se les permite
lawn: césped
open to: abierto a
twelve years old: de doce años
under: menores *(de doce años)*
only when accompanied: sólo si están acompañados

Celebrating Workers

Every year, on the **first Monday** in September, **Labor Day commemorates workers** in America. The **timing** of the **holiday** makes it an ideal **bridge between summer vacations** and the **autumn season** and **new school year**. It is a federal holiday and all banks, schools, **post offices** and **government** offices are **closed** on Labor Day **throughout the country**.

First **celebrated** in New York City in 1882 with a **parade** of 10,000 workers, Labor Day **was made** a legal holiday in all states in 1894 **under** President Grover Cleveland. **Although** the U.S. government was **encouraged to change** the **date** and **adopt** May 1st **along with** the majority of the world, the September date **stuck**, and **remains to this day**.

It is now celebrated **mainly** as a **day of rest** and **even more so** as the unofficial **end** of the summer season. Popular resort areas are **packed with** people **enjoying** one **last three-day weekend** of summer vacation.

Forms of celebration include picnics, barbecues, **fireworks**, and **camping**. Families with **school-age children** take it as the last weekend **to travel before** the **school year begins**.

Leaders of the American Federation of Labor **called** the day a national tribute to the **huge contributions** workers have made to the **strength**, **prosperity** and **well-being** of the United States. The **principles behind** this holiday are as important **today** as they were 112 years **ago**, as **we continue to honor** the workers of America's **past**, present and **future**.

every year: cada año
first Monday: primer lunes
Labor Day: Día del Trabajo
commemorates/to commemorate: conmemora/conmemorar
workers: trabajadores
timing: momento (en que se celebra)
holiday: feriado
bridge: puente
between: entre
summer vacations: vacaciones de verano
autumn season: estación otoñal
new school year: nuevo año escolar
post offices: oficinas de correos
government: gubernamentales
closed: cerradas
throughout the country: a lo largo del país
celebrated: celebrado
parade: desfile
was made: fue hecho
under: bajo (la presidencia de)
although: a pesar de que
encouraged to change: alentados a cambiar
date: fecha
adopt: adoptar
along with: junto con
stuck: quedó
remains to this day: se mantiene hasta el día de hoy
mainly: principalmente
day of rest: día de descanso
even more so: aún más
end: final
packed with: llenas de
enjoying/to enjoy: disfrutando/disfrutar
last: último
three-day weekend: fin de semana de tres días
fireworks: fuegos artificiales
camping: ir de campamento
school-age children: niños en edad escolar
to travel: para viajar
before: antes de
school year: año escolar
begins/to begin: empiece/empezar
leaders: líderes
called/to call: llamaron/llamar
huge contributions: enormes contribuciones
strength: fuerza
prosperity: prosperidad
well-being: bienestar
principles: principios
behind: detrás
today: hoy
ago: hace (112 años)
we continue: continuamos
to honor: honrando
past: pasado
future: futuro

Shakespeare Festivals

poet: poeta
playwright: dramaturgo
widely regarded: generalmente
  considerado
greatest writer: mejor escritor,
  el más grande
language: idioma, lengua
preeminent dramatist: preeminente
  dramaturgo
wrote/to write: escribió/escribir
approximately: aproximadamente
sonnets: sonetos
as well as: así como
works: obras
non-profit groups: groups sin fines
  de lucro
strive to/to strive to: se esfuerzan por/
  esforzarse por
provide: proveer
stimulating: estimulante
atmosphere: ambiente, atmósfera
watch: mirar
participate in: participar en
become immersed: sumergirse
entertain/to entertain: entretienen/
  entretener
enrich/to enrich: enriquecen/
  enriquecer
educate/to educate: educan/educar
brings/to bring: trae/traer
summer: verano
free: gratis
park: parque
welcomed tradition: tradición
  acogida
bringing: trayendo
audiences: públicos
in addition: además
reaches/to reach: alcanza/alcanzar
over: más de
arts education programs: programas
  de educación artística
rely on/to rely on: dependen de/
  depender de, contar con
supporters: quienes apoyan
share/to share: comparten/compartir
belief: creencia, opinión
power: poder
beauty: belleza
should be accessible: debería ser
  accesible
everyone: todos, todo el mundo

William Shakespeare was an English **poet** and **playwright**. He is **widely regarded** as the **greatest writer** of the English **language** and as the world's **preeminent dramatist**. He **wrote approximately** 38 plays and 154 **sonnets, as well as** a variety of other poems.

In the United States, small and large communities celebrate the **works** of Shakespeare through festivals. Both profit and **non-profit groups strive to provide** playgoers a **stimulating** festival **atmosphere** where they can **watch, participate in**, and **become immersed** in experiences that **entertain, enrich**, and **educate**.

The San Francisco Shakespeare Festival **brings** Shakespeare's greatest works to over 30,000 people in the Bay Area each **summer** with **Free** Shakespeare in the **Park.**

Free Shakespeare in the Park has become a **welcome tradition** in the Bay Area, **bringing** professional, free performances of Shakespeare's greatest works to diverse **audiences** for over 20 years.

In addition, each year The San Francisco Shakespeare Festival **reaches** a new audience of **over** 120,000 kids throughout the state with unique **arts education programs**—Shakespeare on Tour, Midnight Shakespeare, and Bay Area Shakespeare Camps.

Non-profit groups **rely on** donations from friends and **supporters** who **share** a **belief** that the **power** and **beauty** of William Shakespeare's work **should be accessible** to **everyone**.

Martin Luther King Day

All through the 1980s, controversy surrounded the idea of a Martin Luther King Day. Members of Congress and citizens had petitioned the President to make January 15, Dr. Martin Luther King, Jr.'s birthday, a federal holiday. Others wanted to make the holiday on the day he died, while some people did not want to have a holiday at all.

On Monday, January 20, 1986, in cities and towns across the country people celebrated the first official Martin Luther King Day. A ceremony which took place at an old railroad depot in Atlanta, Georgia was especially emotional. Hundreds had gathered to sing and to march. Many were the same people who, in 1965, had marched for fifty miles between two cities in the state of Alabama to protest segregation and discrimination of black Americans.

Today, Martin Luther King Day is observed on the third Monday of January each year, around the time of King's birthday, January 15. Schools, offices and federal agencies are closed for the holiday. On this Monday there are quiet memorial services as well as elaborate ceremonies and parades in honor of Dr. King. Speeches are given reminding everyone of Dr. King's lifelong work for peace.

Martin Luther King Day is not only for celebration and remembrance, education and tribute, but also a day of service. All across America people perform service in hospitals and shelters and prisons and wherever people need some help. It is a day of volunteering to feed the hungry, rehabilitate housing, tutor those who can't read, and a thousand other projects for building the beloved community of Martin Luther King's dream.

---

all through: durante todo
controversy: controversia
surrounded/to surround: rodeó/rodear
citizens: ciudadanos
petitioned/to petition: pidieron/pedir, solicitar
to make: que hiciera
federal holiday: día feriado federal
died/to die: murió/morir
some: algunas
did not want: no querían
at all: en absoluto
cities: ciudades
towns: pueblos
first: primer
ceremony: ceremonia
took place/to take place: tuvo lugar/ tener lugar
old railroad depot: vieja estación de trenes
emotional: conmovedora
hundreds: cientos
gathered/to gather: reunido/reunirse
to sing: para cantar
to march: para marchar
same: misma
fifty miles: cincuenta millas
between: entre
to protest: para protestar
observed: observado, cumplido
third: tercer
around the time: alrededor de la fecha
closed: cerrados
quiet: silenciosos, tranquilos
as well as: así como
elaborate: elaboradas
parades: desfiles
speeches: discursos
reminding: recordando
lifelong: de toda la vida
work: obra, trabajo
peace: paz
not only...but also: no sólo... pero también
service: servicio
perform/to perform: lleva a cabo/ llevar a cabo, efectuar (un trabajo)
shelters: refugios
prisons: prisiones, cárceles
wherever: donde sea
need/to need: necesita/necesitar
help: ayuda
volunteering: trabajar como voluntario
to feed: para alimentar
hungry: hambrientos
rehabilitate: rehabilitar
housing: viviendas
read: leer
thousand: mil
projects: proyectos
building: construir
beloved: amada
dream: sueño

Ethnic Celebrations

Various **ethnic groups** in America celebrate days that **carry special meaning** for them. **Jews**, **for example**, **observe** their **high holy days** in autumn, and most **employers** show consideration by **allowing them to take these days off**. Irish Americans celebrate the **patron saint**, Saint Patrick, on March 17. In May, the **townspeople** of Holland, Michigan celebrate their **Dutch ancestry** through a **yearly Tulip Festival**. **Folk fairs** in the American Midwest offer **foods** of ethnic diversity, because people of so many different nationalities **have settled** there. Many different ethnic celebrations **take place**, at different times, all across the United States.

In January and February large **crowds gather** in the **narrow streets** of Chinatown in New York, San Francisco, and other cities where Chinese have **settled,** to celebrate **Chinese New Year**. A huge **cloth dragon sways back and forth through** the streets. **Following** the dragon are people **playing drums** and **dancers carrying paper lion heads** on **sticks**. As they dance, **store** and **business owners come outside** to give them **money**. New Year is the most important **holiday** in China, and Chinese people **all over the world** actively **observe it**.

For **over** 700 years Portuguese people have celebrated the **Feast of the Holy Spirit**. In San Diego, California, this is the **oldest ethnic** religious celebration, **dating back to** the time when the first families settled here in 1884. This 3-day event is San Diego's oldest festival and is **hosted by** the Portuguese community. The celebration **includes** traditional music and dancing, and food and **games** for adults and children. The festival is **held** each year on **Pentecost Sunday**, seven weeks after Easter. It **honors** Queen Isabel, the Portuguese royal who was **known for serving** the **poor** and **feeding** the **hungry** with **bread** from her **own table**.

The festival begins with an **elaborate parade**. Girls **wear crowns** and Renaissance-style **gowns to symbolize** Queen Isabel, while the boys **escorting them** wear **tuxedos**. The **finely dressed** kings and queens **march** to St. Agnes Roman Catholic Church, where the new queen is **crowned**. The crown is the **same one used** since the first festival in 1910.

On May 5, Los Angeles, California is **alive** with color, **laughter** and dancing. More than 500,000 Mexicans and Americans of Mexican **origin** are celebrating Cinco de Mayo.

The celebration takes place in the streets **outside City Hall** where Mexican orchestras and **local bands play** Mexican patriotic **songs**. The streets are **colored** in **red, white** and **green** - the colors of the Mexican **flag**. Young boys are **proud** to be **seen** in Mexican **clothing** and girls wear red and green **ruffled dresses** with **wide skirts**. Famous musicians play popular **tunes** on their guitars while dancers **spin around** and **click** their **castanets**.

A temporary **stage** at the **steps** of City Hall is **decorated** with a **picture** of General Zaragoza, **flanked by** Mexican and American flags. Mexican **dignitaries** are **guests of honor**, **pleased to hear** the **mayor** of Los Angeles **making a speech** in Spanish. **Later**, celebrants **stroll** through the streets to the old section of the city. Others go to **city parks** where **sports events**, dances and **picnics featuring** Mexican food are taking place.

It is an occasion which Mexicans and Americans **share to emphasize** the **friendship between** their two **countries.**

elaborate parade: desfile elaborado
wear crowns: llevan coronas
gowns: vestidos
to symbolize: para simbolizar
escorting them: que las acompañan
tuxedos: esmoquines
finely dressed: elegantemente vestidos
march/to march: marchan/marchar
crowned/to crown: coronada/coronar
same one used: misma usada
alive: viva
laughter: risa
origin: origen
outside: afuera del
City Hall: ayuntamiento
local bands: grupos de música locales
play/to play: tocan/tocar
songs: canciones
colored: coloreados
red: rojo
white: blanco
green: verde
flag: bandera
proud: orgullosos
seen/to see: vistos/ver
clothing: ropas
ruffled dresses: vestidos con volantes
wide skirts: faldas amplias
tunes: melodías
spin around: dan vueltas
click: hacer click
castanets: castañuelas
stage: escenario, tablado
steps: escalinatas
decorated: decorado
picture: foto
flanked by: flanqueada por
dignitaries: dignatarios
guests of honor: huéspedes de honor
pleased to hear: encantados de escuchar
mayor: alcalde
making a speech: dando un discurso
later: más tarde
stroll/to stroll: dan un paseo/ dar un paseo
city parks: parques de la ciudad
sports events: eventos deportivos
picnics: picnics, comidas al aire libre
featuring: presentando
share/to share: comparten/compartir
to emphasize: para enfatizar
friendship: amistad
between: entre
countries: países

Test Your Comprehension

Luck of the Irish, page 66

1. ¿Cuándo y dónde tuvieron lugar las primeras celebraciones estadounidenses del Día de San Patricio?

2. ¿Qué le pasa a la gente que es sorprendida sin estar usando verde en el Día de San Patricio?

Powwows, page 68

1. La palabra powwow se deriva de un término que se refiere ¿a qué cosa?

2. Típicamente, ¿en qué consiste un powwow?

3. ¿Verdadero o Falso? A la gente que no es Nativa Americana no se le permite participar en las actividades de un powwow.

Seasonal Celebrations, page 70

1. ¿Cuáles son los principales festivales de otoño en la región noreste?

2. En el Lago Houghton, Michigan, un festival de invierno ofrece un concurso ¿para qué cosa?

3. La primavera en el suroeste encuentra a los ciudadanos de Okeene, Oklahoma, ¿haciendo qué cosa?

Flavor of America, page 72

1. ¿Qué les pasa a los crustáceos que ganan en la carrera de cangrejos?

2. ¿Dónde encontrarás la enchilada más grande del mundo?

3. ¿Cuánto queso se produce cada año en Little Chute, Wisconsin?

Examina tu comprensión

Parents Appreciation Day, page 75

1. ¿Cuál es la flor oficial del Día de la Madre?

2. ¿Cuál es el origen del Día del Padre?

Celebrating the Worker, page 79

1. ¿Cuándo es el Día del Trabajo?

2. ¿Cuándo y dónde se celebró el Día del Trabajo por primera vez? ¿Cuándo fue legalizado como día festivo en todos los estados?

3. El Día del Trabajo se celebra en forma no oficial como el fin ¿de qué cosa?

Shakespeare Festivals, page 80

1. ¿Quién era William Shakespeare?

2. ¿Qué es Shakespeare en el Parque?

3. ¿Cómo es posible que los grupos sin fines de lucro sean capaces de presentar obras de Shakespeare?

Then join hand in hand, brave Americans all!
By uniting we stand, by dividing we fall.

John Dickinson

People

best known: mejor conocidos	
back: de vuelta	
discovery: descubrimiento	
visionary project: proyecto visionario	
to explore: de explorar	
began/to begin: empezó/empezar	
ended/to end: terminó/terminar	
traveled/to travel: viajó/viajar	
over: más de	
main achievements: principales logros	
include/to include: incluyen/incluir	
gained/to gain: ganó/ganar, lograr	
extensive knowledge: extenso conocimiento	
maps: mapas	
rivers: ríos	
mountain ranges: cadenas de montañas	
plants: plantas	
species: especies	
discovered: descubiertas	
described: descritas	
communications: comunicaciones	
opened/to open: abiertas/abrir	
army: ejército	
claim: reclamo, reivindicación	
strengthened/stregthen: fortalecido/fortalecer	
large body: gran cuerpo	
only woman: única mujer	
birth: nacimiento	
son: hijo	
left/to leave: dejó/dejar	
village: pueblo, aldea	
to journey: para viajar	
often: a menudo	
credited: se le atribuye	
guide: guía	
led/to lead: dirigió/dirigir	
across: a través	
plains: planicies, llanuras	
contributed/to contribute: contribuyó/contribuir	
significantly: significativamente	
success: éxito	
helped/to help: ayudó/ayudar	
met/to meet: encontraron/encontrar	
tribes: tribus	
along the way: a lo largo del camino	
dispelled: disipar	
war party: banda de guerreros	
wrote/to write: escribió/escribir	
party of men: grupo de hombres	
token of peace: señal de paz	
retraced: seguir la misma ruta	
following: siguiendo	
stretches/to stretch: se extiende/extenderse	
winds/to wind: serpentea/serpentear	
high deserts: desiertos altos	
shores: costas	
experience/to experience: viven la experiencia/vivir la experiencia	
learn/to learn: aprenden/aprender	
first hand: de primera mano	

Meriwether Lewis and William Clark are **best known** for their expedition from the Mississippi River to the West Coast and **back**. The expedition, called the Corps of **Discovery**, was President Thomas Jefferson's **visionary project to explore** the American West. It **began** in May of 1804 and **ended** in September 1806. The expedition **traveled over** 8,000 total miles over a period of 2 years, 4 months and 10 days.

The **main achievements** of the expedition **include**:

- The U.S. **gained extensive knowledge** of the geography of the American West in the form of **maps** of major **rivers** and **mountain ranges**.
- 178 **plants** and 122 **species** of animals were **discovered** and **described**.
- Diplomatic relations and **communications** with the Indians were **opened**.
- A precedent for **Army** exploration of the West was established
- The U.S. **claim** to Oregon Territory was **strengthened**.
- A **large body** of literature about the West was established: The Lewis and Clark diaries.

Sacagawea was the **only woman** to travel with the Corps of Discovery. Two months after the **birth** of her **son**, Sacagawea **left** her **village to journey** west with Lewis and Clark. Sacagawea is **often credited** as the **guide** who **led** the Corps **across** the **plains**. She **contributed significantly** to the **success** of the journey. Simply because she was a woman, Sacagawea **helped** with the journey. The explorers **met** many **tribes along the way** and her presence **dispelled** the notion that the group was a **war party**. William Clark **wrote**, "A woman with a **party of men** is a **token of peace**."

Today, the Expedition's path can be **retraced** by **following** the Lewis and Clark National Historic Trail. The Trail **stretches** through 11 states and **winds** over mountains, along rivers, through plains and **high deserts**, and ends at the **shores** of the Pacific Oregon coast. Visitors to the Trail **experience** and **learn first hand** about the Lewis and Clark Expedition.

Mother of Civil Rights

Rosa Parks is **called** "The Mother of the Civil Rights Movement." She is **considered** one of the most important **citizens** of the 20th **century**. By **not giving up** her **seat** to a **white passenger** on a **city bus**, Rosa Parks **started** a **protest** that **redirected** the **course** of history.

In the fifties, **segregation laws** were **prevalent** in the **South**. Black and white people were segregated in **almost every aspect** of **daily life**. Buses **enforced seating policies** that **stated** there were **separate sections** for blacks and whites. White people were given **preferential treatment**.

On December 1, 1955 Rosa Parks **refused to obey** bus **driver** James Blake and would not give up her seat to a white man. She was **arrested**, **tried** and **convicted** of **violating** a city law. Her actions **prompted** the Montgomery Bus Boycott. This boycott **lasted** for **over a year** and was one of the **largest movements against** racial segregation in history. Her actions also brought Martin Luther King, Jr. to the **forefront** of the civil rights movement. In 1956 the U.S. Supreme Court **outlawed** segregation on city buses.

For the **next** forty years Rosa Parks **dedicated** her life to civil rights and **continued** to **fight** for **equal rights** for all people. She **received** many **awards**, **including** the Martin Luther King Jr. Nonviolent Peace Prize and the Presidential Medal of Freedom. Her role in American history **earned her** an **iconic status** in American culture.

Rosa Parks died on October 24, 2005 at age 92. Her life and the **positive changes** she made in America **remain** an **inspiration** to people **everywhere**.

called/to call: llamada/llamar
considered/to consider: considerada/considerar
citizens: ciudadanos
century: siglo
not giving up: no ceder
seat: asiento
white passenger: pasajero blanco
city bus: autobús municpal
started/to start: empezó/empezar
protest: protesta
redirected/to redirect: cambió/cambiar *(la dirección)*
course: curso
segregation laws: leyes de segregación
prevalent: prevalentes
south: sur
almost every aspect: casi todos los aspectos
daily life: vida diaria
enforced/to enforce: hacían cumplir/hacer cumplir *(reglas)*
seating policies: normas de ubicacíon de los pasajeros
stated/to state: declaraban/declarar
separate sections: secciones separadas
preferential treatment: tratamiento preferente
refused/to refuse: rehusó/rehusar
to obey: a obedecer
driver: conductor
arrested/to arrest: arrestada/arrestar
tried/to try: juzgada/juzgar
convicted: condenada
violating: violar
prompted/to prompt: provocó/provocar
lasted/to last: duró/durar
over a year: más de un año
largest movements: movimientos más grandes
against: contra
forefront: vanguardia
outlawed/to outlaw: prohibió/prohibir
next: próximos
dedicated/to dedicate: dedicó/dedicar
continued/to continue: continuó/continuar
fight: lucha
equal rights: igualdad derechos
received/to receive: recibió/recibir
awards: premios
including: incluyendo
earned her: le ganó
iconic status: categoría icónica
positive changes: cambios positivos
remain/to remain: continúan/continuar *(siendo)*
inspiration: inspiración
everywhere: en todas partes

The Founding Fathers

The **Founding Fathers** of the United States, **also known as** the Fathers of our country, are the **political leaders** who **signed** the Declaration of Independence or the United States Constitution, and were **active** in the American Revolution. The American Revolution **refers to** the **period** when the **original thirteen colonies gained independence** from the British.

The 55 **delegates** who **make up** the Founding Fathers were a **distinguished group** of men who **represented** American **leadership**. **Everyone** in the group had **extensive** political experience and **practiced** a **wide range** of **occupations**. **Some** men **continued on** to become an important **part of** American history.

GEORGE WASHINGTON

George Washington is **called** the "Father of the nation." His devotion and **critical role** in the **founding** of the United States **earned him** this title. Washington **led** America's army to **victory** over Britain in the American Revolutionary War. In 1789 he was **elected** the **first** president of the United States. He served two four-year terms from 1789 to 1797. His dedication and **honorable reputation** made him an ideal **figure among early** American politicians.

THOMAS JEFFERSON

Thomas Jefferson was an **influential** Founding Father for his **promotion** of the **ideals** of **Republicanism** in the United States. He was the **third** president of the United States and the **principal author** of the Declaration of Independence. **Major events during** his presidency include the Louisiana Purchase and the Lewis and Clark Expedition.

JAMES MADISON

James Madison is also **considered** one of the most influential Founding Fathers. He is **referred to as** the "Father of the constitution" because he **played** a **bigger role** in **designing** the **document** than **anyone else**. In 1788, he **wrote** over a third of the Federalist Papers, **still** the most **influential commentary** on the Constitution. James Madison was the **fourth** President of the United States (1809–1817). He **drafted** many **basic laws** and was responsible for the first ten **amendments** to the Constitution. For this, he is also known as the "Father of the Bill of Rights."

BENJAMIN FRANKLIN

Benjamin Franklin is one of the **best-known** Founding Fathers of the United States. He is the **only** Founding Father who is a **signatory** of all four of the major documents of the founding of the United States: the Declaration of Independence, the Treaty of Paris, the Treaty of Alliance with France, and the United States Constitution. Most people **think** of him **primarily** as a **scientist.** The famous **kite experiment**, which **verified** the **nature of electricity**, is **told** and **retold** throughout American history. It is just one of many **amazing accomplishments** made by Benjamin Franklin during his **lifetime.**

Franklin was **noted** for his **diversity** of **talents**. He was a **leading** author, politician, **printer**, scientist, **philosopher**, civic activist, and **diplomat**. Franklin was an **extraordinary inventor**. Among his many creations were the **lightning rod**, the **glass harmonica**, the Franklin **stove**, **bifocal glasses**, and **swim fins**.

In 1776, he was a **member** of the **Committee of Five** that drafted the Declaration of Independence, and made several small **changes** to Thomas Jefferson's draft.

At the signing, he is **quoted** as **stating**: "We must all **hang together**, or **assuredly** we shall all hang **separately**."

The Best of Two Worlds

Pepe Stepensky, from Mexico City, **has been living** in San Diego for the **past twenty years**. He is a **driving force** in the San Diego Latino community as the **founder** and director of the **award-winning theater group** "Teatro Punto y Coma." **In addition to** being a **published author** of **poetry** and **short stories,** Pepe, **along with** his **wife** Deborah, **own** and **operate** two **fast food** restaurants and the Cerveza Store in Seaport Village. **Maximizing** his **bilingual talents**, Pepe is a **successful voice-over** artist **performing** Hispanic characters and voiceovers for big and small companies nationwide. Deborah and Pepe have three **children**—Jessica 18, Alejandra 16 and Fernando 9 years old.

Think English (TE): **Tell us** about your **journey** to the United States.

Pepe Stepensky (PS): **I met** my wife in May of 1986 and **asked her to marry me three weeks later**. We got married in August of 1986 and **moved** to San Diego **after** our **wedding**. I was 28 years old. I had a **job offer** and **decided** to **take the chance**. I had one **brother living here** but the **rest** of my family, **including** my **parents**, **stayed** in Mexico.

TE: What were the **biggest challenges** for you **bridging** your culture with your **newly adopted** American culture? What was **most exciting** to you about bridging these cultures?

PS: **I feel** that the American culture is more individualist. Each one **cares** more for **themselves**. The Mexican culture is **about people**, friends, family. You **stay at home until** the day you get married. Your parents **are not counting** the days until you go to college so they can **remodel** your **room**! **On the other hand**, America is the **land of opportunities**. Here, the different **social classes** are not so **far away** like in Mexico. In the United States **anybody** can have the **same things** as others.

TE: **How has being** bilingual **benefitted you**?

PS: Being bilingual has **opened many doors** for me. Being a voiceover talent for the Hispanic **market** was a **great adventure** for me when I **started almost** 15 **years ago**.

TE: Are your children bilingual? How do you **maintain** and keep your Hispanic **heritage alive** with your children **growing up** in America?

PS: **We are having** a **hard time making** our kids **talk to us** in Spanish, but we are **proud** that we did it, and my kids are **perfectly** bilingual. The official language in our house is Spanish. Now that our **first daughter** is **going** to college, she **finally thanked us** because she **realized** how important it was **to know two languages**. We maintained our heritage because **every summer** we go to Mexico **to visit uncles** and **grandparents** and the kids **were able to stay** with them for a **couple of weeks**.

TE: What are your **thoughts** on the incredible **growth** of the Hispanic **population** in the US?

PS: The Hispanic market is the **fastest** growing market in the U.S. We can't **disregard** or **ignore** it. **We need to know** about it, **learn** about it and work **towards considering** them a very important part of the American culture.

TE: **What advice would you give** to a **fellow** Hispanic American **starting out** in this **country**?

PS: **Integrate. Try to understand** your new country, but **never forget** your **roots**. **Make sure** your children know where they **come from**, and **teach them** your language.

TE: What are you **most proud of** as a Hispanic American?

PS: I'm proud of being binational, bilingual and bicultural. **What else can I ask for**? I have the **best of two worlds**!

Frank Lloyd Wright

Frank Lloyd Wright is **considered** the most **influential architect** of his time. He **influenced** the **entire course** of American architecture and he **remains**, **to this day**, America's most famous architect.

Frank Lloyd Wright **designed** about 1,000 **structures** and over 400 of these were **built**. He **described** his architecture as one that "**proceeds**, **persists**, **creates**, according to the nature of man and his **circumstances** as they both **change**."

As an independent architect, Wright **became** the **leader** of a style known as the **prairie house**. Prairie houses had **sloping roofs, clean skylines** and **extended lines** that **blend** into the **landscape.** These **designs** were considered **to complement** the land **around** Chicago where they were built. Wright **practiced** what is known as organic architecture, an architecture that is designed to naturally **fit into** the **surroundings**. Houses in **wooded regions, for instance, made heavy use** of wood. Desert houses made use of **stone**, and houses in **rocky areas** were built **mainly** of **cinder block**. He was also **well known** for making use of **innovative building materials**. Wright **often** designed furniture as well. Some of the **built-in furniture remains** in the houses today.

Wright built 362 houses, about 300 of which are still **standing.** Oak Park, Illinois, a Chicago **suburb,** has the **largest collection** of Wright houses, as well as Wright's home and **studio**. Some of the houses are **open** for **public tours**. **Walking** tours are a wonderful **way to experience** Wright's architecture and **see** the houses as they fit into the **surrounding** landscape.

---

considered: considerado
influential architect: arquitecto influyente
influenced/to influence: influyó/influir
entire course: rumbo completo
remains/to remain: sigue siendo/ seguir siendo
to this day: hasta el día de hoy
designed/to design: diseñó/diseñar
structures: construcciones
built/to build: construidas/construir
described/to describe: describió/ describir
proceeds/to proceed: procede/ proceder
persists/to persist: persiste/persistir
creates/to create: crea/crear
circumstances: circunstancias
change/to change: cambian/cambiar
became/to become: se convirtió/ convertirse
leader: líder
prairie house: casa de la pradera
sloping roofs: techos inclinados
clean skylines: líneas del horizonte bien definidas, elegantes
extended lines: líneas extendidas
blend/to blend: mezcla con/mezclar con
landscape: paisaje
designs: diseños
to complement: complementar
around: alrededor
practiced/to practice: practicaba/ practicar
fit into: encajar en
surroundings: entorno
wooded regions: regiones boscosas
for instance: por ejemplo
made heavy use: usaron mucha
stone: piedra
rocky areas: áreas rocosas
mainly: mayormente, principalmente
cinder block: bloque de cemento
well known: conocido
innovative building materials: materiales de construcción innovadores
often: a menudo
built-in furniture: muebles empotrados
remains/to remain: permanecen/ permanecer
standing: están en pie
suburb: barrio residencial periférico
largest collection: colección más grande
studio: estudio
open: abiertas
public tours: visitas guiadas al público
walking: a pie
way: manera
to experience: de experimentar, de tener la experiencia
see: ver
surrounding: de alrededor

Rags to Riches

Andrew Carnegie's life was a **true** "**rags to riches**" **story**. He was born to a **poor Scottish** family that immigrated to the United States. Carnegie was **devoted** to **hard work** from a **young age**. At age thirteen, Carnegie went to work in a **cotton mill**. He then **moved quickly through** a series of different jobs with Western Union and the Pennsylvania **Railroad**.

By the 1870s Carnegie had **become** a **powerful businessman** and **founded** the Carnegie Steel Company. By the 1890s, the company was the largest and most **profitable** industrial **enterprise** in the world. In 1901 he **sold** his company to JP Morgan's U.S. Steel and **retired** as the world's **richest** man. Carnegie **devoted** the **remainder** of his life to **philanthropy**.

Today, he is **remembered** as an **industrialist**, millionaire, and philanthropist. He **believed** in the "**Gospel of wealth**," which **meant** that wealthy people were **morally obligated to give** their **money back to** others in society.

In 1902 he founded the Carnegie Institution **to fund scientific research** and with a $10 million donation **established** a **pension fund** for **teachers**.

When Carnegie was a young man he **lived** near Colonel James Anderson, a rich man who **allowed** any **working boy to use** his personal **library for free**. **At that time**, free public libraries did not exist. Carnegie **never forgot** Colonel Anderson's generosity. Carnegie used his money **to support** education and **reading**. He gave money to **towns** and **cities to build** more than 2,500 public libraries. He also gave $125 million to a foundation called the Carnegie Corporation **to aid** colleges and other schools.

By 1911, Carnegie had **given away** 90 percent of his fortune. **During** his **lifetime**, he **gave away** over $350 million.

true: verdadera
rags to riches: del pobre que hace fortuna
story: historia
poor: pobre
Scottish: escocesa
devoted: devoto
hard work: trabajo duro
young age: joven
cotton mill: fábrica de algodón
moved quickly through: avanzó rápidamente por
railroad: ferrocarril
become/to become: convertido/convertirse
powerful businessman: poderoso hombre de negocios
founded/to found: fundado/fundar
profitable: rentable, provechosa
enterprise: empresa
sold/to sell: vendió/vender
retired/to retire: retiró/retirarse
richest: más rico
devoted/to devote: se dedicó/dedicarse
remainder: resto
philanthropy: filantropía
remembered: recordado
industrialist: industrial, empresario
believed/to believe: creía/creer
Gospel of wealth: evangelio de la riqueza
meant/to mean: significaba/significar
morally obligated: moralmente obligados
to give: a dar
money: dinero
back to: de vuelta a
to fund: para patrocinar
scientific research: investigación científica
established/to establish: estableció/establecer
pension fund: fondo de pensiones
teachers: maestros
lived/to live: vivió/vivir
allowed/to allow: permitía/permitir
working boy: chico que trabajaba
to use: usar
library: biblioteca
for free: gratis
at that time: en esos tiempos
never forgot: nunca olvidó
to support: para apoyar
reading: lectura
towns: pueblos
cities: ciudades
to build: para construir
to aid: para ayudar
given away/to give away: regalado/regalar
during: durante
lifetime: vida
gave away/to give away: regaló/regalar

America Takes Flight

Orville and Wilbur Wright **are credited as** the two Americans to **build** the world's **first successful airplane**. On December 17, 1903, the "Wright flyer" **flew** for 12 **seconds** and 120 **feet**.

The Wright brothers **did not go** to **college**; however they had **intuitive scientific** and **technical abilities**. They **built** their own bicycles and **operated** a bicycle **repair** and **sales shop**. The **profits** from their bicycle **business funded** their **airplane-building venture**.

The brothers flew their **test planes** in Kitty Hawk, North Carolina. It was a **small town** that had **steady winds**. They could **glide** and **land safely** on the area's **sand dunes**.

The brothers continued to **develop** more **complicated** planes over the next **few years**. The Wright Company was **formed** to build and sell their airplanes.

You can see the famous airplane, the "Wright flyer," at the National Air and Space Museum in Washington, D.C.

Another famous American **aviator** is Amelia Mary Earhart. Amelia Earhart was a **renowned** American aviation **pioneer** and **women's rights activist**. **In addition to breaking** many aviation **records,** she **wrote best-selling books** about her flying experiences and **helped form** the women's pilot organization, The Ninety-Nines.

In 1928, she was the first woman to fly as a **passenger across** the Atlantic Ocean. In 1932, she became the first woman to fly solo across that **same** ocean. For this flight, she became the first woman **to receive** the Distinguished Flying Cross.

In 1937, while **attempting** a flight **around the world**, Earhart **disappeared** over the central Pacific Ocean. Her disappearance is **considered**, to this day, to be a **mystery**.

Amelia Earhart's actions have **inspired** generations of women **to follow** their **dreams** and do things **never done** by women **before**.

Dr. Seuss

Dr. Seuss **helped millions** of **kids learn** how **to read**. He **entertained children** and adults **alike**. His **books** were famous for their **silly rhymes** and **whimsical characters**. Dr. Seuss **wrote** and **illustrated nearly** 50 books during his **lifetime**.

Dr. Seuss was **born,** as Thedore Geisel, in Springfield, Massachusetts, on March 2, 1904. He **graduated** from Dartmouth College in 1925 and **continued** his education at Oxford University.

During World War II, Geisel joined the Army and was **sent to** Hollywood where he wrote **documentaries** for the **military**. During this time, he also **created** a **cartoon** called Gerald McBoing-Boing. This cartoon **won him** an Oscar.

In the **spring** of 1954, a **report** was **published discussing illiteracy** among **schoolchildren**. The report **suggested** that **boring** books were **causing** children **to have trouble** reading. This **news prompted** Geisel's **publisher to send** Geisel a list of 400 **words** important for children to learn. The publisher **asked** Geisel to **shorten** the list to 250 words and **use them** to write an **entertaining** children's book. **Using** 220 of the words given to him, Geisel published *The Cat in the Hat*. The book was an **instant success**.

Winner of the Pulitzer Prize in 1984 and three Academy Awards, Theodor Geisel is **considered** the 20th century's most famous author for children.

Theodor Geisel **died** on September 24, 1991, but Dr. Seuss **lives on**, **inspiring** generations of children of **to explore the joys** of reading.

helped/to help: ayudó/ayudar
millions: millones
kids: niños
learn/to learn: aprender
to read: leer
entertained/to entertain: entretuvo/ entretener
children: niños
alike: por igual
books: libros
silly: tontas
rhymes: rimas
whimsical: caprichosos, fantásticos
characters: personajes
wrote/to write: escribió/escribir
illustrated/to illustrate: ilustró/ilustrar
nearly: casi
lifetime: vida
born/to be born: nació/nacer
graduated/to graduate: se graduó/ graduarse
continued/to continue: continuó/ continuar
sent to/to send to: enviado a/enviar a
documentaries: documentales
military: fuerzas armadas
created/to create: creó/crear
cartoon: dibujo animado
won him: *(por el cual)* ganó
spring: primavera
report: informe
published/to publish: publicado/ publicar
discussing/to discuss: que trataba/ tratar
illiteracy: analfabetismo
schoolchildren: escolares
suggested/to suggest: sugería/sugerir
boring: aburridos
causing/to cause: causaban/causar
to have trouble: tuvieran problemas
reading/to read: leer
news: noticias
prompted/to prompt: movió/mover *(a alguien a hacer algo)*
publisher: editor
to send: a enviar
words: palabras
asked/to ask: le pidió/pedir
shorten/to shorten: que acortara/ acortar
use them/to use: las usara/usar
entertaining: entretenido
using/to use: usando/usar
instant success: éxito inmediato
winner: ganador
considered/to consider: considerado/ considerar
died/to die: murió/morir
lives on: continúa viviendo
inspiring/to inspire: inspirando/ inspirar
to explore: a explorar
the joys: las alegrías

Author and Preservationist

John Muir was **born** in Scotland in 1838. His family **immigrated** to Wisconsin in 1849. He **briefly attended** college but did not **finish**. **Instead** he began 40 years of **walking** and **exploring** the **wilderness** of North America. His **journals produced** some of the best **nature writing** in the English language. His **works include** *The Mountains of California, Our National Parks, My First Summer in the Sierra, Steep Trails,* and others. His **letters**, **essays**, and **books telling of** his adventures in nature **have been read** by millions and are **still** popular today.

However, Muir's writing was **not just for enjoyment.** John Muir was one of the first **modern environmental activists** and **preservationists**. His direct activism and the attention his writings **received helped protect** the Yosemite Valley and other wilderness areas. His **articles** and books **describing** Yosemite's **natural wonders inspired** public **support establishing** Yosemite as the first national park in 1890.

Another great **accomplishment** is the Sierra Club, which he **founded.** The Sierra Club is one of the most important conservation organizations in the United States. His writings and philosophy were a **driving force** in the creation of the modern environmental movement.

For John Muir, **sleeping outside under the stars** was one of life's **great pleasures.** He **kept track of** his experiences by **recording them** in his journals. Here is what he wrote on July 19, 1869, when he **woke up** in the Sierra Nevada Mountains of California:

"**Watching** the **daybreak** and **sunrise.** The **pale** rose and **purple sky changing** softly to yellow and white, **sunbeams pouring through** the **peaks** and over the Yosemite domes."

Dr. Jonas Salk

Jonas Salk was born on October 28th, 1914, in New York City. His **parents** were Russian-Jewish immigrants who **fled** their **home country** for a **new life** in the United States. After **graduating high school** at the age of 15, Salk went to college **to pursue** a **law degree**. **Somewhere along the way**, he **changed his mind** and **decided** to pursue a degree in medicine. **Luckily** for the world, Jonas Salk **chose** medicine!

Salk **enrolled** in the medical school at New York University. He **began research** on the **flu virus**, **gathering knowledge** that would **lead to** his **discovery** of the **polio vaccine**. In 1947, Salk **accepted** an appointment to the Pittsburgh Medical School. He **started** working with the National Foundation for Infantile Paralysis and **saw** the opportunity to develop a vaccine **against** polio. He **devoted** the next eight years to this work.

In 1955, Jonas Salk's years of research finally **paid off**. The **summertime** was a time of **fear** and **anxiety** for many parents. Summer was the **season** when **thousands** of children became infected with the **disease** of polio. Parents' **worst** fear was **forever eliminated** when it was **announced** that Dr. Jonas Salk had developed a vaccine against the disease. Salk was **hailed** as a **miracle worker** and he **became famous overnight**. He **refused** to **patent** the vaccine, which made him even more **loved** by the people. He had **no desire to profit** personally from the discovery. His **ultimate wish** was to see the vaccine **distributed as widely as possible**, to as many people as possible. In countries where Salk's vaccine **has remained in use**, the disease has nearly been eliminated.

In 1963, Salk **founded** the Jonas Salk Institute for Biological Studies, a center for medical and scientific research. He **died** on June 23, 1995. His **legacy lives on** forever and his contributions to the world of science and health are **still utilized** today.

parents: padres
fled/to flee: escaparon/escapar
home country: país natal
new life: nueva vida
graduating/to graduate: graduarse
high school: secundaria
to pursue: para seguir *(una carrera)*
law degree: título o diploma en leyes
somewhere along the way: en algún sitio del camino
changed/to change: cambió/cambiar
his mind: de opinión
decided/to decide: decidió/decidir
luckily: afortunadamente
chose/to choose: eligió/elegir
enrolled/to enroll: se registró/registrarse
began/to begin: empezó/empezar
research: investigación
flu virus: virus de la gripe
gathering/to gather: recogiendo/recoger
knowledge: conocimientos
lead to: llevar a
discovery: descubrimiento
polio vaccine: vacuna contra la polio
accepted/to accept: aceptó/aceptar
started/to start: empezó/empezar
saw/to see: vio/ver
against: contra
devoted/to devote: se dedicó/dedicarse
paid off/to pay off: valió la pena/valer la pena
summertime: verano
fear: miedo
anxiety: ansiedad
season: estación
thousands: miles
disease: enfermedad
worst: peor
forever: para siempre
announced/to announce: anunciado/anunciar
hailed/to hail: saludado/saludar
miracle worker: hacedor de milagros
became famous overnight: se hizo famoso de un día para otro
refused/to refuse: se rehusó/rehusarse
patent: patentar
loved: amado
no desire: ningún deseo
to profit: de sacar provecho
ultimate wish: máximo deseo
distributed/to distribute: distribuida/distribuir
as widely as possible: tan ampliamente como fuera posible
has remained in use: se ha mantenido en uso
founded/to found: fundó/fundar
died/to die: murió/morir
legacy: legado
lives on: continúa vivo
still: todavía
utilized/to utilize: utilizadas/utilizar

Angel of the Battlefield

Clara Barton is **best known** as being the **founder** of the American Red Cross and for **serving** as a **nurse** on Civil War **battlefields**. Her **compassionate work** during the Civil War **would inspire praise** of her as "the **true heroine** of the age, the angel of the battlefield."

During the **early years** of the Civil War, she and a **few friends** began **to distribute first-aid supplies** to field hospitals, camps and battlefields. **In addition to** distributing supplies, she **worked tirelessly taking care of injured soldiers**.

At the **end** of the war, Barton **assisted** the government in **finding** information on **missing** soldiers. She **helped identify** and **mark almost** 13,000 **graves** at Andersonville, Georgia.

In 1881 her most **enduring** work began, the **establishment** of the American Red Cross. She **convinced** the government **to identify** the Red Cross as a governmental agency that would **provide aid** for **natural disasters**. Throughout the 1880s, victims of **fire**, **earthquake**, **drought**, tornado, and **flood** received aid and assistance from the Red Cross. Clara **learned** the importance of **educating** victims **to take care of** themselves so they would **be able to rebuild** their **lives** again after Red Cross workers had **left.** This concept of **teaching** first aid would **later** be **realized** in the formation of first-aid classes. First-aid classes are a very important part of the American Red Cross's service today.

Miss Barton continued to **work in the field** until she was **well into** her 70s. She died in 1912 at age 90 in her home. The mission of her life can be **summed up** in her **own words**, "You must **never** so much as **think** whether you like it or not, whether it is **bearable** or not; you must never think of anything except the **need**, and how **to meet it**."

Let There Be Light

Thomas Alva Edison is **considered** one of the greatest, most prolific inventors in history. He has over 1,093 U.S. **patents** in his name. His **inventions** and **devices** greatly **changed** and **influenced** life all over the world.

The invention that **first made** him famous was the **phonograph** in 1877. The cylinder phonograph was the first **machine** that could **record** and **reproduce sound**. Its invention **created** a sensation and brought Edison international **fame**.

In 1877 and 1878, Edison invented and **developed** the carbon microphone used in all **telephones along with** the Bell **receiver** until the 1980s. The carbon microphone was also used in **radio broadcasting** through the 1920s.

Edison is most famous for the **electric light bulb**. **Contrary to popular belief**, he didn't invent the light bulb, but **rather** he **improved** upon a 50-year-old idea.

The problem other inventors had **encountered** was the ability to **make it work** for **long periods** of **time**. Edison **solved** this problem and created a light bulb that **sustained** light for 40 **straight hours**. More importantly, he created a system that **allowed** homes and businesses to be **supplied** with electricity.

The **success** of electric light **brought** Thomas Edison to **new levels** of fame and **wealth.** His electric companies continued to **grow** and in 1889 they **merged** to form Edison General Electric. In 1892 Edison General Electric merged with its competitor, Thompson-Houston. Edison was **dropped** from the **name**, and the company became General Electric.

Thomas Alva Edison died in West Orange, New Jersey on October 18,1931. **After** his death, Edison became a **folk hero** of **legendary status**. His inventions have **profoundly affected** and **shaped** the **modern society** that we **know today**.

considered: considerado
patents: patentes
inventions: inventos
devices: aparatos, mecanismos
changed/to change: cambiaron/cambiar
influenced/to influence: influyeron/influir
first: primero
made/to make: hizo/hacer
phonograph: fonógrafo
machine: máquina
record: grabar
reproduce: reproducir
sound: sonido
created/to create: creó/crear
fame: fama
developed/to develop: desarrolló/desarrollar
telephones: teléfonos
along with: junto con
receiver: receptor
radio broadcasting: transmisión por radio
electric light bulb: bombilla eléctrica
contrary to popular belief: contrario a la creencia popular
rather: más bien
improved/to improve: mejoró/mejorar
encountered/to encounter: encontrado/encontrar
make it work: hacerla funcionar
long periods: largos períodos
time: tiempo
solved/to solve: solucionó/solucionar
sustained/to sustain: mantenía/mantener, sostener
straight hours: horas consecutivas
allowed/to allow: permitía/permitir
supplied/to supply: suministrados/suministrar
success: éxito
brought/to bring: trajo a/traer a
new levels: nuevos niveles
wealth: riqueza
grow/to grow: creciendo/crecer
merged/to merge: fusionaron/fusionar
dropped/to drop: abandonado/abandonar, dejar
name: nombre
after: después de
folk hero: héroe popular
legendary status: de categoría legendaria
profoundly affected: afectado profundamente
shaped/to shape: moldeado/moldear
modern society: sociedad moderna
know/to know: conocemos/conocer
today: hoy

are becoming/to become: se están volviendo/volverse	

are becoming/to become: se están volviendo/volverse

largest minority group: grupo minoritario más grande

adding/to add: agregando/agregar

value: valor

society: sociedad

enriching/to enrich: enriqueciendo/enriquecer

government: gobierno

throughout: a través de, a lo largo de

listed/to list: listados/listar

famous firsts: primicias famosas

contributions: contribuciones

world: mundo

fill/to fill: ocupan/ocupar

top positions: los mejores puestos

currently: actualmente

serves/to serve: sirve/servir

Attorney General: Abogado General

Cuban-born: nacido en Cuba

Secretary of Commerce: Secretario de Comercio

Congress: congreso

the first ... ever to hold: la primera ... *(en la historia)* en ocupar *(un puesto)*

tenure: permanencia

focused/to focus: enfocó/enfocar

health: salud

workshop: taller

organized/to organize: organizó/organizar

led/to lead: llevó/llevar, conducir a

creation: creación

science: ciencia

medicine: medicina

another: otra

also: también

developing/to develop: desarrollando/desarrollar

plasma rocket: cohete de plasma

female: mujer

first of four: primera de cuatro

shuttle missions: misiones en transbordadores especiales

Hispanics **are becoming** the **largest minority group** in the United States. Hispanic Americans are **adding** great **value** to American **society** and **enriching** U.S. **government** and culture. **Throughout** this article are **listed** some of the "**famous firsts**" made by Hispanic Americans. These people have made great **contributions** to the United States and the **world**.

Hispanics **fill top positions** in the U.S. government. As of 2005, Mexican-American Alberto Gonzáles **currently serves** as U.S. **Attorney General** and **Cuban-born** Carlos Gutiérrez as **Secretary of Commerce**.

Joseph Marion Hernández was the first Hispanic American to serve in the United States **Congress**. He served from September 1822 to March 1823. From 1990 to 1993, Antonia Coello Novello served as the U.S. Surgeon General. She was first Hispanic and **the first** woman **ever to hold** this position. During her **tenure** as Surgeon General, Novello **focused** her attention on the **health** of women, children and minorities. A **workshop** that she **organized led** to the **creation** of the National Hispanic/Latino Health Initiative.

The world of **science** and **medicine** is **another** area where Hispanic Americans have greatly contributed. In 1986 Franklin Chang-Díaz became the first Costa Rican astronaut. Chang-Díaz is **also** the director of the Advanced Space Propulsion Laboratory at NASA's Johnson Space Center, where he has been **developing** a **plasma rocket**. The first **female** Hispanic astronaut was Ellen Ochoa, whose **first of four shuttle missions** was in 1991.

Luiz Walter Alvarez is the first Hispanic American **to receive** a Nobel Prize in **physics**. He received this **award** in 1968, for **discoveries** about subatomic particles.

Since the 1950s, a number of Hispanic American **musicians** and **performers** have **gained widespread popularity**, including Julio Iglesias, Jennifer López, Gloria Estefan and the group Los Lobos.

Lucrezia Bori, a Spanish soprano, became the first Hispanic American **to debut** at the Metropolitan Opera in 1912. After 1935 she was a director of the Metropolitan Opera Association. She was **distinguished** for her **stage presence** as well as her **singing voice**.

The first Hispanic American to be **inducted** into the Rock and Roll **Hall of Fame** was Carlos Santana in 1998. Santana is **considered** a **guitar-playing legend** and he has been a leader in the music industry for over 30 years.

Many Hispanic **athletes** have **made their mark** in American **sports**. In 1973 Roberto Clemente of Puerto Rico became the first Hispanic American inducted into the Hall of Fame. He was also the first Hispanic **player to serve** on the Players Association Board and to reach 3,000 **hits**. John Ruiz became the **first-ever** Hispanic **heavyweight boxing champ**. He **won** the title **defeating** Evander Holyfield in 2001.

A number of **painters** and **writers** have **further enriched** American culture, such as Hispanic artists John Valadez, Martín Ramírez, Frank Romero and Arnaldo Roche. Oscar Hijuelos is the first Hispanic to win the Pulitzer Prize for fiction. Hijuelos **earned** the Pulitzer for his book, *The Mambo Kings Play Songs of Love* . In this book he **tells the story** of Cuban musicians in New York in the early 1950s.

As more and more Hispanic Americans are **rising to the ranks** and making their mark in their **preferred fields**, the 21st century will **observe** even greater Hispanic contributions to U.S. society and culture. September 15 to October 15 is National Hispanic Heritage Month in the United States. Hispanic Heritage Month **celebrates** and **recognizes** **past** and **present achievements** of Hispanic Americans and **encourages future ones.**

to receive: recibir
physics: física
award: premio
discoveries: descubrimientos
since: desde
musicians: músicos
performers: intérpretes, actores
gained/to gain: logrado/lograr, ganar
widespread popularity: popularidad generalizada
to debut: debutar
distinguished/to distinguish: distinguida/distinguir
stage presence: presencia en el escenario
singing voice: voz para el canto
inducted: ser aceptado como miembro
Hall of Fame: salón de la fama
considered/to consider: considerado/ considerar
guitar-playing legend: leyenda en la guitarra
athletes: atletas
made their mark: hicieron su marca
sports: deportes
player: jugador
to serve: en servir
hits: golpes
first-ever: primero en la historia
heavyweight boxing champ: campión de boxeo en peso pesado
won/to win: ganó/ganar
defeating/to defeat: venciendo/vencer
painters: pintores
writers: escritores
further enriched: enriquecido aún más
earned/to earn: ganó/ganar
tells/to tell: cuenta/contar
the story: la historia
as more and more: a medida que más y más
rising to the ranks: ascendiendo a las posiciones
preferred fields: áreas preferidos
observe: observar
celebrates/to celebrate: celebra/celebrar
recognizes/to recognize: reconoce/ reconocer
past: pasados
present: presentes
achievements: logros
encourages/to encourage: promueve/ promover
future ones: logros futuros

Test Your Comprehension

Trail of Discovery, page 88

1. ¿Por qué quería Thomas Jefferson que Lewis y Clark salieran de expedición?

2. ¿Quién fue la única mujer que viajó con los Cuerpos de Descubrimiento?

3. ¿Cómo ayudó y contribuyó al viaje?

Founding Fathers, page 90

1. ¿Qué son los padres fundadores?

2. ¿A quién se le llama el Padre de la Patria?

3. ¿Quién fue el autor principal de la Declaración de la Independencia?

4. ¿Qué experimento científico hizo famoso a Benjamín Franklin?

Mother of Civil Rights, page 89

1. ¿Qué se rehusó a hacer Rosa Park?

2. ¿Cuándo se prohibió la segregación en los autobuses urbanos?

Frank Lloyd Wright, page 94

1. ¿Por qué estilo de casas era famoso Wright?

2. Describe este estilo.

Examina tu comprensión

Rags to Riches, page 95

1. ¿Qué significaba el "evangelio de la riqueza" para Carnegie?

2. ¿Qué inspiró a Carnegie a construir y financiar las bibliotecas públicas gratuitas?

3. ¿Cuánto dinero regaló Carnegie a lo largo de su vida?

America Takes Flight, page 96

1. ¿Cómo pagaron los hermanos Wright sus aventuras construyendo aviones?

2. ¿Por qué los hermanos Wright probaban sus aviones en Kitty Hawk, Carolina del Norte?

3. En 1928 y 1932 Amelia Earhart se volvió famosa, ¿por qué razón?

Dr. Jonas Salk, page 99

1. ¿Qué descubrió Jonas Salk?

2. ¿Cuál fue su "máximo deseo" con referencia a esta vacuna?

Angel of the Battlefield, page 100

1. ¿Por qué se le llamaba el "Ángel del campo de batalla" a Clara Barton?

2. ¿Qué trabajo hizo Clara Barton al final de la guerra?

The successful man will profit from his mistakes
and try again in a different way.

Dale Carnegie

Business

Introduction to Taxes

How does the United States **pay** to **operate** our government?

The United States must pay for all of the things **needed to run** a government. The government must pay for our **national parks**, **schools**, **roads**, the **military**, **government employees**, and much more. The government has a **system** where people and companies pay a **percentage** of their **income** to the government. This is **called** the income tax.

Who is **responsible** for **collecting** the taxes?

The **Internal Revenue Service** (IRS) **enforces** the tax **laws**. The Internal Revenue Service is also responsible for processing our **tax returns**, collecting **taxes**, and for **giving** the money collected to the **U.S. Treasury**.

To whom does the Internal Revenue Service give our **tax dollars**?

The IRS gives the money collected to the U.S. Treasury, who pays various government **expenses**. The President of the United States and the Congress are responsible for the **federal budget**. The budget is **how much** the government **plans** to **spend** on various programs and services. When the government spends **more** money, it must **raise** more money through taxes. When the government spends less money, it can **afford to** lower taxes.

Who must pay taxes?

1. Every organization, person, **non-profit**, or company, must **report their income** and **calculate** their tax. Some organizations **do not have to pay** tax, but they **still have to report** to the government that they have **tax-exempt status**.

2. You **are taxed** on any money you **earn**. This includes salary from an employer, **interest on savings**, **profits on investments**, **pensions**, and other income.

3. Everyone must pay taxes **throughout the year**. This **is called** "pay as you go." This usually means your income taxes **are taken out of** your paycheck and **sent directly to** the federal government by your employer. At the **end of the year**, if you paid more than what you owe, the government **refunds** the amount paid **over what**

you owed. This is called a **tax refund**. If you have not paid **enough to cover** what you owe, you must pay the **amount due by** April 15th of the **following year**. If you don't pay the taxes due, the government **will charge** you **interest** and **penalties**.

4. People who make more money have a **higher tax rate**, and people who make less money have a **lower** tax rate. Your tax rate will change **depending on** how much money you made that year. This system is called a progressive tax system.

5. People **are free to arrange** their **financial affairs in order to get tax benefits**. **For example**, you can **reduce** your **total income** if you **contribute money** to retirement accounts, such as a 401(k) or IRA plans. There are many other **types** of tax benefits. Tax benefits are how Congress **rewards** people for making **certain** types of decisions. **The goal** of **tax planning** is **to choose** which tax benefits **make the most sense** for you.

throughout the year: a lo largo del año

is called/to call: se llama/llamar

are taken out of: se deducen

sent/to send: enviados/enviar

directly to: directamente a

end of the year: final del año

refunds/to refund: reembolsa/reembolsar, devolver dinero

over: sobre

what you owed: lo que debías

tax refund: reembolso de impuestos, devolución de cuotas ingresadas

enough: bastante

to cover: para cubrir

amount: cantidad

due by: vence en *(fecha)*

following year: año siguiente

will charge/to charge: cobrará/cobrar

interest: interés

penalties: multas

higher: más alta

tax rate: tipo de gravamen

lower: más baja

depending on/to depend on: dependiendo de/depender de

are free: son libres

to arrange: de ordenar o arreglar

financial affairs: asuntos financieros

in order to get: de manera de obtener, para recibir

tax benefits: beneficios impositivos

for example: por ejemplo

reduce: reducir

total income: ingresos totales

contribute/to contribute: aportas/aportar

money: dinero

types: tipos

rewards/to reward: premia/premiar

certain: ciertos

the goal: el objetivo

tax planning: planear los impuestos

to choose: elegir

make the most sense: tienen mayor sentido

Entrepreneurship

Many immigrants **move** to the United States **to work towards** a **better life** for **themselves** and their families. **Entrepreneurship** is often **the route** they **take**, or **hope** to take.

It is often said that starting a **business** is an American **dream**. With the **right product** or service, the U.S. is the **best place** in the world **to launch** a **new company**. The **trouble** is that many new entrepreneurs **lack** the **language**, business **skills**, and **start-up money** to successfully **manage** and **grow** their businesses.

STARTING OUT

Fortunately, there is **help to get you started**. There are numerous organizations helping Spanish-speaking immigrants who have an **entrepreneurial drive**.

In many other cultures, you can start a business at **any time** and **worry** about the **planning later**. In the U.S. culture, you **need to get** all the planning and permits **done first**.

Some of the best places to start are SBA, SCORE and the Hispanic Chamber of Commerce.

- Small Business Association (www.sba.gov). The SBA is a **governmental agency** that **offers all levels** of assistance, **business loans** and **grants** for small businesses. The SBA is a **strong advocate** of **minority audiences**.

- SCORE. SCORE is a subdivision of the SBA. SCORE offers **free online** or **face-to-face** business **counseling** and **low cost** seminars and **workshops**. Online you will find a list of resources specifically for minority entrepreneurs. To make it **even easier**, all of their information **is offered** in English and Spanish.

- Hispanic Chamber of Commerce (www.ushcc.com). **To advocate**, **promote** and **facilitate** the **success** of Hispanic businesses. They provide **technical assistance** to Hispanic business associations and entrepreneurs.

START-UP COSTS

Access to **capital** can be a **concern** for Hispanic business owners.

In addition to loans through governmental agencies, **more and more** banks are **setting up** divisions that **focus entirely** on loans for the Hispanic/Latino communities in the U.S.

Wells Fargo has a **long tradition** of providing **financial services** to Latinos. On their website it states: "Wells Fargo is **committed** to helping Latino owned businesses grow and **prosper**." In 1997, Wells Fargo launched Latino Business Services **to support** and **build relationships** with the Latino-owned businesses in our communities. Wells Fargo also **celebrates outstanding** Latino entrepreneurs with **award** grants.

Smaller community banks also offer small business loans for minority businesses. Do some **research** to learn about banks in your area that **pride themselves** on their relationships with the Latino community.

LOW OVERHEAD

Many people **decide** to start businesses that don't need a lot of startup money.

Miguel Peña **began selling custom boots** and **hats** after a **construction injury**. He **sold** his boots and hats at **swap meets** and to friends. Success on that level gave him the **desire to open** a **tiny store** in 1989. Today, he **operates** stores in Arizona.

Lucy Acedo **tested interest** in an **antique shop** by having frequent **garage sales** to sell her **treasures**. She **invested** around $500 **to acquire collectible dishes** and **knick-knacks** at **estate** and garage sales. She's **managed to keep** the business **running** for 4 ½ years.

The United States **truly is** a **land of opportunity**. With the **abundance** of business **resources** offered, it is possible to start your own business. If you plan to start your own business, make **the most** of what is **offered** to you and **memorize** this American **idiom**: "**Where there's a will, there's a way!**"

---

capital: capital *(dinero)*
concern: preocupación
in addition to: además de
more and more: más y más
setting up/to set up: estableciendo/ establecer
focus/to focus: se centran/centrarse
entirely: enteramente, por entero
long tradition: larga tradición
financial services: servicios financieros
committed/to commit: comprometido/comprometerse
prosper/to prosper: prosperar/ prosperar
to support: para apoyar
build: construir
relationships: relaciones
celebrates/to celebrate: celebra/ celebrar
outstanding: sobresalientes
award: premio
research: investigación
pride themselves/to pride oneself: se enorgullecen/enorgullecerse
decide/to decide: deciden/decidir
began/to begin: empezó/empezar
selling/to sell: vendiendo/vender
custom boots: botas a medida
hats: sombreros
construction injury: lesión causada trabajando en construcción
sold/to sell: vendió/vender
swap meets: encuentros para intercambiar
desire: deseo
to open: de abrir
tiny store: tienda minúscula
operates/to operate: maneja/manejar
tested/to test: probó/probar
interest: interés
antique shop: tienda de antigüedades
garage sales: ventas de garaje
treasures: tesoros
invested/to invest: invirtió/invertir
to acquire: para adquirir
collectible dishes: platos de colección
knick-knacks: baratijas
estate: patrimonio
managed/to manage: consiguió/ conseguir
to keep...running: mantener... funcionando
truly is: realmente es
land of opportunity: tierra de oportunidades
abundance: abundancia
resources: recursos
make the most: aprovecha...al máximo
offered/to offer: ofrece/ofrecer
memorize/to memorize: memoriza/ memorizar
idiom: dicho
Where there's a will, there's a way!: ¡Querer es poder!

population: población
integrating/to integrate: intengrándose/integrarse
systems: sistemas
however: sin embargo
say/to say: dicen/decir
not using banks: no usan bancos
cash: dinero en efectivo
preferred method: método preferido
managing/to manage: manejar/ manejar
finances: finanzas
remains/to remain: se mantiene/ mantenerse
lack of identification: falta de identificación
undocumented: sin documentos
banking: el sector bancario
concept: concepto
laborers: trabajadores
without: sin
income: ingresos
reluctant: reticentes, reacios
set up: abrir
account: cuenta
legal residency: residencia legal
simply: simplemente
unsure: no seguros
about: sobre
works/to work: funciona/funcionar
has not started/to start: no ha empezado a/ empezar
often come: a menudo vienen
rural areas: áreas rurales
villages: pueblos
access: acceso
limited: limitado
nonexistent: inexistente
established/to establish: establecido/establecer
relationship: relación
to start: empezar
new country: nuevo país
fully speak: hablan completamente
language: idioma
living: vivir
cash-only: sólo al contado
risks: riesgos
law enforcement officials: agentes de la ley
criminals: delincuentes
view/to view: ven/ver
easy targets: blancos fáciles
carry/to carry: llevan/llevar

Banking in America

The nation's Hispanic **population** is **integrating** into the social and cultural **systems**. **However,** many people **say** they are **not using banks** and **cash** is the **preferred method** for **managing** their **finances**.

Cash **remains** popular because of a **lack of identification** for new or **undocumented** immigrants. Also, cultural differences make **banking** a foreign **concept** to many.

For some **laborers without** documentation, all their **income** is in cash.

Some are **reluctant** to **set up** an **account** because they might not have **legal residency**, while others are **simply unsure about** how the banking process **works**.

Another reason the Hispanic community **has not started** using banks is that they **often come** to the United States from **rural areas** in Latin American countries. In these small **villages access** to banking is **limited** or **nonexistent**. Many immigrants haven't **established** a banking **relationship** even in Mexico. It is difficult for them **to start** their banking in a **new country** where they don't **fully speak** the **language**.

Living in a **cash-only** world has its **risks. Law enforcement officials** say **criminals view** Hispanics as **easy targets** because they are known to often **carry** cash.

Banks **across** the nation are **welcoming** the Hispanic population and **setting up** programs specifically for Hispanics and new immigrants.

Bank of America started a **pilot program** in the Los Angeles area **late last year** that **issues credit cards** in California to non-citizens who don't have **Social Security numbers**. The **goal** of the card is **to introduce customers** to banking and **help build** a **credit history.**

Citigroup has had a similar program for years and Wells Fargo & Co. officials have said they are **considering** such a card.

Community banks are **tapping** the Hispanic **market** by **offering video tapes** that **explain topics** such as **insurance, investing, public schools** and **starting a business**.

Many banks are offering **cost effective alternatives** for **money wires** and making it **easier** and **cheaper** to wire money home. Mitchell Bank in Milwaukee **caters** to an increasingly Mexican customer base. The bank offers the first two wire transfers free, and then charges $2.50 for each additional wire. This is a **significant savings compared to** private wire services.

Many immigrants don't **realize** that you can **open** a bank account without a Social Security number. Banks nationwide **accept** identification issued by Mexican **consulates** to customers who want to open an account but don't have Social Security numbers.

All **throughout** the U.S. banks have been working very hard **in order to promote** their services and **let** the Hispanic population **know** there are many possibilities **besides** cash. The Latin American Council is working **to educate** people on the **value** of **building** a credit history, having a savings account and making investments. These are **things** that will help new immigrants **assimilate** into their **community**.

across: a lo largo de
welcoming: dando la bienvenida
setting up: estableciendo
pilot program: programa piloto
late last year: a finales del año pasado
issues: emite/emitir
credit cards: tarjetas de crédito
Social Security numbers: números de seguridad social
goal: objetivo
to introduce: introducir
customers: clientes
help build: ayudar a construir
credit history: historia de crédito
considering/to consider: considerando/considerar
tapping/to tap: aprovechando/aprovechar
market: mercado
offering/to offer ofreciendo/ofrecer
video tapes: cintas de video
explain topics: explican temas
insurance: seguros
investing: inversiones
public schools: escuelas públicas
starting a business: montar un negocio
cost effective: rentables, beneficiosas
alternatives: alternativas
money wires: giros telegráficos
easier: más fáciles
cheaper: más baratas
caters/to cater: atiende/atender
significant savings: ahorros considerables
compared to: comparados con
realize/to realize: se dan cuenta/darse cuenta
open: abrir
accept/to accept: aceptan/aceptar
consulates: consulados
throughout: a lo largo de
in order to promote: para promover
let ... know: hacer ... saber
besides: aparte de
to educate: para educar
value: valor
building: construir
things: cosas
assimilate: asimilarse
community: comunidad

Negotiating Your Salary

For many **job seekers**, salary negotiation can be the most **intimidating part** of the employment process. It can be even more **nerve-wracking** if you are a foreign professional who **is unsure about** the **rules** of salary negotiation in the United States.

While it may **feel** like an **uncomfortable** situation, U.S. employers are prepared for **potential hires** to **negotiate** compensation. People often have the tendency to be **grateful** for that **first offer** and **fail to** negotiate, says psychology professor Melanie Domenech-Rodriguez.

By using some simple negotiating techniques, you can **increase** your annual salary.

• **Research** your **market value** — Before your interview, **gather** information about the **current** market value for similar positions.

• **Reach out** to current employees at the company or colleagues in the **same field** for information on **pay ranges**.

• **Check** comparison websites like www.Salary.com that **allow** you **to search** salary ranges by profession and location.

• **Review** salary information from the U.S. Bureau of Labor Statistics.

Remember, many companies **pay a premium** for **bilingual employees**. **Depending** on the industry, you could **earn as much as** 20 percent **more than** colleagues who don't speak Spanish.

Never be the first one to **discuss** salary — During the interview process, **always** let the employer be the one to **bring up** compensation. If you **broach the subject** first, you **risk** looking **as though** you are more interested in your paycheck than the **job itself**. If you **propose** an amount **before hearing** the employer's offer, you could **price yourself** well **below** what they were **willing** to pay.

Once you hear their initial offer, **stay silent** —When the employer does propose a salary amount, you shouldn't **rush to respond**. This simple tactic lets the employer know you are not **overly enthusiastic** about the offer.

4. Consider (and negotiate!) other types of compensation — Ask about other aspects of the offer **such as** medical and life insurance, 401(k) plans, **vacation time**, **moving expenses**, **flex time** and other benefits. These extras may effectively increase your compensation, or they can be used as **additional points** of negotiation later.

5. Take time to think — You shouldn't **feel pressured to accept** or **decline** an offer **on the spot**. Thank the recruiter for the offer and request a day or two to consider it.

6. Ask for more than you **expect to get** — Negotiators **around the world** know the concept of **meeting in the middle**. By asking for a **higher** salary **initially**, you are **creating** a win-win situation – one where **both parties** are able **to give up** something and still **win**. This **is called** a **win-win situation**.

It is always best to negotiate in person, so make an appointment **to meet with** the company representative. Briefly **remind** them:

- That you are **excited** about the opportunity

- How you **plan** on contributing to their success

- The **special skills** you bring, **including** bilingualism/biculturalism

You are then ready to make your **counter-offer**. Although you will be asking for more than you actually expect, make sure that the amount is **within the realm** of possibility based on your market research.

If you have another offer **on the table**, it's okay **to mention it**, **as long as** you are **tactful**. Never **pretend** that you have other offers if you don't.

If you have **gauged** the market **accurately**, the employer should **suggest** a "meet in the middle" figure or **at least** improve their initial offer. In cases where the salary figure is **firm**, suggest additional **perks** or benefits that would make the offer more **appealing** to you.

7. Get it in writing — Once you've **come to an understanding**, your **last step** is to **make sure** the company **provides** a **written employment agreement** covering not just salary, but **all the points** you negotiated. Do not **skip** this step—the person you negotiated with could leave the company or later **forget** exactly what they **agreed to verbally**.

Congratulations, you just **negotiated your way** to a higher salary!

consider/to consider: considera/considerar
such as: tales como
vacation time: tiempo de vacaciones
moving expenses: gastos de mudanza
flex time: horario flexible
additional points: puntos adicionales
take time: tómate tiempo
feel pressured: sentirse presionado/a
to accept: a aceptar
decline: rehusar, declinar
on the spot: en el momento, en el acto
expect/to expect: esperas/esperar
to get: recibir
around the world: alrededor del mundo
meeting in the middle: encontrarse en el medio
higher: más alto
initially: inicialmente
creating/to create: creando/crear
both parties: ambos partidos
to give up: ceder
win: ganar
is called/to call: se llama/llamar
win-win situation: situación donde todos ganan
to meet with: encontrarse con, reunirse con
remind/to remind: recuerda/recordar
excited: entusiasmado/a
plan/to plan: planeas/planear
special skills: habilidades especiales
including: incluyendo
counter-offer: contraoferta
within the realm: dentro de la esfera
on the table: sobre el tapete
to mention it: mencionarla
as long as: siempre y cuando
tactful: con tacto
pretend/to pretend: pretendas/pretender
gauged/to gauge: calculado/calcular
accurately: con precisión
suggest/to suggest: sugerir/sugerir
at least: por lo menos
firm: firme
perks: ventajas
appealing: atractiva
get it in writing: obtenlo por escrito
come to an understanding: llegaste a un acuerdo
last step: último paso
make sure: asegurarse
provides/to provide: provee/proveer
written employment agreement: acuerdo de empleo por escrito
all the points: todos los puntos
skip/to skip: te saltees/saltearse
forget/to forget: olvidar/olvidar
agreed to verbally: acordaron verbalmente
congratulations: felicitaciones
negotiated your way: negociaste tu camino

Retirement Plans

In the United States, **many** employers **offer** a **company-sponsored retirement plan** for **employees called** a 401(k) plan. **Knowing** some basic information about the 401(k) plan **will help you** do **further research to make** the **best decision** for you and your family.

What is a 401(k) Plan?

A 401(k) plan is a company-sponsored **qualified** retirement plan for employees. Your contributions will be **deducted** from your **paycheck before** taxes are **withheld**.

You will have the option **to decide how much** you want **to contribute** to the plan each **payday**. The money you contribute to the plan is not **subject to** federal and most **state income taxes** until you **withdraw** the **funds**.

Once you are **eligible** to **start participating** in your company's 401(k) plan, **you will be given** a list of **stocks**, **bonds** and/or **money market** funds in which **you can invest**. There are limits **regarding** the **amount** you can invest.

Your contributions will be deducted from your paycheck **before** taxes are withheld. Depending on your income and **tax bracket**, this pretax deduction can **be like getting** a 25-percent **rate of return** on your **investment**. These contributions are then invested into the funds **you select**.

Your company matches your contribution to the 401(k) plan.

If you are lucky enough to work for a company that provides the benefit of a **company match**, it's like **earning free money**. **For example**, if you **choose** to contribute 2% of your **salary**, your company also contributes 2%. Your employer **will match** a maximum **amount**.

Withdrawing Money from a 401(k)

For people 70½ **years old or older**, the law currently requires that you **begin** withdrawing **money** from your 401(k). You can **defer** this withdrawal **rule** if you are **still** a **full-time** employee with the company sponsoring your 401(k). If you are 59½ or older, you may begin withdrawals **without** any **early withdrawal penalty**. You are also **exempt** from this penalty if you are over age 55 and have been **terminated** by your company or if you **become totally disabled**.

About 85 **percent** of 401(k) plans **allow** employees **to take loans against** the money in their **account**, up to a maximum of 50 percent of their **savings**. The money you **borrow is not subject to** the 10 percent penalty **as long as** you **pay it back** (with interest) **within the time established** by your employer's plan.

If you do take a loan from your 401(k), you will have up to 5 years **to repay** the loan. But if you **leave** your job, it **must be repaid within** 30 days. Any amount that you **fail to** repay is subject to the 10 percent early withdrawal penalty and taxes. And the interest? The interest you pay **goes directly** into your account—you are paying it to yourself!

Get Started

A 401(k) plan is an important part of **retirement planning**. **You should learn** everything you can from your employer about the plan that is offered. **Gather** information on **vesting**, **contribution limits**, and matching funds. Research all available information on the funds offered for investing. **Track** your investments **regularly** and **ask for assistance** if you feel your investment options **aren't performing** satisfactorily.

years old or older: de edad o mayor
begin/to begin: empieces/empezar
money: dinero
defer/to defer: diferir/diferir
rule: regla
still: todavía
full-time: de tiempo completo
without: sin
early withdrawal penalty: penalización por retiro temprano *(de dinero)*
exempt: exento
terminated/to terminate: despedido/despedir
become/to become: te vuelves/volverse
totally: totalmente
disabled: incapacitado
about: alrededor de
percent: por ciento
allow/to allow: permiten/permitir
to take: tomar
loans: préstamos
against: contra
account: cuenta
savings: ahorros
borrow/to borrow: tomas prestado/tomar prestado
is not subject to: no está sujeto
as long as: siempre y cuando, mientras que
pay it back: devuelvas
within the time established: dentro del plazo establecido
to repay: para devolver *(dinero)*
leave/to leave: dejas/dejar
must be repaid within: debe ser devuelto dentro
fail to/to fail to do something: no consigues/no conseguir hacer algo
goes/to go: va/ir
directly: directamente
retirement planning: planificación de jubilación
you should learn: deberías aprender
gather/to gather: junta/juntar
vesting: adquisición de derechos de pensión
contribution limits: límites de contribución
track/to track: controla/controlar
regularly: regularmente
ask for/to ask for: pide/pedir
assistance: asistencia, ayuda
aren't performing/to perform: no están rindiendo/rendir

subtle: sutiles
not-so-subtle: no tan sutiles
between: entre
the way: la forma
employment interviews: entrevistas de trabajo
conducted/to conduct: se llevan a cabo/ llevar a cabo, conducir
top ten tips: mejores diez consejos
avoid: evitar
misconceptions: ideas equivocadas
pitfalls: dificultades
job: trabajo
acing: lograr resultados fenomenales, triunfar
take credit/to take credit: atribúyete el mérito/atribuirse el mérito
accomplishments: logros
expects you: espera que tú
"toot you own horn": literalmente: "toques tu propia bocina", hables de tus logros
can be awkward: puede resultar incómodo o embarazoso
group-oriented: con orientación grupal
crucial part: parte crucial
discussing: (el) discutir
viewed/to view: visto/ver
arrogant: arrogante
egotistical: egotista
in fact: de hecho
point out/to point out: indicas/indicar
solo successes: logros individuales
will assume/to assume: asumirán/asumir
to talk about: de (las) que hablar
eye contact: contacto ocular
picturing you as: te imaginarán como
co-worker: compañero/a de trabajo
expect/to expect: esperan/esperar
look them in the eye: mirarlos a los ojos
act: actuar
shows confidence: muestra confianza
failing: el dejar de
could be interpreted: podría ser interpretado
sign: señal, indicación
untruthful: mentiroso, falso
get to the point: ve al grano
focus/to focus: enfócate/enfocarse
relevant facts: hechos relevantes
busy: ocupados
time is short: hay poco tiempo
to shine: brillar
brief time: breve tiempo
in front of them: frente a ellos
personal issues: cuestiones personales
to break the ice: para romper el hielo
tell me: dime
are not asking/to ask: no están preguntando/preguntar
childhood: infancia
to hear: escuchar
the jobs you've had: los trabajos que has tenido
past: pasado

There are some **subtle**—and some **not-so-subtle**—differences **between the way employment interviews** are **conducted** in the United States and in Latin America.

Here are the **top ten tips** from Hispanic job board LatPro.com to help you **avoid** possible **misconceptions** and cultural **pitfalls** so you can get the **job** you want!

Top Ten Tips for **Acing** your U.S. Job Interview

1. Take Credit for your Professional Accomplishments

An employer **expects you** to **"toot your own horn,"** says Graciela Kenig, founder and president of LatinoWorkforce.com. This **can be awkward** for Latinos, who are more community and **group-oriented**, but it's a **crucial part** of the U.S. interview.

Discussing your individual accomplishments won't be **viewed** as **arrogant** or **egotistical**. **In fact**, if you don't **point out** your **solo successes**, employers **will assume** you don't have significant contributions **to talk about**.

2. Make Eye Contact

Interviewers will be **picturing you** as a potential **co-worker** during the interview. They **expect** you **to look them in the eye** and **act** like a colleague. In the U.S. making good eye contact **shows confidence**; **failing** to look your interviewer in the eye will not only make them uncomfortable, it **could be interpreted** as a **sign** that you are being evasive or **untruthful**.

3. Be Direct

In the U.S. interview you should **get to the point** quickly and **focus** only on the **relevant facts**. Getting directly to the matter at hand may seem rude or abrupt to a Latino, but it won't to the person doing the interview. They are **busy**, **time is short**, and you need **to shine** during the **brief time** you have **in front of them**.

4. Focus on Professional, not Personal Issues

Interviewers may ask a question just **to break the ice,** says Nelson De Leon, bilingual recruiting consultant and the owner and founder of America At Work.com. When an interviewer asks you to "**tell me** something about yourself," they **are not asking** about your **childhood**, your dogs or your family. They want **to hear** about you in relation to **the jobs you've had** in the **past** and the job you want.

5. Get Rid of the "Yes Syndrome"

The Yes Syndrome is something De Leon identifies as an idiosyncrasy of Hispanic culture. As an interviewer is talking, the recruit may be **nodding his head**, saying yes **over and over**, but that doesn't necessarily mean they've **understood** everything. It does mean they've **heard**; they are **listening**, and they won't interrupt for fear of seeming rude. "**It's okay** to **ask questions**," says De Leon. It **does not make you look stupid**, as some **fear**. It makes you look and **sound engaged** in the interview.

6. Don't Be Passive

If you are **too humble** or too reserved, you may appear **uninterested** in the job, warns De Leon. Once you start asking questions, it shows you have a **good grasp** of the job **at hand.** The **smartest** people don't give the best answers, they ask the best questions, showing potential employers they can **identify** problems.

7. Beware Tú versus Usted

Latinos are **aware** of the **formality** of "usted," but because English only uses "you," be **conscious** that you **don't get too familiar** with your interviewer. While a recruit should not be subservient, there should still be respect. If you **happen to be** interviewing in Spanish, **stick with** "usted" during the interview. Don't lapse into using "tú" for the entire corporate culture.

8. Dress Conservatively

Even if the **day-to-day dress** of regular employees **is casual**, you should **choose** conservative **business attire** for your interview. A professional appearance **shows** that you **respect** the interviewer and **are serious about** the available position. Avoid anything that **will detract** from the interview, **including** too much **jewelry**, perfume or **aftershave**.

9. Don't be Discouraged if the Interviewer Seems Impersonal

Employers who don't ask about **your background**, your family, your kids and your church **are not being rude**, and it **does not mean** they **don't like you** as a potential employee. In the U.S., many personal questions like these are **prohibited** during an interview.

10. Research the company before your interview – and don't forget your Hispanic connections!

It's a **big world**, but cultural connections can make the world s**eem smaller. In addition to** more traditional research methods, reaching out to fellow Latinos can **give you valuable insight** into a company. Within the **close-knit** Hispanic community, **chances are good** that you can **find** someone who has already interviewed with or **worked for** a particular company. **All you have to do** is ask!

---

get rid of: deshazte
nodding his head: asintiendo con la cabeza
over and over: una y otra vez
understood/to understand: entendido/ entender
heard/to hear: escuchado/escuchar
listening/to listen: escuchando/escuchar
it's okay: está bien
ask questions: hacer preguntas
does not make you look stupid: no te hace lucir como un estúpido
fear/to fear: temen/temer
sound/to sound: sonar/sonar
engaged: interesado
passive: pasivo
too humble: demasiado humilde
uninterested: desinteresado
good grasp: buena comprensión
at hand: a mano *(ese trabajo)*
smartest: más inteligente
identify: identificar
beware: ten cuidado
aware: conscientes
formality: formalidad
conscious: consciente
don't get too familiar: no trates ... con excesiva confianza
happen to be: si por casualidad estás
stick with: cíñete al
dress conservatively: vístete de forma conservadora
day-to-day dress: vestimenta diaria
is casual: es informal
choose/to choose: elegir/elegir
business attire: ropa de negocios
shows/to show: muestra/mostrar
respect/to respect: respetas/respetar
are serious about: tienes intenciones serias respecto a
will detract: reste mérito
including: incluyendo
jewelry: joyas, alhajas
aftershave: loción para después del afeitado
don't be discouraged: no te desanimes
seems/to seem: parece/parecer
your background: tu origen
are not being rude: no están siendo groseros
does not mean: no significa
don't like you: no les gustas
prohibited: prohibidas
research/to research: investiga/investigar
don't forget: no olvides
connections: conexiones
big world: mundo grande
seem smaller: parezca más pequeño
in addition to: además de
give you valuable insights: darte una valiosa perspectiva
close-knit: muy unida
chances are good: hay buenas posibilidades
find/to find: encontrar/encontrar
worked for: trabajó para
all you have to do: todo lo que tienes que hacer

Test Your Comprehension

Introduction to Taxes, page 108

1. ¿Quién es responsable de recaudar los impuestos?

2. ¿A quién da el Servicio de Impuestos Internos nuestro dinero de los impuestos?

3. ¿Qué pasa si no pagas impuestos?

Entrepreneurship, page 110

1. ¿Qué le hace falta a muchos empresarios nuevos para hacer crecer su negocio?

2. Además de préstamos a través de agencias gubernamentales, ¿a dónde más puedes obtener un préstamo?

3. ¿Qué son los gastos generales bajos?

Banking in America, page 112

1. ¿Por qué muchos inmigrantes prefieren dinero al contado en vez de usar un banco?

2. ¿Por qué es riesgoso vivir en un mundo sólo al contado?

3. El Banco de América empezó un programa que emite tarjetas de crédito en California a no-ciudadanos que no tienen número de seguridad social. ¿Cuál es la finalidad de esta tarjeta?

Negotiating Your Salary, page 114

1. Dependiendo de tu industria, ¿cuánto más podrías ganar como un empleado bilingüe?

2. Una vez que el empleador te da su oferta incial de salario, ¿qué sugiere el artículo que hagas?

3. Una vez que te has puesto de acuerdo en un salario, ¿cuál es el último paso que no debes saltearte?

Examina tu comprensión

Retirement Plans, page 116

1. ¿Qué es un Plan 401(k)?

2. ¿A qué no está sujeto el dinero que contribuyes al plan?

3. ¿Cuál es una parte importante del planeamiento para la jubilación?

Mastering the Interview, page 118

1. ¿Verdadero o falso? Discutir tus logros personales se verá como arrogante o egotista.

2. Hacer un buen contacto con la mirada, ¿qué demuestra?

3. Hacer preguntas durante la entrevista, ¿qué hace?

4. ¿Si estás teniendo la entrevista en español, debes usar "tú" o "usted"?

5. ¿Por qué no se hacen muchas preguntas personales durante una entrevista?

¡Información Importantes!

Los artículos *Negotiating Your Salary* y *Mastering the Interview* fueron proporcionados por **LatPro.com,** el sitio más visitado por hispanos y profesionales bilingües en busca de trabajo. Desde 1997 LatPro ha ayudado a hispanos en busca de trabajo a encontrar empleo en las mejores compañías a lo largo de los Estados Unidos y América Latina. Además de avisos de trabajo actuales, este sitio de empleo (ganador de varios premios y disponible en inglés, español y portugués) ofrece amplio asesoramiento para hispanos que buscan trabajo. Visite **LatPro.com** por más artículos relacionados a su carrera, consejos para su curriculum vitae y recursos para profesionales latinos.

The future belongs to those
who believe in the beauty of their dreams.

Eleanor Roosevelt

Empowerment

Citizenship

With the exception of Native Americans, the United States is a nation of people who **left** their **home country looking for** a **better life**. The **population** of the United States is **made up of** a **mixture** of people from different countries and is **sometimes called** a "melting pot." **Although** your **neighbor** or **co-worker** may have been **born** in the United States, **at some point**, that person's family left their home country and **came** to the United States.

Living in the United States doesn't **automatically** make one an American citizen. Residents of the United States can be **aliens**, **nationals**, or **citizens**.

- **Aliens:** Aliens are people **who have left** a foreign country to live in the United States. They have **some of the same freedoms** and **legal rights** as U.S. citizens, but they **cannot vote** in **elections**.

- **Nationals:** American nationals are **natives** of American territorial possessions. They have all the legal protections which citizens have, but they **do not have** the full **political rights** of U.S. citizens.

- **Citizens:** Persons born in the U.S. are citizens of the United States. Persons born in other countries who **want to become** citizens must **apply for** and **pass** a **citizenship test**. Those who become citizens **in this manner** are **naturalized** citizens.

Over time, most immigrants become U.S. citizens. The process, **however**, is not an **easy** one. It **involves learning** how **to speak**, **read**, and **write ordinary** English; learning about the history and government of the United States and **patiently wading through** a bureaucratic process.

Community-based organizations and local government agencies have **developed** materials and **techniques** to help immigrants become **full participants** in our **society**.

---

with the exception of: con la excepción de
left/to leave: dejó/dejar
home country: país natal
looking for/to look for: buscando/ buscar
better life: vida mejor
population: población
made up of: compuesta por
mixture: mezcla
sometimes: a veces
called/to call: llamada/llamar
although: aunque, si bien
neighbor: vecino
co-worker: compañero/a de trabajo
born: nacido
at some point: en algún momento
came/to come: vino/venir
living: *(el)* vivir
automatically: automáticamente
aliens: extranjeros
nationals: nacionales
citizens: ciudadanos
who have left: quienes han dejado
some of the same: algunas de las mismas
freedoms: libertades
legal rights: derechos legales
cannot vote: no pueden votar
elections: elecciones
natives: nativos
do not have: no tienen
political rights: derechos políticos
want/to want: quieren/querer
to become: convertirse
apply for: solicitar
pass: aprobar
citizenship test: examen de ciudadanía
in this manner: de esta manera
naturalized/to naturalize: naturalizados/naturalizar
over time: con el tiempo
however: sin embargo
easy: fácil
involves/to involve: supone/suponar
learning: *(el)* aprender
to speak: hablar
read: leer
write: escribir
ordinary: común
patiently: pacientemente
wading through: abrirse camino a través de
developed/to develop: han desarrollado/desarrollar
techniques: técnicas
full participants: participantes de pleno derecho
society: sociedad

Civic Participation

Participation in America's **civic life** is something that **may at first seem** like a **luxury** for immigrants. As people **become rooted** in their **adopted country**, most immigrants become citizens. **Beyond that, voter registration**, voting, and other forms of civic participation **vary**. Even **as they become** a **larger portion** of our population, new Americans are **under-represented** in our civic life.

This **is beginning to change**! There are a **number** of groups **around** the **country** who **help** immigrants **understand** our civic culture and help them **get involved**. Some groups **regularly** hold voter registration **drives**. In the process, they are helping to **transform** our civic culture. As the number of new citizens **continues to grow**, our civic culture will grow **as well**—**adapting** to **desires** and **needs** of immigrants who have become Americans by **choice**.

The **following** organizations **provide outstanding** civic participation programs and information:

- National Association of Latino Elected Officials: www.naleo.org
- Democracy Collaborative: www.democracycollaborative.org

QUICK FACTS

Hispanic Immigrants and the Electorate
- **Over** 5.9 million Latinos participated in the presidential election in 2000.
- In the **last decade**, the number of **voting-age** Latinos **rose** by 47%. Latinos **as a percentage** of the voters **nationwide** went from 5% in 1996 to 7% in 2000.

Immigrants as **Volunteers** and **Philanthropists**
- Hispanic Americans 45 and **older** volunteer the **most hours** per month. They are the **most likely** to provide help to immigrants in this country and **send** money to help people in other countries.
- In 2001 Hispanic Americans sent **remittances** to Latin America and the Caribbean totaling $23 billion.

Immigrants in the **Military**
- 1.1 million—the number of Latino **veterans** of the U.S. **armed forces**.
- **About** 63,000 people of Hispanic origin were on **active duty** in 2002 in the U.S.

civic life: vida civil
may at first seem: puede parecer al principio
luxury: lujo
become rooted: se arraiga, echa raíces
adopted country: país adoptivo
beyond that: más allá de eso
voter registration: registro de votantes
vary/to vary: varían/variar
as they become: a medida que ellos se convierten
larger portion: porción mayor
under-represented: poco representados
is beginning to change: está empezando a cambiar
number: número
around: alrededor
country: país
help/to help: ayudan/ayudar
understand: entender
get involved/to involve: involucrarse/involucrar
regularly: regularmente
drives: campañas
transform: transformar
continues/to continue: continúa/continuar
to grow: crecer
as well: también
adapting/to adapt: adaptándose/adaptar
desires: deseos
needs: necesidades
choice: elección
following: siguientes
provide/to provide: proveen/proveer
outstanding: sobresalientes
over: sobre
last decade: última década
voting-age: en edad de votar
rose/to rise: aumentó/aumentar
as a percentage: como porcentaje
nationwide: en todo el país
volunteers: voluntarios
philanthropists: filántropos
older: mayores
most hours: mayor número de horas
most likely: más propensos
send: enviar
remittances: dinero, pago
military: ejército, fuerzas armadas
veterans: veteranos
armed forces: fuerzas armadas
about: alrededor de, aproximadamente
active duty: (estar de) servicio activo

Empowerment with Education

Latinos are one of our nation's **largest** ethnic minorities and the **fastest-growing segment** of our population.

Between 2000 and 2005 the Hispanic population in the United States **grew from** 12.5 percent of the **overall** population **to about** 14 percent. **All indications** are that this **trend will continue**. **As of** 2005, there were over 42 million Hispanics living in the United States. The U.S. Census Bureau **estimates** that number **will increase** to 63 million by 2030.

As the Hispanic population continues to increase, education is a **key issue**. **Although** a growing segment of the Hispanic population is achieving **educational excellence**, reports from the U.S. Census Bureau **reveal** a **startling discrepancy** in the educational **attainment** of Hispanics **compared to** other groups:

- In 2000, 36 percent of Hispanic high school graduates ages 18 to 24 **enrolled in colleges** and universities, compared to 44 percent of non-Hispanic whites.
- In 2000, Hispanic students **accounted for** 7 percent of students enrolled at **4-year institutions**.
- About 12 percent of Hispanic adults **currently** have a **bachelor's degree, compared with** 30.5 percent of non-Hispanic whites.

There are **several** organizations that **might help you** in your **search** for **scholarships** or **financial aid. In order to most effectively plan** your search, you should **contact** the necessary organizations **up to a year in advance**. Your **first step** should be **to decide** on a **few schools** and contact their financial aid **offices, asking about** any scholarships or financial aid they offer to **minority students**.

Be sure to explore all financial aid and scholarship possibilities, **not just** those opportunities **targeted specifically** towards minorities. The federal government has several major financial aid **packages**, **work-study programs**, and **grants**. You may contact their educational **hotline** at 1-(800) 433-3243.

The Hispanic Scholarship Fund (HSF) is the nation's **leading organization** supporting Hispanic higher education. HSF **was founded** in 1975 with a vision of **strengthening the country** by **advancing** college education among Hispanic Americans. **In support of** its mission **to double the rate of** Hispanics **earning** college degrees, HSF provides the Latino community with **more** college scholarships and educational **outreach support than any other** organization in the country. **In addition**, HSF **launched** the Hispanic Scholarship Fund Institute **to create public partnerships** in support of its work. **During** its 31-year history, HSF **has awarded** more than 78,000 scholarships to Latinos from all 50 states, Puerto Rico, the U.S. Virgin Islands and Guam. HSF **scholars have attended** more than 1,700 colleges and universities. To read more, go to www.hsf.net.

The Hispanic College Fund **provides talented** and **underprivileged** Hispanic **youth** with mentors, **resources** and scholarships. For more information, go to www.hispanicfund.org.

The Hispanic Bar Association of D.C. is a separate **non-profit entity**. First- and second-year law students attending D.C.-area law schools are **eligible to apply** for the fellowship. To read more, go to www.hbadc.org.

The Association of Latino Professionals in Finance and Accounting (ALPFA) provides many programs and **benefits** to **aspiring** Latino students interested in **accounting**, **finance** or related **career** professions. **To learn more**, go to www.alpfa.org.

Community Colleges

world of opportunity: un mundo de oportunidades
across: a lo largo de
specialty: especialidad
credit classes: clases *(que otorgan)* créditos
non-credit: *(clases)* que no otorgan créditos
a host of: un montón de
options: opciones
there are over: hay más de
open admissions policies: políticas de admisión abierta
low tuitions: matrículas de bajo costo
represent/to represent: representan/representar
rich diversity: rica diversidad
include/to include: incluyen/incluir
mix of ages: mezcla de edades
variety: variedad
ethnic: étnicos
backgrounds: orígenes
numerous: numerosos
entire: enteros
focused: enfocados
are provided/to provide: se proveen/proveer
service: servicio
low cost: bajo costo
free: gratis
for example: por ejemplo
are offered/to offer: se ofrecen/ofrecer
all levels: todos los niveles
morning: mañana
evening: noche
as an added bonus: y además, como una ventaja extra
free babysitting: cuidado gratis de bebés o niños
in addition: además
job training: capacitación laboral
finding a job: conseguir un trabajo
also: también
offers/to offer: ofrece/ofrecer
to assist: ayudar
filling out/to fill out: llenar/llenar
application forms: impresos de solicitud
passing/to pass: aprobar/aprobar
citizenship: ciudadanía
test: examen
interview: entrevista

There is a **world of opportunity** at community colleges **across** the United States. You can choose from **specialty** career training, college-**credit classes**, English as a Second Language, **non-credit** classes, and **a host of** fun personal enrichment **options**.

There are over 1200 public and independent community colleges in the United States educating over 11.6 million students. Through **open admissions policies** and **low tuitions**, the students **represent** the **rich diversity** of the United States. Classes **include** a **mix of ages** along with a **variety** of **ethnic** and socioeconomic **backgrounds**.

English as a Second Language (ESL)
Numerous community colleges have **entire** departments **focused** on English as a Second Language. These classes **are provided** as a **service** to the community for a **low cost**, or **free**.

For example, in the San Diego Community College District all ESL classes are free. Classes **are offered** in **all levels** from **morning** to the **evening**. **As an added bonus**, they also provide **free babysitting** through the Community-Based English Tutoring Program. **In addition**, a Vocational English as a Second Language (VESL) series is offered for **job training** or **finding a job**. The San Diego district **also offers** citizenship classes **to assist** in **filling out application forms** and **passing** the **citizenship test** and **interview**.

College and Workforce Training Credits

Attaining credits **that transfer** for a **baccalaureate degree** continues to be the goal for a **large segment** of the community college population. Many **success stories** got their **start** at community colleges, including **members of Congress**, **astronauts**, actors, scientists, **business leaders** and philanthropists.

Many others receive an **Associate Degree**, which is a **two-year certificate**. The five **hottest** community college programs are **registered nursing**, **law enforcement**, **licensed practical nursing**, **radiology**, and **computer technologies**.

Personal Enrichment

Have you ever **wanted to learn** about **photography** or **wines**? **How about** mastering using your **personal home computer**, or **feeling more savvy** with your personal **finances**? Community colleges offer an **exciting range** of non-credit classes **to enrich** your life and world.

So what are you **waiting for**? **Contact** your local community college today, and ask them **to mail** their course listing to find your **personal goldmine** of opportunity.

Go to www.aacc.nche.edu or call 202-728-0200 **to find a location** in your **neighborhood**.

Helping Children Succeed

When **parents** are **involved** in their **children's education**, kids **do better** in **school**. In **numerous studies**, **researchers report** the importance for parents **to be actively involved** in their child's education. Why is **parental involvement** important?

- The family makes **critical contributions** to **student achievement** from preschool through high school. A home **environment** that **encourages** learning is **more important** to student achievement than **income**, **education level** or cultural **background**.

- **Reading aloud** to children is the most important activity that parents can do **to increase** their child's **chances** of **reading success**.

- When children and parents **talk regularly** about school, children **perform** better **academically**.

- Three kinds of parental involvement at home are **consistently associated with** higher student achievement: actively organizing and **monitoring** a child's time, helping with **homework** and **discussing school matters**.

- **The earlier** that parent involvement begins in a child's educational process, **the more powerful** the effects.

- **Positive results** of parental involvement **include improved** student achievement, **reduced absenteeism**, and improved **behavior**.

COMMUNICATING WITH TEACHERS

Good communication **between** parents and **teachers** has many **benefits**. When parents and teachers **share information**, children learn more and parents and teachers **feel more supported**. Good communication **can help create** positive **feelings** between teachers and parents.

---

parents: padres, progenitores
involved: involucrados
children's education: educación de sus hijos
do better: tienen más éxito, les va mejor
school: escuela
numerous studies: numerosos estudios
researchers: investigadores
report/to report: informan/informar
to be actively involved: estar involucrados de forma activa
parental involvement: participación de los padres
critical contributions: contribuciones fundamentales
student achievement: logro de los estudiantes
environment: ambiente
encourages/to encourage: fomenta/ fomentar, animar
more important: más importante
income: ingresos
education level: nivel de educación
background: origen, historia, contexto
reading aloud: *(el)* leer en voz alta
to increase: para aumentar
chances: oportunidades, posibilidades
reading success: éxito en la lectura
talk/to talk: hablan/hablar
regularly: regularmente, con regularidad
perform/to perform: se desempeñan/ desempeñarse
academically: académicamente
consistently: de forma consistente
associated with: asociados con
monitoring: controlar
homework: tareas, deberes
discussing: discutir
school matters: asuntos de la escuela
the earlier... the more powerful: cuanto más temprano... más poderoso
positive: positivos
results: resultados
include/to include: incluyen/incluir
improved: mejorado
reduced absenteeism: ausentismo reducido
behavior: comportamiento
between: entre
teachers: maestros
benefits: beneficios
share/to share: comparten/compartir
information: información
feel/to feel: se sienten/sentirse
more supported: más apoyados
can help: pueden ayudar a
create/to create: crear/crear
feelings: sentimientos

Parent-teacher communication can be **hard** when parents feel **uncomfortable** in school and **don't speak** English well. **Fortunately**, both parents and teachers have **developed ways** to make communication **easier**.

Here are some ideas to help **overcome** the language **barrier**.

- **Spend time** at the school. A mother **speaks** Spanish and her child's teacher does not. The mother feels **comfortable** at the school, but uncomfortable working in the **classroom**. She **still helps** with school events by doing things like **decorating** the school. Helping out in the school **lets everyone see** that **she cares about** her child and the school. She **stays involved** and **knows what is going on**.

- **Find someone** who speaks your language. Find another parent or teacher in the school who speaks Spanish and is bilingual. They can **listen** to parents' **concerns** or **translate** during parent-teacher conferences. **Another option** is **to bring** a bilingual friend or family member to school to help with translation.

- **Ask** about **language classes** at the school. **Sometimes** schools can help parents learn the new language. One parent **took** English as a Second Language (ESL) lessons **right in her** child's school.

- **Volunteer** at home. At some schools, you can help with a **class project** at home. Teachers **will appreciate** your involvement and your children **will see** that you care about their school.

Teachers **agree** with the importance of parent's participation with their schools. Teachers **have suggested** that **greater support** from parents and the community would make education a **high priority**.

One teacher **said**, "If every family **valued** education and **let their children know** that, there would be a **completely** different **attitude** towards education. Parents are their child's **first teachers** and **should never stop playing that role**."

hard: dura, difícil
uncomfortable: incómodos
don't speak: no hablan
fortunately: afortunadamente
developed ways: desarrollado formas
easier: más fácil
overcome: superar
barrier: barrera
spend time: pasa tiempo
speaks/to speak: hable/hablar
comfortable: cómoda
classroom: salón de clase
still helps: ayuda de todas maneras
decorating: decorar
lets everyone see: hace que todos vean
she cares about: a ella le importa
stays/to stay: se mantiene/mantenerse
involved: involucrada
knows/to know: sabe/saber
what is going on: qué está pasando
find someone: encuentra a alguien
listen: escuchar
concerns: preocupaciones
translate/to translate: traducir/traducir
another option: otra opción
to bring: traer
ask/to ask: pregunta/preguntar
language classes: clases de idiomas
sometimes: a veces
took/to take: tomó/tomar *(clases)*
right in her: en la escuela misma de su
volunteer: trabaja como voluntario/a
class project: proyecto para la clase
will appreciate/to appreciate: apreciarán/apreciar
will see/to see: verán/ver
agree: están de acuerdo
have suggested/to suggest: han sugerido/sugerir
greater support: mayor apoyo
high priority: prioridad alta
said/to say: dijo/decir
valued/to value: valorizara/valorizar
let their children know: hacerles saber a sus hijos
completely: completamente
attitude: actitud
first teachers: primeros maestros
should never stop: nunca deberían dejar de
playing that role: jugar ese papel

Maximizing Your Talents

requests: pedidos
bilingual employees: empleados bilingües
growing/to grow: aumentando/ aumentar
greatest need: mayor necesidad
consumer services industry: industria de servicios al consumidor
such areas as: tales áreas como
retailing: ventas
communications: comunicaciones
banking: banca
to fill positions: llenar puestos
call center staff: personal de un centro de llamadas
medical: *(personal)* médico
legal: legal
administrative staff: personal administrativo
receptionists: recepcionistas
the need: la necesidad
can vary: puede variar
depending on: dependiendo de
in general: en general
most highly requested: más solicitado
language: lengua
due to: debido a
million-plus: más de...millones
still growing: todavía está aumentando
however: sin embargo
there is: existe, hay
increasing need: necesidad creciente
due to: debida a
usually: generalmente, comúnmente
first choice: primera opción
will continue to be: continuarán siendo
Spanish-speaking: hablantes de español
to find: para encontrar
business: negocios
background: experiencia, historia
fluent: hablan con fluidez
recruiters: personas que reclutan
resourceful: llenos de recursos, ingeniosos
employers: empleadores
have joined/to join: se han unido a/ unirse, hacerse socio
now: ahora
participate/to participate: participan/ participar

Requests for **bilingual employees** are **growing** in the United States. The **greatest need** for bilingual employees is in the **consumer services industry** in **such areas as retailing**, **communications**, and **banking**. Bilingual employees are needed **to fill positions** as **call center staff**, **medical** and **legal administrative staff**, and **receptionists**.

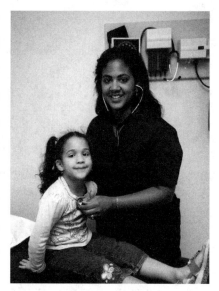

The need for bilingual employees **can vary depending on** what area of the country a company serves. **In general**, Spanish is the **most highly requested language**, **due to** the 40 **million-plus** Hispanic population, which is **still growing**. **However**, **there is** an **increasing need** for Chinese and Vietnamese on the West Coast and for French and Portuguese on the East Coast, **due to** increasing populations from these immigrant groups.

Spanish is **usually** the **first choice** for companies requesting a bilingual employee. As the Hispanic population grows, there is, and **will continue to be**, a need for **Spanish-speaking** employees.

FINDING THE BILINGUAL EMPLOYEE

To find employees who have a **business background** and are **fluent** in Spanish, some **recruiters** have become **resourceful**. **Employers have joined** and **now participate** in such organizations as the Latin American Association, the Hispanic Chamber of Commerce and the National Society of Hispanic MBAs.

All of these organizations are a **valuable** resource **since** they not only have fluent Spanish speakers, but also **candidates** with the **required** educational background and **business skills** needed.

TESTING FOR LANGUAGE AND CULTURAL **UNDERSTANDING**

Many employees **say** they are bilingual, **but** are they bilingual in **financial transactions** or **technical terminology**? **To verify** that a bilingual employee **not only** speaks a second language fluently **but also** speaks with knowledge of the **proper vocabulary** for the **position**, many recruiters **test** candidates **during** the **interview** process.

Even though a **prospective** employee **might be fluent** in the language needed, **it does not mean** they have the **necessary skills** required for the position. Prospective employees not only have to be fluent in Spanish, but they also must speak English, **along with** having **previous work experience**.

THE FUTURE

As the **purchasing power** of immigrants across the United States grows, companies **are recognizing** that they must have a **workforce** that **reflects** their **consumer bases**. Bilingual employees **must have both** language and **cultural awareness**. Employers are **looking for** the **best talent** they can for any position **that is open**, and **they know** that the employee that is fluent in a second language **does create an advantage**.

---

all of these: todas estas
valuable: valioso
since: ya que
candidates: candidatos
required: requeridos
business skills: capacidades o habilidades en negocios
testing: pruebas
understanding: comprensión
say/to say: dicen/decir
but: pero
financial transactions: transacciones financieras
technical terminology: terminología técnica
to verify: para verificar
not only...but also: no sólo...pero también
proper vocabulary: vocabulario apropiado
position: posición, puesto
test/to test: examinan/examinar
during: durante
interview: entrevista
even though: aunque, aun cuando
prospective: potencial
might be fluent: puede que hable con fluidez
it does not mean: eso no significa
necessary skills: habilidades necesarias
along with: junto con
previous work experience: previa experiencia de trabajo
purchasing power: poder de compra
are recognizing/to recognize: están reconociendo/reconocer
workforce: trabajadores
reflects/to reflect: refleja/reflejar
consumer bases: bases de consumidores
must have: deben tener
both: ambos
cultural awareness: conciencia cultural
looking for/to look for: buscando/ buscar
best talent: mejor talento
that is open: que esté abierto/a
they know/to know: ellos saben/saber
does create an advantage: crea una ventaja

during: durante	
immigration process: proceso de inmigración	
someone: alguien	
may need help: puede necesitar ayuda	
understanding: para comprender	
laws: leyes	
while: mientras que, aunque	
can feel: puede parecer	
overwhelming: abrumador, aplastante	
daunting: desalentador	
proper research: investigación adecuada	
will find/to find: encontrarás/encontrar	
abundance: abundancia	
along the way: en el camino, durante el proceso	
lawyer: abogado	
graduated/to graduate: recibido/recibirse	
licensed: autorizado	
to practice law: para ejercer la abogacía	
regulated/to regulate: regulado/regular	
obtain: obtener	
legal status: estatus legal	
represent you: representarte	
court: tribunal, corte	
following ways: siguientes maneras	
analyze: analizar	
facts of your case: hechos de tu caso	
explain: explicar	
benefits: beneficios	
you may be eligible: a los que puedes tener derecho	
recommend: recomendar	
best ways: mejores maneras	
complete: completar	
submit: presentar	
applications: solicitudes	
stay current: estar al corriente	
that affect you: que te afectan	
avoid: evitar	
delays: retrasos	
discuss: discutir	
status: estatus	
speak for you: hablar por tí	
file: presentar	
appeals: apelaciones	
waivers: renuncias, dispensas	
utilize: utilizar	
how do you find: cómo encuentras	
online: en línea	
directory: directorio, guía	
who are members: que son miembros	
free legal services: servicios legales gratuitos	
self-help: autoayuda	

Legal Resources

During the **immigration process,** you or **someone** in your family **may need help understanding** the many immigration **laws.** **While** the process **can feel overwhelming** and **daunting,** with the **proper research** you **will find** there is an **abundance** of legal resources and organizations to help you **along the way**.

An immigration **lawyer** has studied the immigration laws of the United States and has **graduated** from law school. He or she is **licensed to practice law** and is **regulated** by the State and Federal Government. He or she can help you **obtain legal status** from the Department of Homeland Security or **represent you** in Immigration **Court**.

An immigration lawyer can help you in the **following ways**:

- **Analyze** the **facts of your case** thoroughly.
- **Explain** all the **benefits** for which **you may be eligible**.
- **Recommend** the **best ways** to obtain legal status.
- **Complete** and **submit** your **applications** properly.
- **Stay current** on the new laws **that affect you**.
- **Avoid delays** and problems with your case.
- **Discuss** the **status** of your case with you.
- **Speak for you** and represent you in court.
- **File** necessary **appeals** and **waivers**.
- **Utilize** the system to your advantage.

How do you find an immigration lawyer or the necessary resources to assist you?

Visit www.ailalawyer.com, the **online directory** of attorneys **who are members** of the American Immigration Lawyers Association.

On this web site you will find **free legal services** provided by state. You will also find national and community resources and **self-help** materials. http://www.usdoj.gov/eoir/probono/probono.htm

Used with the permission of the American Immigration Law Foundation

Public Benefits

Many immigrants, **even when eligible** for **public benefits**, **do not apply** for **fear** that **accepting** benefits **will have consequences** for their immigration **status** or that of **someone** in their family. Even when immigrants are **aware of** their **rights**, local agencies **sometimes mistakenly deny** benefits to immigrants **who are entitled** to them, or **ask for** information that **may discourage** an **applicant** from **obtaining** the benefit. Immigrants **with limited** English **proficiency face additional barriers** when service provider agencies **fail to make** appropriate **language translation services available** to their clients.

National and local organizations and **advocacy groups** have been **filling the gap** in **assisting** immigrants **to navigate** the **various** and **continuously changing** public benefits laws and policies. Immigrants come to this country **ready to work**, and many work in **low-wage**, **undesirable jobs**. Immigrants **should have access to** public benefits that **they pay for** with their **taxes**.

Today and **throughout history**, immigrants **contribute far more** to the American **economy** and culture than **they receive** in benefits.

The **following** organizations **provide outstanding** public benefit programs, activities, and information.

- Center for Public Policy Priorities : www.cppp.org
- Coalition on Human Needs: www.chn.org/issuebriefs/immigrants.asp
- Center on Budget and Policy Priorities: www.cbpp.org/pubs/immpub.htm
- The Finance Project: www.financeprojectinfo.org
- National Immigration Law Center: www.nilc.org

Used with the permission of the National Immigration Forum

---

even when eligible: aún cuando reúne los requisitos
public benefits: beneficios públicos
do not apply/to apply: no solicitan/solicitar
fear: miedo
accepting: aceptar
will have/to have: tendrá/tener
consequences: consecuencias
status: estado, estatus, categoría
someone: alguien, alguno
aware of: conscientes de
rights: derechos
sometimes: a veces
mistakenly: de manera equivocada
deny/to deny: niegan/negar
who are entitled: que tienen derecho
ask for/to ask for: piden/pedir
may discourage: puede desalentar
applicant: solicitante
obtaining/to obtain: obtener/obtener
with limited ... proficiency: con manejo limitado de ...
face/to face: enfrenta/enfrentar
additional barriers: barreras adicionales
fail: no *(hacer algo)*
to make...available: poner... a disposición
language translation services: servicios de traducción de idiomas
advocacy groups: grupos de apoyo
filling the gap: llenando el hueco
assisting/to assist: ayudando/ayudar, asistir
to navigate: a navegar
various: varios
continuously changing: cambiando constantemente
ready to work: prontos para trabajar
low-wage: bajo salario
undesirable: no deseables
jobs: trabajos
should have access to: deberían tener acceso a
they pay for: ellos pagan
taxes: impuestos
throughout history: a través de la historia
contribute/to contribute: contribuyen/contribuir
far more: mucho más
economy: economía
they receive: lo que reciben
following: siguiente
provide/to provide: proveen/proveer
outstanding: sobresaliente, destacado

Owning Your Own Home

Since a **large number of** immigrants have **come to** the United States **in the last** 10 years and because many of them **begin** their **working careers** in **low-paying jobs**, many **do not yet own** homes. The **cost of housing** presents a **significant financial barrier** for many people. Yet, as a group, immigrants **steadily pursue** homeownership.

Financial institutions are beginning to **realize** the **huge potential** immigrants **represent** for the housing market. In the last few years, many **have made commitments** to reach out to immigrant populations and are **providing** immigrants with the skills they need **to gain access to** the housing market.

These efforts are beginning to **pay off**, as immigrants are **increasingly achieving** the American **dream** of homeownership.

According to recent reports, Hispanics **still face** significant barriers to achieving the American dream of owning a home. **In response to** this problem, the Congressional Hispanic Caucus Institute (CHCI) **launched** the National Housing Initiative (NHI).

The NHI **benefits** areas with large Hispanic populations and **will employ up to** 4 **mid-career** professionals **to create** and **implement specialized housing initiatives** for the purpose of increasing homeownership opportunities for Latinos **across the country**.

Homeownership is one of the best ways **we have to help empower** families to achieve financial security and help communities **attain greater stability**. For this reason, CHCI reports that they are **proud** to launch this exciting and important **endeavor** to help address the housing **needs** of Latinos everywhere. It is through an initiative such as this that Hispanics **will continue to assume** greater **leadership roles** in all **sectors of society**.

For more information on CHCI and its leadership **development** programs and scholarship awards, please visit www.chciyouth.org or call toll-free 1-800 EXCEL DC.

Parent-Teacher Association

As the largest **volunteer child advocacy association** in the nation, the **National Parent-Teacher Association** (PTA) **reminds** our country of its obligations to children. The PTA **provides** parents and families with a **powerful voice to speak on behalf of** every child **while** providing the **best tools** for parents **to help** their children be **successful students**.

The National PTA **does not act alone**. Working in cooperation with many national education, **health**, **safety**, and child advocacy groups and federal agencies, the National PTA **collaborates** on projects that **benefit children** and that bring **valuable resources** to its **members**.

The PTA is the nation's original parent group in schools, **influencing** millions of parents, **past and present**, to get involved in their children's education. A national, nonprofit organization, **neither** the organization **nor** its leaders **receive any financial benefit** from PTA activities. The PTA is **composed of** 6 million volunteers in 23,000 local units. **Run by** volunteers and **led by** volunteers, the PTA is **accountable to** parents and schools. The PTA gives parents what they want—a **way to help** their children succeed.

JOIN THE PTA

The PTA is **open to all** adults who **care** about children and schools. The **main thing** parents want from schools is to help their child **succeed academically**, emotionally, and personally. The PTA **bridges** the gap **between** homes and schools. **By getting involved** with the PTA, the child **who benefits most** is one's own. **They work hard** to bring mothers, fathers, teachers, school administrators, grandparents, mentors, **foster parents**, other **caregivers**, and **community leaders** into the association.

Talk with the **school principals** in your town **to find out** how you may **partner** with the schools and be one of the members of a **powerful** organization that **makes a difference every day**.

volunteer child advocacy association: asociación voluntaria de apoyo al niño
National Parent-Teacher Association: Asociación Nacional Padres y Maestros
reminds/to remind: recuerda/recordar
provides/to provide: provee/proveer
powerful voice: voz poderosa
to speak on behalf of: para hablar en nombre de
while: mientras que
best tools: mejores herramientas
to help: para ayudar
successful students: estudiantes exitosos
does not act alone: no actúa solo
health: salud
safety: seguridad
collaborates/to collaborate: colabora/colaborar
benefit children: benefician a los niños
valuable resources: recursos valiosos
members: miembros
influencing/to influence: influyendo/influir
past and present: pasados y presentes
neither... nor...: ni... ni...
receive/to receive: reciben/recibir
any financial benefit: ningún beneficio financiero
composed of: compuesto de
run by: operado por
led by: dirigido por
accountable to: responde a
way to help: manera de ayudar
open to all: abierta a todos
care/to care: se preocupan/preocuparse
main thing: cosa principal
succeed academically: tengan éxito académico
bridges/to bridge: supera/superar, salvar, servir de puente
between: entre
by getting involved: al involucrarse
who benefits most: que más se beneficia
they work hard: ellos trabajan duro
foster parents: padres adoptivos *(temporales)* de acogida
caregivers: cuidadores
community leaders: líderes comunitarios
talk with/to talk with: habla con/hablar con
school principals: directores de las escuelas
to find out: para averiguar
partner: trabajar conjuntamente
powerful: poderosa
makes a difference: produce un impacto positivo
every day: cada día

being involved: estar involucrado	
benefits: beneficios	
many: muchos	
levels: niveles	
allows you to: te permite	
get to know: conocer	
neighbors: vecinos	
integrate: integrarse	
into your immediate surroundings: en tu entorno inmediato	
also: también	
identify: identificar	
utilize: utilizar	
resources: recursos	
helps/to help: ayuda/ayudar	
to build: a construir	
society: sociedad	
values/to value: valora/valorar	
diversity: diversidad	
respects/to respect: respeta/respetar	
dignity: dignidad	
rights: derechos	
of all people: de toda la gente	
libraries: bibliotecas	
offer/to offer: ofrecen/ofrecer	
free: gratis	
internet access: acceso a internet	
computer classes: clases de computación	
wonderful: maravillosos	
magazines: revistas	
books: libros	
as well as: así como	
test preparation: preparación para exámenes	
church: iglesia	
ESL classes: clases de inglés como lengua secundaria *(ESL=English as a Second Language)*	
designed/to design: diseñadas/diseñar	
adjust: acomodarse	
found: que se encuentran	
medium-sized cities: ciudades medianas	
here: aquí	
childcare: cuidado de niños	
summer programs: programas de verano	
concerts: conciertos	

You and Your Community

Being involved in your community has **benefits** on **many levels**. On a local level it **allows you to get to know** your **neighbors** and **integrate** better **into your immediate surroundings**. It **also** helps you **identify** and **utilize** the many **resources** available for you and your family. On a national level your involvement **helps to build** a **society** that **values diversity** and **respects** the **dignity** and **rights of all people**.

Local Communities

- **Libraries**—Many libraries **offer free internet access** and **computer classes**. They also offer ESL classes, **wonderful** children's programs, **magazines** and **books** in Spanish, **as well as** citizenship **test preparation** books and resources.

- **Church**—Local churches often offer free **ESL classes** as well as other classes **designed** to help immigrants **adjust** to life in the United States.

- **Community Centers**—Community Centers, also called Parks and Recreation departments, are **found** in most **medium-sized cities** and offer an abundance of resources for you and your family. **Here** you can find adult and children's programs, **child care**, **summer programs**, local **concerts** and community festivals.

- **Volunteer**—A **great way to meet new people** and make a difference in your community is to volunteer. **Even if you are not yet fluent** in English, this is a great way **to practice** your English. Volunteer **options** include: working at local **homeless shelters**, **assisting** adults or children to **learn to read** with **literacy programs**, **litter patrol** with **environmental programs**, or helping out at local festivals or **fundraisers**.

National Communities

- National Council of La Raza is a **nonprofit** organization **established** in 1968 **to reduce poverty** and discrimination and **improve life opportunities** for Hispanic Americans.

- LULAC—The Mission of the League of United Latin American Citizens is **to advance** the **economic condition**, educational **attainment**, political **influence**, **health** and civil **rights** of the Hispanic population of the United States.

There are many options for community involvement **right outside your door**. **Take a class**, **listen to** a concert in the park, **help organize** the **next** Cinco De Mayo festival. **Take the time** to **be involved** and **make the most** of your community.

volunteer: voluntario
great way: excelente manera
to meet new people: hacer nuevas amistades
even if: aun si
you are not yet fluent: no hablas aún con fluidez
to practice: practicar
options: opciones
homeless shelters: refugios para personas sin techo
assisting: el ayudar
learn to read: aprender a leer
literacy programs: programas de alfabetismo
litter patrol: patrullas que recogen basura
environmental programs: programas para el medio ambiente
fundraisers: *(eventos)* para recaudar fondos
nonprofit: sin fines de lucro
established: establecida
to reduce: para reducir
poverty: la pobreza
improve life opportunities: mejorar las oportunidades de vida
to advance: hacer avanzar
economic condition: condición económica
attainment: logro
influence: influencia
health: salud
rights: derechos
right outside your door: justo al otro lado de tu puerta
take a class: tome una classe
listen to/to listen to: escucha/ eschuchar
help organize: ayuda a organizar
next: próximo
take the time: tómate el tiempo
be involved: estar involucrado
make the most: aprovecha al máximo

Hispanics in the Workplace

Because the Hispanic population is **growing** so rapidly in the U.S., there are **opportunities** for **graduates across many fields**. Employers are **recognizing the need to hire** individuals who **understand** the **language** and culture of this growing segment of the population, and there are opportunities in many professions. **Unfortunately**, individuals of Hispanic **heritage** may still have to **overcome negative stereotypes** during their **job search,** but it is important to remember that being bicultural is a definite competitive advantage. Job seekers should **highlight** the **unique benefits** their **background** can provide to an employer, including international experience, **language skills** and cultural **insight**.

What Are Employers Doing?

To **make the most** of their **minority recruiting efforts**, the most successful employers use a variety of methods and **diligently work** to **promote** these initiatives on campus.

Many employers are **reaching out** to Hispanic students by **sponsoring career fairs** and other events on campus, attending **recruiting events** and even offering **scholarships** to Hispanic students. Companies are also **connecting with** students through **professional societies** such as the Society of Hispanic Professional Engineers and the Association of Latino Professionals in Finance and Accounting.

Where to Look for Your First Job

Students should be **searching** the Internet **job boards**, both the big ones as well as **niche boards** that match **either** their career functions, locations **or** ethnic background. LatPro.com, for example, is a niche **diversity job board** for Hispanic and bilingual professionals.

Industries Where Hispanics **Are Under-Represented**

Despite promising **advances** in many areas, Hispanics continue to be under-represented in a variety of professions. The **fields** we **hear** employers **mentioning** most include science, information technology, **engineering** and **healthcare** (especially **nurses** and **physicians** with Spanish language skills).

The reasons are varied and **complex,** but multicultural students **are not entering** these fields in **great enough numbers**. We can **encourage** students **to pursue** these fields by increasing scholarships **to ease** the **financial burden** of advanced education, **as well as** promoting **mentorship** opportunities **to expose** young Latinos/Latinas to these career options **early on**.

What are employers looking for?

Many employers **want to see that** students are **involved** in organizations related to their profession, especially those **focused on** supporting Hispanic professionals **within** a **specific field**. **For example**, accounting students and graduates **should consider joining** the Association of Latino Professionals in Finance and Accounting. Other organizations include the Society of Hispanic Professional Engineers, the National Association of Hispanic Nurses, and many others. These organizations are an excellent **source** for **networking** opportunities and **job leads**. An **online listing** can be found at: http://www.latpro.com/network.

Another source of networking opportunities would be Hispanic Chambers of Commerce. Every resource should be used, especially for **newly** graduating students **in search of** their first jobs.

It is important for Hispanic students to learn how organizations **value** a diverse workforce. Employers **can better inform** students about **corporate diversity initiatives** by using multiple **strategies** such as promoting **employee referral programs** and **affinity** organizations within the company, sponsoring scholarships for Hispanic students, **advertising** on diversity job boards, and **supporting** Hispanic professional organizations **within their field**.

Recruiting Hispanic employees requires the employer to understand the benefit that a diverse workforce brings to the business **bottom line**. Minority **candidates** want to know that they are being recruited for their skills and the value they will bring to an organization, versus being a **number** in a **diversity hiring effort**.

complex: complejas
are not entering: no están entrando
great enough numbers: cantidad suficiente
encourage: animar
to pursue: a ejecer
to ease: que quite, que alivie
financial burden: carga económica
as well as: así como
mentorship: servir como mentor
to expose: para exponer
early on: desde el principio
want to see that: quieren ver que
involved: involucrados
focused on: enfocadas a
within: dentro
specific field: campo específico
for example: por ejemplo
should consider joining: deberían considerar unirse
source: fuente
networking: establecer contactos
job leads: ofertas de trabajo
online listing: listado en línea
newly: nuevos, recientes
in search of: en busca de
value/to value: valoran/valorar
can better inform: pueden informar mejor
corporate diversity initiatives: iniciativas de la empresa respecto a la diversidad
strategies: estrategias
employee referral programs: programas de recommendación de empleados
affinity: afinidad
advertising/to advertise: hacer publicidad/hacer publicidad
supporting/to support: apoyando/apoyar
within their field: dentro de su área
bottom line: resultado final, balance
candidates: candidatos
number: número
diversity hiring effort: esfuerzo por emplear grupos diversos

Test Your Comprehension

Citizenship, page 124

1. Los residentes de los Estados Unidos pueden ser extranjeros, nacionales o ciudadanos. ¿Quiénes son extranjeros y cuáles son sus derechos?

2. ¿Quiénes son los nacionales y cuáles son sus derechos?

Community Colleges, page 128

1. ¿Cuántas instituciones terciarias comunitarias hay en los Estados Unidos?

2. ¿Qué es un associate degree?

3. ¿Cuáles son los programas de instituciones terciarias comunitarias más populares?

Empowerment with Education, page 126

1. ¿Cuál es la minoría étnica más numerosa de la nación y el segmento de más rápido crecimiento de nuestra población?

2. Cuando busques ayuda financiera o becas, ¿cuál debería ser tu primer paso?

3. Durante sus 31 años de historia, ¿HSF ha otorgado cuántas becas a latinos?

Helping Children Succeed, page 130

1. Verdadero o Falso – Cuando los padres están involucrados en la educación de sus hijos, ¿a los hijos les va mejor en la escuela?

2. ¿Qué pasa cuando los padres y maestros comparten información?

3. ¿Cuáles son algunas ideas para ayudar a superar la barrera del idioma y participar de manera más activa en la escuela de tu niño/a?

Examina tu comprensión

Bilingual Resources, page 132

1. ¿Qué industrias tienen mayor necesidad de empleados bilingües?

2. ¿Cómo verifica un empleador que el empleado bilingüe habla con fluidez y conoce el vocabulario adecuado para el puesto?

3. Los posibles empleados necesitan hablar español con fluidez así como ¿qué otra cosa?

Legal Resources, page 134

1. ¿Qué es un abogado de inmigración?

2. ¿Cómo puede ayudar un abogado de inmigración a un nuevo inmigrante a los Estados Unidos?

Owning Your Own Home, page 136

1. ¿Cuál es la tasa de propiedad de vivienda para hispanos en los Estados Unidos?

2. Ser propietario de vivienda está considerado como una de las mejores formas de ayudar a posibilitar ¿el qué?

You and Your Community, page 138

1. ¿Cuál es son algunos de los beneficios de estar involucrado con tu comunidad?

2. ¿Qué puedes encontrar en los Departamentos de Parques y Recreación?

3. ¿Cuál es una gran forma de hacer nuevas amistades y crear un cambio en tu comunidad?

A page of history is worth a pound of logic.

Oliver Wendell Holmes

History

Independence Day

There are 50 **states** in the Union. The **first** 13 states were Connecticut, New Hampshire, New York, New Jersey, Maryland, Virginia, Pennsylvania, Rhode Island, Massachusetts, Georgia, Delaware, North Carolina, and South Carolina. The **last** state **to join** the Union was Hawaii.

Congress **voted** for the United States **to become independent** from Great Britain on July 2, 1776. **However**, **we celebrate** Independence Day on July 4th. This is because it **took** two days for Congress to vote **to accept** an official Declaration of Independence. This document was **written** by Thomas Jefferson and **edited** by Congress. It **explained** why the American colonies were **separating** from their British **ruler**. The 4th of July is **now** **considered** the **birthday** of America. We celebrate with **parades, fireworks**, patriotic **songs**, and **live readings** of the Declaration of Independence.

The **decision to break from** the British was not an **easy choice** for many colonists. **However**, Great Britain's "**repeated injuries**" **against** the Americans **convinced** many **to join** the **rebellion**. After years of **difficult fighting**, the colonists went on **to win** their **freedom**.

---

states: estados
first: primeros
last: último
to join: en unirse
voted/to vote: votó/votar
to become independent: se independizara
however: sin embargo
we celebrate/to celebrate: nosotros celebramos/celebrar
took/to take: llevó/llevar, tomar
to accept: el aceptar
written/to write escrito/escribir
edited/to edit: editado/editar
explained/to explain: explicaba/explicar
separating/to separate: separando/separar
ruler: gobernante
now: ahora
considered/to consider: considerado/considerar
birthday: cumpleaños
parades: desfiles
fireworks: fuegos artificiales
songs: canciones
live readings: lecturas en vivo
decision to break from: decisión de separarse de
easy choice: fácil elección
however: sin embargo
repeated injuries: repetidos daños
against: en contra de
convinced/to convince: convencieron/convencer
to join: de unirse
rebellion: rebelión
difficult fighting: difícil lucha
to win: ganar
freedom: libertad

Stars and Stripes

We call the American **flag** the "**Stars** and **Stripes**." Congress **chose** the stars and stripes **design** for our flag on June 14, 1777. Congress **explained** the colors: **red stands for hardiness** and valor, **white** for **purity** and **innocence**, and **blue** for **vigilance**, **perseverance**, and **justice**.

The white stars on the flag **represent** the United States as **being like** "a **new constellation**" in the **sky**. The nation was **seen** as a new constellation because the **republican system** of government was new and different in the 1770s. In the republican system of government, leaders **work to help** all of the country's people. They **do not act** to help only a **few** special citizens. **Since** the people **choose** these leaders, the people **hold the power** of government.

Each star represents a **state**. This is why the number of stars **has changed over the years** from 13 to 50. The number of stars **reached** 50 in 1959. In that year, Hawaii **joined** the United States as the 50th state.

The stars represent the Founding Fathers' **view** of the American **experiment** in democracy. To them, the **goal** of a republic **based** on **individual freedom** was a noble idea. Stars are **considered** a symbol of the **heavens** and the **high**, ambitious vision of the Founding Fathers.

In 1818, Congress **decided** that the number of red and white stripes on the flag **should always be** 13. This would **honor** the original states, **no matter how many** new states would join the United States later.

---

we call/to call: nosotros llamamos/ llamar
flag: bandera
stars: estrellas
stripes: rayas
chose/to choose: eligió/elegir
design: diseño
explained/to explain: explicó/explicar
red: rojo
stands for/to stand for: representan/ representar
hardiness: robustez, resistencia
white: blanco
purity: pureza
innocence: inocencia
blue: azul
vigilance: vigilancia
perseverance: perseverancia
justice: justicia
represent/to represent: representan/ representar
being like: ser como
new: nueva
constellation: constelación
sky: cielo
seen: vista
republican system: sistema de república
work to help: trabajan para ayudar
do not act: no actúan
few: pocos
since: ya que
choose/to choose: elige/elegir
hold the power: mantienen el poder
state: estado
has changed over the years: ha cambiado con los años
reached/to reach: alcanzó/alcanzar
joined/to join: se unió/unirse
view: visión
experiment: experimento
goal: meta, objetivo
based: basada
individual freedom: libertad individual
considered/to consider: consideradas/ considerar
heavens: cielos
high: alta
decided/to decide: decidió/decidir
should always be: debería ser siempre
honor: honrar
no matter how many: no importa cuántos

The Electoral College

place: lugar

school: escuela

process: proceso

designed: diseñado

writers: escritores, autores

to select: para seleccionar

came from/to come from: vino de/
venir de

compromise: compromiso

between: entre

being elected: ser electo/a

chosen: elegido

combining: combinando

vote/to vote: vota/votar

meet/to meet: se reúnen/reunirse

to choose: para elegir

today: hoy, hoy en día

officially: oficialmente

first in line: primero en la línea
fue sucesión

to take over: para hacerse cargo/
hacerse cargo, asumir el cargo,
tomar el mando

happened/ to happen: pasado/
pasar, ocurrir, suceder

times: veces

died in office: murió *(estando)* en
el poder

killed/to kill: muertos/matar

resigned/to resign: renunció/
renunciar

The Electoral College is not a **place** or a **school**. The Electoral College is a **process** that was **designed** by the **writers** of the Constitution **to select** presidents. It **came from** a **compromise** **between** the President **being elected** directly by the people and the President being **chosen** by Congress. **Combining** these ideas, the American people **vote** for a "college" of electors, who then **meet to choose** the President. **Today**, the people of each of the 50 states and the District of Columbia vote for the electors in November. The electors then **officially** vote for the President in December.

The Vice President is **first in line to take over** as President. This has **happened** nine **times** in U.S. history. Four presidents **died in office**, four presidents were **killed** in office, and one president, Richard Nixon, **resigned** from office.

Supreme Law of the Land

The U.S. Constitution **has lasted longer** than any **other country's** constitution. It is the **basic legal framework establishing** the U.S. government. **Every** person and every agency and department of government must **follow** the Constitution. This is why it is **called** the "**supreme law of the land.**" **Under** this system, the **powers** of the national government are **limited** to those **written** in the Constitution. The **guiding principle behind** this system is **often called** the **rule** of law.

It **is not easy** for the Constitution to be **changed**. Changes to the constitution are called Amendments. **First**, **two-thirds** of the Senate and two-thirds of the House of Representatives must vote **to approve** an amendment. Then, **three-fourths** of the states must approve the amendment.

The first amendments to the Constitution were **added** in 1791. These original ten amendments are called the Bill of Rights. Since the Bill of Rights **passed**, 17 more amendments **have been added**. The 27th amendment is the **most recent addition**. It was added in 1992 and **addresses** how Senators and Representatives are **paid**. **Interestingly**, Congress **first discussed** this Amendment **back in** 1789.

has lasted longer: ha durado más tiempo
other: otro
country's: de ... país
basic legal framework: marco legal básico
establishing/to establish: que establece/establecer
every: toda
follow: seguir
called/to call: llamada/llamar
supreme law of the land: ley suprema del país
under: bajo
powers: poderes
limited/limit: limitados/limitar
written/to write: escritos/escribir
guiding principle: principio rector o guía
behind: detrás de
often called: a menudo llamado
rule: regla
is not easy: no es fácil
changed/to change: cambiada/cambiar, alterar
first: primero
two-thirds: dos tercios
to approve: para aprobar
three-fourths: tres cuartos
added/to add: agregados/agregar
passed/to pass: aprobado/aprobar
have been added: han sido agregados
most recent addition: adición más reciente
addresses/to address: trata de/tratar
paid/to pay: pagados/pagar
interestingly: interesantemente
first discussed: discutió por primera vez
back in: en (*refiriéndose a un tiempo anterior*)

Divisions of Power

The **writers** of the Constitution **created** a process that **divides** the government's **power among** three **branches**: Executive, Judicial, and Legislative. These branches **operate under** a **system** of **checks** and **balances**. This **means** that each branch can **block**, or **threaten to** block, the action of **another** branch. This way, no one branch can **grow too powerful** and **harm** the **liberties** of **citizens**.

Congress is a legislative branch. The **main job** of Congress is **to make federal laws**. Congress is divided into two parts—the **Senate** and the House of Representatives. By dividing Congress into two parts, the Constitution **put** the checks and balances idea **to work within** the legislative branch. Each part of Congress **makes sure** that the other does not **become** too powerful. These two "check" each other because **both** must **agree** for a law to be **made**.

Specific powers are **assigned** to each of these **chambers**. **Only** the Senate has the power **to reject** a **treaty signed** by the President. Only the House of Representatives has the power **to begin considering** a **bill** that makes Americans **pay taxes**. **Also**, only the House of Representatives has the power to make a President **go to trial** for a **crime against** the United States.

A federal law is a **rule** that all people **living** in the United States **must follow**. Every law begins as a **proposal** made by a member of Congress. Tax proposals must begin in the House of Representatives. Other types of proposals can be made by any senator or representative. When the Senate or House begins **to debate** the proposal, it is **called** a bill. If the President **signs** the bill, it becomes a federal law.

The nation is **divided** into 435 Congressional **districts**. The people of each district are **represented** by a **member** of the House of Representatives.

The **people** of each state also **vote** for two U.S. senators. There are 100 senators (two **from each** state). The **term of office** for members of the House of Representatives is two years. The term for senators is six years.

One reason the Senate was **created** was **to make** states with **fewer** people **equal** in power to states with many people. With two senators representing each state, states with **small populations** have the same Senate representation as states with **large** populations.

The writers of the Constitution **wanted** senators to be **independent** of **public opinion**. A **longer**, six-year term **would give them** this **protection.** The Constitution **puts no limit** on the number of terms a senator may **serve**.

rule: regla
living: viviendo
must follow: deben seguir
proposal: propuesta
to debate: a debatir
called/llamar: llamado/to call
signs/to sign: firma/firmar
divided/dividir: dividida/
  to divide
districts: distritos
represented/to represent:
  representados/representar
member: miembro
people: personas
vote: votar
from each: de cada
term of office: mandato
one reason: una razón
created/to create: creado/crear
to make: para hacer
fewer: pocas
equal: igual, mismo
small populations: poblaciones
  pequeñas
large: grande
wanted/to want: querían/
  querer
independent: independientes
public opinion: opinión pública
longer: más largo
would give them: les daría
protection: protección
puts no limit: no pone límites
serve: servir

History of the White House

The President's **official home** is the White House. The first White House was **built between** 1792 and 1800 in Washington, D.C. President George Washington **helped choose** its **exact location** and **supervised** its construction, but **never actually lived** there. America's second president, John Adams, was the first **to live** in the White House. Fourteen years after construction, the White House was **burned** by British **troops during** the **War** of 1812. Another **destructive fire took place** there in 1929, when Herbert Hoover was president.

When the Constitution **established** our nation in 1789, the city of Washington, D.C. **did not exist**. **At that time**, the capital was New York City. Congress **soon began discussing** the location of a **permanent** capital city. **Within** Congress, representatives of northern states **fought bitterly against** representatives of **southern** states. Each side **wanted** the capital **to be in** their region. **Finally**, with the Compromise of 1790, the **North agreed to let** the capital be in the South. **In return**, the North was **relieved** of some of the **debt** that they **owed** from the Revolutionary War.

The **building** was not officially **known as** the White House **until** 1901, when Theodore Roosevelt was president. **Before then**, it was also called the "President's Palace," the "President's House," and the "Executive Mansion." The **current look** of the White House comes from a **renovation** that **happened** when Harry Truman was president.

The Bill of Rights

Freedom of speech is a very important **civil liberty**. The **first** section of the Bill of Rights, the First Amendment, **guarantees** this freedom. Speech **can mean writing**, **performing**, or other ways of **expressing yourself**. Americans have the basic right **to express** their **views** on any **subject**. This is **true even if** the government **disagrees** with these views.

When the Constitution was **first written**, it did not **focus** on individual **rights**. The **goal** was **to create** the system and **structure** of government. Many Americans wanted a specific list of **things** the government **could not do**. James Madison **responded** with a list of individual rights and limits of government. Some of these **included** citizens' rights **to practice** their religion **freely**, to speak and **publish** freely, and to **complain publicly** about anything they wanted. The list was in the form of changes, or amendments, to the Constitution. These amendments were **ratified** in 1791. They soon **became known as** the Bill of Rights.

The Bill of Rights guarantees the rights of individuals and **limits** government **power**. The first eight amendments **set out** individual rights, such as the freedom of expression; the **right to bear arms**; freedom from **search without warrant**; freedom to not be **tried** twice for the **same crime**; the right to not **testify against yourself**; the right **to trial by a jury** of **peers**; the right to an **attorney**; and protection against **excessive fines** and **unusual punishments**.

One **reason** that millions of immigrants **have come to** America is this guarantee of rights. The Fifth Amendment guarantees everyone in the United States **equal protection under** the law. This is **true no matter** what color your **skin** is, what **language** you speak, or what religion you practice.

freedom of speech: libertad de expresión
civil liberty: derecho civil
first: primera
guarantees/to guarantee: garantiza/garantizar
can mean: puede significar
writing: escribir
performing: actuar
expressing yourself: expresarse uno mismo
to express: de expresar
views: opiniones
subject: tema
true: asi
even if: aun si
disagrees/to disagree: está en desacuerdo/estar en desacuerdo
first written: inicialmente escrito
focus/to focus: enfocó/enfocarse
rights: derechos
goal: meta, objetivo
to create: crear
structure: estructura
things: cosas
could not do: no podía hacer
responded/to respond: respondió/responder
included/to include: incluían/incluir
to practice: de practicar
freely: libremente
publish: publicar
complain publicly: quejarse públicamente
ratified/to ratify: ratificados/ratificar
became known as: fueron conocidas como
limits/to limit: limitan/limitar
power: poder
set out/to set out: expusieron/exponer
right to bear arms: derecho a portar armas
search without warrant: registro sin orden (de registro)
tried/to try: juzgado/juzgar
same crime: mismo crimen
testify against yourself: testificar en contra de uno mismo
to trial by a jury: a juicio ante jurado
peers: pares
attorney: abogado
excessive fines: multas excesivas
unusual punishments: castigos poco usuales
reason: razón
have come to: han venido a
equal protection under: igualdad de protección ante
true: verdad
no matter: sin distinción de
skin: piel
language: idioma

United States Presidency

The **writers** of the Constitution **argued over** how much **power** the **new** President should have. They **decided** that the President's powers should be **limited** in many ways, but that the President should be Commander-in-Chief of the **military**. **During** the Revolutionary War, George Washington, **known as** the "**father of our country**" had been **Supreme Commander** of the military. From this position, he **led** the U.S. **forces** to **victory**. This **helped make him** a **unanimous choice** to be the **first** President and Commander-in- Chief.

Washington was a **brave** military general, a **respected** leader of the American Revolution, and our first President. His leadership was very important **during** America's transition from **war** and revolution to **stability under** the new government. **After** his victory **over** the British army, Washington **retired**. He **reluctantly left** retirement and helped lead the **effort to create** a Constitution for the United States.

The President is **both** the head of state and the head of the Executive branch of the government. Presidential powers **include** the **ability** to **sign treaties** with other countries and **select** ambassadors to represent the United States **abroad**. As **head** of the executive branch, the President **names** the top leaders of the federal departments. **However**, the Senate has the power to **reject** the President's choices. This **limit** on the power of the President is an example of **checks and balances**.

Early American leaders **felt** that the head of the British government, the **king**, had too much power. Because of this, they limited the powers of the head of the new U.S. government. They decided that the President would have to be **elected** by the people **every four years**.

The writers of the Constitution wanted the President to be an **experienced** leader with a **strong connection** to the United States. The **eligibility requirements make sure** that this **happens.** A **candidate** for president must be a **native-born**, not a **naturalized citizen,** be **at least** 35 **years old**, and have **lived** in the U.S. for at least 14 years. The **youngest** person in American history to become president was Theodore Roosevelt. Roosevelt **entered** the White House when he was 42 years old.

The first U.S. President, George Washington, only **ran** for president **twice**. Washington felt that one person **should not serve** as president for a very **long time**. **Following** this tradition, no future president served for **more than** two terms until Franklin Roosevelt. Roosevelt was elected to four terms. **Not long after** he **died**, the Constitution was **amended** so that a president could only serve two full terms.

The American Revolution

European **countries began taking control** of areas of America in the 1500s. These European-controlled areas were **called** colonies. England's **first successful** American colony was Virginia. Virginia began in 1607 as a **small camp** at Jamestown. Later, Pennsylvania was **founded** as a **home** for a **religious group**, the Quakers. The Dutch colony of New Netherlands was **captured** by British **forces** in 1664 and **renamed** New York. The 13 American colonies **would later unite** into one country, but the history of **each one** was **quite distinct**.

The Mayflower **left** from Plymouth, England, on September 6, 1620. After 65 days **crossing** the **ocean**, the **ship landed** in **what is now** the state of Massachusetts. **Soon after**, the Pilgrims **signed** an **agreement** called the Mayflower Compact. In it, the Pilgrims **agreed to unite** into a "Civil Body Politic." The Compact did not **set up** a governing system, as the Constitution later would. It **did contain** the idea that the people **freely agreed to live under** the government. The **power** of this government **came directly** from the people.

In 1774, representatives from 12 of the colonies **met** in Philadelphia, Pennsylvania, for the First Continental Congress. They **protested** British **laws** that **treated them unfairly**. They also began to **organize** an **army**. After **fighting began between** the colonists and the British army, a Second Continental Congress met. This group **appointed** Jefferson and others **to create** the Declaration of Independence.

This document **stated** that if a government **does not protect** the **rights** of the people, the people can create a **new** government. **Following** this idea, the colonists **broke from** their British rulers and **formed** a new country.

The Declaration of Independence, **adopted** July 4, 1776, is **based on** ideas about freedom and basic individual rights that all men and women are created **equal** and have the **right to life**, **liberty**, and the **pursuit** of **happiness**. Thomas Jefferson and the Founding Fathers **believed** that people are **born** with natural rights that no government can **take away**. Government **exists** only **to protect** these rights. Because the people **voluntarily give up** power to a government, they can **take back** that power. The British government **was not protecting** the rights of the colonists, so they took back their power and **separated** from Great Britain.

The American colonists' **anger** had been **building** for **years** before the Revolutionary War began. The Americans **fought** this war because they **wanted** freedom from British **rule**. The fighting of the war **ended** in 1781, **after** the Battle of Yorktown. The Americans, with French **help**, **won** this battle. It was not **until** 1783 that the British **fully accepted** United States independence.

Patrick Henry was a **fiery leader** of the American Revolution. Before U.S. independence, he **spoke out for** colonial rights within the Virginia legislature. He is famous for his **commitment** to the **cause** when he said "**Give me liberty or give me death**." Henry **represented** Virginia in **both** the First and Second Continental Congresses. He **helped push** the colonies **toward** independence. In 1775, when the Revolutionary War began, Henry **convinced** Virginia **to join** the colonists' **side**. **Later** he became the **first governor** of Virginia.

The Underground Railroad

noted/to note: notó/notar, fijarse
train: tren
ran without tracks: andaba sin vías
railroad: ferrocarril
transported slaves: transportaba
  esclavos
network: red
led by secret: dirigida por secretos
growing: creciente
called: llamada
thousands: miles
found/to find: encontraron/encontrar
runaway: fugitivos
sought refuge: buscaron refugio
hide/to hide: escondían/esconder
escaped: escapados
teach them: les enseñaban
codes: códigos
phrases: frases
to help: para ayudar
find: encontrar
next safe house: próxima casa segura
continued/to continue: continuaba/
  continuar
reached/to reach: alcanzaban/alcanzar
born into: nacida en
strength of character: fuerza de carácter
able to: capaz de
herself: ella misma
hundreds: cientos
obtain: obtener
after living: después de vivir
learned/to learn: supo/saber
separated/to separate: separada/separar
sold/to sell: vendida/vender
planned/to plan: planeó/planear
neighbor: vecino
told her: le dijo, le contó
traveled/to travel: viajó/viajar
back: parte de atrás
wagon: carro, carreta, vagón
covered/to cover: cubierta/cubrir
sack: bolsa
made her way: se abrió camino
described/to describe: describió/
  describir
heaven: cielo
cooked/to cook: cocinó/cocinar
sewed/to sew: cosió/coser
to save: para ahorrar
money: dinero
to rescue: para rescatar
gain: ganar, lograr
to alert: para alertar
danger: peligro
nurse: enfermera
sick: enfermos
wounded: heridos
taught/to teach: enseñó/enseñar
newly freed: recientemente liberados
care: cuidar
ship: barco
honored/to honor: honró/honrar
accomplishments: logros
postage stamp: sello postal

In 1786, George Washington **noted** the existence of an invisible **train** that **ran without tracks**. This **railroad transported slaves** to freedom through a **network** of "stations" **led by secret** "conductors." By 1831, this **growing** freedom network was **called** the "Underground Railroad." **Thousands** of slaves **found** freedom through this human train in the 1800s.

Runaway slaves from the South **sought refuge** in states where slavery was prohibited. Conductors on the railroad would **hide escaped** slaves in their homes and **teach them** secret **codes** and **phrases to help** them **find** the **next safe house** along the railroad. This **continued** until they **reached** freedom.

One of the most famous conductors along the Underground Railroad was Harriet Tubman. Harriet was **born into** slavery, but through her **strength of character**, she was **able to** help **herself** and **hundreds** of others **obtain** freedom. **After living** in Maryland for 25 years as a slave, Harriet **learned** she was going to be **separated** from her family and **sold**, so she **planned** her escape. A **neighbor told her** of two houses where she would be safe. She **traveled** to the first house in the **back** of a **wagon covered** with a **sack**, and then **made her way** to Philadelphia on her own. Harriet **described** freedom as "**heaven.**"

In Philadelphia, Harriet **cooked** and **sewed to save** enough **money to rescue** her family. She eventually helped 300 slaves **gain** freedom. Harriet used music, Bible verses, and folklore **to alert** escaped slaves of **danger** and give them directions to safe houses.

During the Civil War, Harriet was a **nurse** to **sick** and **wounded** Union soldiers. She also **taught newly freed** men and women how to **care** for themselves. In World War II, a **ship** was named in her memory, and in 1995, the federal government **honored** her **accomplishments** with a **postage stamp**.

A Time of Crisis

October 29, 1929, "Black Tuesday," was a **dark day** in history, **officially setting off** the Great Depression. The **stock market crashed** and **unemployment skyrocketed**. Many people **became homeless**. In 1932, Franklin Delano Roosevelt was **elected** president and he **promised** a "New Deal" for the American people. Congress **created** The Works Progress Administration (WPA), which **offered** work **relief** for **thousands** of people.

The **end** to the Great Depression **came about** in 1941 with America's **entry** into World War II. America **sided with** Britain, France and the Soviet Union **against** Germany, Italy, and Japan. The **loss of lives** in this war was **staggering**.

President Franklin Roosevelt **called** December 7, 1941, "a **date** which **will live in infamy**." On that day, Japanese **planes attacked** the United States Naval Base at Pearl Harbor, Hawaii. The **bombing killed more than** 2,300 Americans. The attack **took the country by surprise**.

"**AIR RAID** ON PEARL HARBOR THIS IS NOT A **DRILL**."

The **ranking** United States **naval officer** in Pearl Harbor **sent** this **message** to all major Navy commands and **fleet units**. Radio stations **receiving** the **news interrupted** regular **broadcasts to announce** the tragic news to the American public. Most people **knew** what the attack **meant** for the U.S. even before Roosevelt's official announcement the next day. The U.S. **would declare** war on Japan.

The U.S. was **already close** to joining the war, but had **committed** to **neutrality**, only committing to **sending** war **supplies on loan** to Great Britain, France, and Russia. Within days, Japan, Germany, and Italy declared war on the United States. December 7, the "date which will live in infamy," **brought us into** World War II.

---

dark day: día oscuro
officially: oficialmente
setting off: desencadenando, provocando
stock market crashed: bolsa de valores quebró
unemployment: desempleo
skyrocketed: se disparó
became homeless: se quedó sin techo
elected/to elect: elegido/elegir
promised/to promise: prometió/prometer
created/to create: creó/crear
offered/to offer: ofrecía/ofrecer
relief: alivio
thousands: miles
end: fin
came about/to come about: ocurrió/ocurrir, suceder
entry: entrada
sided with: se puso del lado de
against: contra
loss of lives: pérdida de vidas
staggering: pasmosa
called/to call: llamó/llamar
date: fecha
will live in infamy: vivirá en la infamia
planes: aviones
attacked/to attack: atacaron/atacar
bombing: bombardeo
killed/to kill: mató/matar
more than: más de
took the country by surprise: tomó al país por sorpresa
air raid: ataque aéreo
drill: ejercicio *(militar)*
ranking: de rango superior
naval officer: oficial de marina
sent/to send: envió/enviar
message: mensaje
fleet units: flotas
receiving/to recieve: que recibían/recibir
news: noticias
interrupted/to interrupt: interrumpieron/interrumpir
broadcasts: transmisiones
to announce: para anunciar
knew/to know: sabía/saber
meant/to mean: significaba/significar
would declare/to declare: declararía/declarar
already close: ya cerca
committed/to commit: comprometido/comprometer
neutrality: neutralidad
sending: enviar
supplies: abastecimientos, suministros
on loan: en préstamo
brought us into: nos llevó a

Spanish-American War

When Cuban **rebels began** a **violent revolution against** Spanish **rule** in 1895, and a **mysterious** explosion **sunk** the *U.S.S. Maine* in the Havana **harbor**, the U.S. **entered** into a **war** with Spain. The war **took place** from April to August 1898. **Only** 113 days after the **outbreak** of war, the Treaty of Paris, which **ended** the **conflict,** gave the United States **ownership** of Puerto Rico, the Philippines, and Guam.

The war **served** to **further cement relations** between the American North and South. The war gave **both sides** a common **enemy** for the **first time** since the **end** of the Civil War in 1865. Many **friendships** were **formed** between **soldiers** of both northern and southern states during their **tours of duty**. This was an important **development** since many soldiers in this war were the **children** of Civil War **veterans** on **both sides**.

The Spanish–American War is **significant** in American history because it **enabled** the United States **to emerge** as a **power** on the **world stage**. The war **marked** American **entry** into world **affairs.** **Over the course** of the **next century**, the United States **had** a large **hand in** various conflicts **around** the world. The United States entered a **lengthy** and **prosperous period** of rapid **economic growth**, population growth, and **technological innovation** which **lasted through** the 1920s.

Women's Right to Vote

Presidents Andrew Jackson, James Polk, and John Tyler, **like many** Americans of the Western Expansion **era** (1829 – 1859), **embraced** the notion of **enlarging** the "**empire for liberty**." **In other words**, they wanted **to expand** the **borders** of America **westward**.

While some **pioneers headed** west to California, others **attempted** to expand the idea of what "liberty" in America **meant**. Abolitionists **opposed laws** that **kept** African Americans **enslaved**, and **advocates** of **women's suffrage argued** that **wives**, **mothers** and **daughters** should **play** a more significant role in **society** by **voting**, **holding office**, and **working outside the home**.

During this **time**, the **right** of women in the United States to vote was **debated**.

Today, women in the United States can vote, **own property**, and hold political office, but it was not always this way. 150 years ago, women **did not have** the same privileges as men in many ways, and they had **to fight** for their rights. In July of 1848, a group of women and men **interested** in **discussing** the position of women in American society **met** at the Seneca Falls Convention in New York.

The assembled group also **considered** and voted on a **number** of resolutions. The number one **point** that was met with **strong opposition**, but was eventually **passed**, was the **following**: "**Resolved**, That it is the **duty** of the women of this country **to secure** to **themselves** their **sacred right to vote**."

The fight for women's **equal** rights was a **long**, **hard battle**. After the **signing** of "The Declaration of Rights and Sentiments" in 1848, it **took** 72 years of **organized struggle** before most women **won** the right to vote when the Nineteenth Amendment to the U.S. Constitution was passed in 1920.

like many: como muchos
era: época
embraced/to embrace: adoptaron/adoptar
enlarging: aumentar
empire for liberty: imperio para la libertad
in other words: en otras palabras
to expand: extender
borders: fronteras, límites
westward: en dirección oeste
while: mientras
pioneers: pioneros
headed/to head: se dirigieron/dirigirse
attempted/to attempt: intentaron/intentar
meant/to mean: significaba/significar
opposed laws: se opusieron a leyes
kept/to keep: mantenían/mantener
enslaved/to enslave: esclavizados/esclavizar
advocates: defensores, partidarios
women's suffrage: sufragio de las mujeres
argued/to argue: sostenían/sostener
wives: esposas
mothers: madres
daughters: hijas
play: jugar, tener (un rol)
society: sociedad
voting: votar
holding office: ocupar cargos
working outside the home: trabajar fuera del hogar
during: durante
time: período
right: derecho
voiced/to voice: manifestado/manifestar
own property: ser dueñas de propiedad
did not have: no tenían
to fight: que pelear
interested: interesados
discussing: discutir
met/to meet: se reunieron/reunirse
considered/to consider: consideró/considerar
number: número
point: punto
strong opposition: fuerte oposición
passed/to pass: aprobado/aprobar
following: siguiente
resolved: resuelto
duty: deber
to secure: asegurarse
themselves: a sí mismas
sacred: sagrado
right to vote: derecho a votar
equal: igualdad
long, hard battle: batalla larga y dura
signing: firma
took/to take: llevó/llevar, demorar
organized struggle: lucha organizada
won/to win: ganaran/ganar, lograr

Test Your Comprehension

Independence Day, page 146

1. ¿Cuántos estados hay en los Estados Unidos?

2. ¿Qué celebramos el 4 de Julio?

Stars and Stripes, page 147

1. ¿Cuáles son los colores de nuestra bandera?

2. ¿Qué significan las estrellas de la bandera?

3. ¿Cuántas estrellas hay en nuestra bandera?

4. ¿Cuántas barras hay en nuestra bandera y de qué color son?

5. ¿Qué representan las barras de la bandera?

Electoral College, page 148

1. ¿Quién es eligen al presidente de los Estados Unidos?

2. ¿Quién se convierte en presidente si el presidente muere o renuncia?

Supreme Law of the Land, page 149

1. ¿Qué es la Constitución?

2. ¿Como se llaman los cambios en la Constitución?

Examina tu comprensión

Divisions of Power, page 150

1. ¿Cuáles son las tres ramas de nuestro gobierno?

2. ¿Cuál es la rama legislativa de nuestro gobierno?

3. ¿Quiénes hace las leyes federales en los Estados Unidos?

4. ¿Quiénes eligen a los miembros del Congreso?

5. ¿Cuántos senadores hay en el Congreso?

The Bill of Rights, page 153

1. ¿De dónde proviene la libertad de expresión?

2. ¿Qué es el Bill of Rights?

3. ¿Los derechos de quiénes están garantizados por la Constitución y el Bill of Rights?

United States Presidency, page 154

1. ¿A qué presidente se le llama el "Padre de la Patria"?

2. ¿Por cuánto tiempo se elige al presidente?

3. ¿Cuáles son algunos de los requisitos para ser candidato a presidente?

4. ¿Cuántos mandatos completos puede ejercer un presidente?

The clearest way into the universe
is through a forest wilderness.

John Muir

Geography

World Heritage Sites

A UNESCO World Heritage Site is a **specific site** that is **listed** by the international World Heritage Program. The program **works to conserve places** of cultural or natural **importance** and preserve each site for **future generations.**

In the United States, there are 22 world heritage sites. Seventeen of these are **natural geographical areas** of **particular interest** or importance.

CARLSBAD CAVERNS, NEW MEXICO: Carlsbad Caverns National Park is home to more than 80 **limestone caves**. The nation's **deepest** cave, at 1,597 feet, is found here.

CHACO CULTURE, NEW MEXICO: The Anasazi, or "Ancient Ones," **built** large **multistory stone villages** and an **impressive** 400-mile **road system** in Chaco canyon. Chaco canyon **houses** the **densest** and most exceptional concentration of pueblos in the American Southwest.

TAOS PUEBLO, NEW MEXICO: Pueblo de Taos is the best preserved of the pueblos in the U.S. Taos is a great **example** of the traditional **architecture** of the pre-Hispanic period. Today Taos is **inhabited** by the Taos Pueblo Indians, and it is still an **active community**.

EVERGLADES NATIONAL PARK, FLORIDA: The Everglades are **formed by** a river of fresh water 6 **inches deep** and 50 **miles wide** that **flows slowly across marshes, pine forests**, and **mangrove islands**. More than 300 **species** of **birds live** in the park **as well as alligators, manatees**, and Florida **panthers**.

GRAND CANYON, ARIZONA: The Grand Canyon, created by the Colorado River, is 277 miles long, **ranges** in **width** from 0.25 to 15 miles and **attains** a **depth** of more than a mile.

SMOKY MOUNTAINS, NORTH CAROLINA/TENNESSEE: "Place of Blue **Smoke**" was the **name given** by the Cherokee Indians to these Appalachian Highlands. The forest here **exudes** water vapor and **oily residues** which **create** a **smoke-like haze** that **surrounds** the **peaks** and **fills** the **valleys**.

HAWAII VOLCANOES NATIONAL PARK: It is thought that the Hawaiian islands were **created** when **molten rock pushed through** Earth's **crust**, **forming** volcanoes. The park's two most impressive volcanoes are Kilauea and Mauna Loa.

MAMMOTH CAVE, KENTUCKY: Mammoth Cave is the world's most extensive cave system, with 345 miles of **passages**. Water **seeping into** the cave creates stalactites, stalagmites, and white crystal formations. **Rare** and **unusual** animals are found here, such as **blind fish** and **colorless spiders**. They **demonstrate** adaptation to the total **darkness** and **isolation**.

CAHOKIA MOUNDS STATE HISTORIC SITE, ILLINOIS: The Cahokia site was the **regional center** for the Mississippian Indian culture. Cahokia **features** the largest prehistoric **earthen constructions** in the Americas. This site is a testament to the **sophisticated engineering skills** of Mississippian culture.

MESA VERDE NATIONAL PARK, COLORADO: The Anasazi **established** villages on the **high**, **flat land** of southwestern Colorado. In the late 1100s they began constructing multistory stone apartment houses, **tucked on ledges** and **under** rock **overhangs**.

OLYMPIC NATIONAL PARK, WASHINGTON: The park **encompasses not only snow-capped** Mount Olympus, glaciers, **alpine meadows**, and **rocky** Pacific Mountain **coastline**, **but also** one of the few **temperate rain forests** in the world.

WATERTON-GLACIER INTERNATIONAL PEACE PARK, MONTANA: The two parks **sustain** a **surprisingly** diverse habitat, **including wolves, bears**, and **mountain lions**. It features a **wide variety** of wild flowers and **wildlife.**

REDWOOD NATIONAL PARK, CALIFORNIA: Redwood National Park **contains** the **tallest living** things on Earth: **evergreen trees** that **grow** to 350 feet.

GLACIER BAY NATIONAL PARK AND PRESERVE, ALASKA: The park is made up of a **huge chain** of **tidewater** glaciers and a dramatic **range** of **landscapes**, from rocky terrain **covered** by ice to **lush** temperate rain forest. Brown and black bears, **mountain goats, whales**, **seals**, and eagles can be **found within** the park.

it is thought/to think: se piensa/pensar
created/crear: creadas/to create
molten rock: roca fundida
pushed/to push: empujó/empujar
through: a través de
crust: corteza
forming: formando
passages: pasajes, pasadizos
seeping into: filtrándose dentro de
rare: raro, poco frecuente
unusual: poco comunes
blind fish: peces ciegos
colorless spiders: arañas sin color
demonstrate/to demonstrate: demuestran/demostrar
darkness: oscuridad
isolation: aislamiento
regional center: centro regional
features/to feature: ponen de relieve/ poner de relieve
earthen constructions: construcciones de tierra o barro
sophisticated: sofisticadas
engineering skills: habilidades de ingeniería
established/to establish: establecieron/establecer
high: alta
flat land: tierra llana
tucked on ledges: metidas en las cornisas
under: bajo
overhangs: salientes
encompasses/to encompass: abarca/ abarcar
not only...but also: no sólo...pero también
snow-capped: cubierto de nieve
alpine meadows: prados alpinos
rocky: rocosa
coastline: litoral, costa
temperate rain forests: bosques templados pluviales
sustain/to sustain: sostienen/sostener
surprisingly: sorprendente
including: incluyendo
wolves: lobos
bears: osos
mountain lions: pumas
wide variety: amplia variedad
wildlife: fauna y flora, vida silvestre
contains/to contain: contiene/contener
tallest: más alto
living: vivientes, vivos
evergreen trees: árboles de hoja perenne
grow/to grow: crecen/crecer
huge chain: cadena enorme
tidewater: marea
range: gama
landscapes: paisajes
covered: cubierto
lush: frondosa
mountain goats: cabras de monteses
whales: ballenas
seals: focas
found within: encontradas dentro

Majestic Mountains

highest: más altas
located/to locate: ubicadas/ubicar
home: hogar
peaks: picos
reaches/to reach: alcanza/alcanzar
height: altura
approximately: aproximadamente
ocean floor: fondo del océano
above sea level: sobre el nivel del mar
generally given: generalmente dadas
hiker's paradise: paraíso para el excursionista
trails: senderos
ranging/to range: que varían/variar
short: cortos
walks: paseos, caminatas
strenuous treks: agotadoras caminatas
long enough: suficientemente largas
to require: como para requerir
overnight camping: acampar por la noche
bears: osos
live/to live: viven/vivir
park: parque
as well as: así como
deer: ciervo
elk: alce
tall: de alto
largest known: más grande conocido
free-standing: suelto, libre, sin sujeción
exposed granite: granito expuesto
top: cima
allows/to allow: permite/permitir
spectacular views: vistas espectaculares
nature: naturales, en la naturaleza
prominent: prominente
range: cadena de montañas
glaciers: glaciares
main feature: rasgo principal

The **highest** mountains in the U.S. are **located** in four states: Alaska, California, Colorado and Washington. Alaska is **home** to 19 of the 20 highest **peaks** in the U.S. and Colorado is home to 16 of the 50 highest peaks in the U.S.

Mount McKinley or Denali in Alaska is the highest mountain peak in North America. At its peak it **reaches** a **height** of **approximately** 20,320 feet.

The United States is home to the world's highest mountain, from its base on the **ocean floor**. Mauna Kea, on Hawaii is 33,474 feet high but only 13,796 feet are **above sea level**. Heights of mountains are **generally given** as heights above sea level.

The Great Smoky Mountains are a **hiker's paradise** with over 800 miles of **trails ranging** from **short walks** to **strenuous treks** that are **long enough to require overnight camping**. Sixteen-hundred **bears live** in the **park as well as deer** and **elk**.

Stone Mountain Park is Georgia's most popular attraction. The mountain is 825 feet **tall**. It is the world's **largest known free-standing** piece of **exposed granite**. The 1.3-mile trail to the **top** of the mountain **allows spectacular views**. There are also 15 miles of **nature** trails for hiking.

At 7962 feet, Mount Olympus is the tallest and most **prominent** mountain in the Olympic Mountain **range** of Western Washington. Mount Olympus has eight **glaciers** and is the **main feature** of Olympic National Park.

MOUNTAINS AND YOU

Mountains **play** an important role in our lives! **Climbers** and tourists **visit** mountains for the **scenery**. **Farmers graze** their animals on them. Water **authorities** make **reservoirs** and **pump** the water to towns and cities. Forestry companies **grow** coniferous forests and **harvest wood** from them.

Tourism has many **advantages**; however, it can have a **serious impact** on the **environment**. As more and more people visit the mountains, the **chances** of the environment being permanently **damaged** become ever greater.

When hiking, **check** to **make sure** the trail you have **chosen** is **open** for use. Make sure it is dry and you always **stay** on the trail. **Mountain biking** and even hiking on **wet** trails **causes damage** that can be irreparable. You should also have **proper footwear** so you can hike through **puddles**. **Walking around** a puddle **widens** the trail and causes erosion.

If you are camping **on or near** a mountain, camp on a **durable surface** such as **rock**, **sand** or **dry grass**. This **minimizes** impact and doesn't **scare** away wildlife.

Finally, don't **pick** the **flowers**! **Leaving** flowers and plants **in place** is very important for **seeding**. If it's **blooming**, and you **take** the **seed away** it won't get **pollinated**, it's no longer a **food source** for **bees**. **Draw** it, **photograph** it or **smell** it, but don't pick it!

play/to play: juegan/jugar
climbers: escaladores, alpinistas
visit/to visit: visitan/visitar
scenery: paisaje
farmers: granjeros, agricultores
graze: llevar a pastar
authorities: autoridades
reservoirs: embalses represas
pump/to pump: bombean/bombear
grow/to grow: cultivan/cultivar
harvest/to harvest: recogen/recoger
wood: madera
advantages: ventajas
serious impact: grave impacto
environment: medio ambiente
chances: oportunidades
damaged: dañado
check/to check: verifica/verificar
make sure/to make sure: asegurarte/ asegurarse
chosen/to choose: elegido/elegir
open: abierto
stay/to stay: permanezcas/permanecer
mountain biking: ciclismo de montaña
wet: mojados
causes/to cause: causa/causar
damage: daño
proper footwear: calzado adecuado
puddles: charcos
walking around: caminar alrededor
widens/to widen: amplía/ampliar
on or near: sobre o cerca de
durable surface: superficie durable
rock: roca
sand: arena
dry grass: pasto seco
minimizes/to minimize: minimiza/ minimizar
scare/to scare: asusta/asustar
pick/to pick: recojas/recoger
flowers: flores
leaving: dejar
in place: en su lugar
seeding: proceso de dejar caer semillas
blooming: floreciendo
take...away/to take away: llevas/llevarse
seed: semilla
pollinated/to pollinate: polinizada/ polinizar
food source: fuente de alimento
bees: abejas
draw/to draw: dibuja/dibujar
photograph/to photograph: fotografía/fotografiar
smell/to smell: huele/oler

North American Deserts

Four **desert regions make up** the North American Deserts: the Great Basin, the Mojave, the Sonoran, and the Chihuahuan.

GREAT BASIN DESERT

The Great Basin Desert is the **largest** desert in the U.S. and **covers over** 190,000 **square** miles. It covers the **northern three-quarters** of Nevada, **western** and **southern** Utah, the **southeastern corner** of Oregon and the southern **third** of Idaho.

The Great Basin is **considered** a **cold** desert. A cold desert is one with **daytime** temperatures **below freezing** for part of the year. **Sagebrush** covers **vast** areas of the Great Basin Desert. This is mainly a **shrub** desert with few **cacti. Compared with** the other deserts of North America, the Great Basin Desert has a limited **range** of plants and animals.

SONORAN DESERT

The Sonoran desert is considered the biologically **richest** desert in the world. It **receives** much of its **moisture** during the **summer** "monsoon" **season, making** it a subtropical desert. **Freezing** conditions can be **expected** for a few nights in **winter**.

The northern part of this desert is in Arizona and California, but it pushes far down into Mexico on both sides of the Gulf of California. It is **broken up** by numerous **mountain ranges**. In the Southwest these mountain ranges are **referred** to as "**sky islands**" due to their **isolation** by valleys.

MOJAVE DESERT

The Mojave is the **smallest** of the North American deserts. It **occupies** a **large portion** of southern California and smaller parts of southwestern Utah, southern Nevada, and northwestern Arizona. It is **named after** the Mojave tribe of Native Americans. The Mojave Desert's **boundaries** are usually **defined** by the **presence** of Joshua Trees. These are the most popular and **well known** plant of the Mojave Desert.

The Mojave Desert receives **less than** 6 inches of rain a year, which makes it the **driest** of the North American deserts. A small California **community** located in the Mojave Desert once went 767 days **without rain**! The Mojave Desert is home to the Mojave National Preserve and the **hottest** place in North America: **Death Valley**. The **all-time record high** was **recorded** here at 134 **degrees**.

ANIMALS OF THE DESERT

Animals that live in the desert have **to adapt** to **lack** of water, extreme temperatures, and **shortage** of food. **To avoid daytime** heat, many desert animals are nocturnal. They **burrow** beneath the surface or **hide** in the **shade**. Many desert animals do not **drink** water at all; they get water from their food or the **moisture** in the plants. The most commonly known animals in North American deserts are the coyote and the **jack rabbit**.

The coyote is a **member** of the dog family and **closely related** to the wolf. The coyote is a fast-running carnivore and **feeds** mainly on small **mammals**. The coyote is one of the **few wild** animals whose communication is frequently **heard**. At night, coyotes **howl** and **emit** a series of short, **high-pitched** yips. Howls are **used** to **keep in touch** with other coyotes in the area.

Jackrabbits are large, **long-legged**, **long-eared hares**. Hares are **similar to rabbits**, but larger. The fur on their long **ears** is **marked** with black **spots**. They are very **fast-moving** mammals and can **run** up to 45 **miles per hour**. Jackrabbits are strict vegetarians. They eat a great variety of **herbs** and shrubs. It is **estimated** that nearly 2 million jackrabbits are **hunted** each year in California.

Other animals **found** in American deserts include **rattlesnakes**, **bighorn sheep**, **roadrunners**, and antelope.

less than: menos de
driest: más seco
community: comunidad
without rain: sin lluvia
hottest: más caliente
Death Valley: Valle de la Muerte
all-time record high: la temperatura más alta de todos los tiempos
recorded/to record: registrado/registrar
degrees: grados
to adapt: que adaptarse
lack: falta
shortage: escasez
to avoid: para evitar
daytime: diurno
burrow/to burrow: cavan/cavar, hacer madrigueras en
hide/to hide: se esconden/esconderse
shade: sombra
drink/to drink: toman/tomar
moisture: humedad
jackrabbit: liebre
member: miembro
closely related: pariente cercano
feeds/to feed: se alimenta/alimentarse
mammals: mamíferos
few: pocos
wild: salvajes
heard/to hear: oída/oír
howl/to howl: aúllan/aullar
emit/to emit: emiten/emitir
high-pitched: agudos
used/to use: usan/usar
keep in touch: mantenerse en contacto
long-legged: de patas largas
long-eared: de orejas largas
hares: liebres
similar to: similares a, parecidas a
rabbits: conejos
ears: orejas
marked: manchadas
spots: manchas
fast-moving: que se mueve rápido
run/to run: correr
miles per hour: millas por hora
herbs: hierbas
estimated/to estimate: se calcula/calcular
hunted/to hunt: cazados/cazar
found/to find: encontrados/encontrar
rattlesnakes: serpientes de cascabel
bighorn sheep: borrego cimarrón
roadrunners: correcaminos

The Great Lakes

The **Great Lakes**—Superior, Michigan, Huron, Erie, and Ontario—are a group of five lakes on the U.S.-Canadian **border**. They are the largest **fresh water** system on Earth.

Covering more than 94,000 square miles, the Great Lakes **hold** about **one-fifth** of the **world's** fresh water **supply** and **nine-tenths** of the U.S. supply.

The geography of the Great Lakes **shoreline flourishes** with diverse plant and animal life. The shoreline systems include **sandy beaches**, **sand dunes** and **wetlands**.

The most common shoreline in the Great Lakes region is the sand beach. The beaches are a great **place** for humans to **swim** and a great place for **birds** and other small other animals to **find food**. Beaches are **rich feeding grounds** for **shorebirds**. A variety of **beetles**, **spiders**, and birds like to feed upon the **driftwood** and other debris that **collects** on the beach.

The sand dunes of the Great Lakes are the largest freshwater coastal dunes in the world. The Indiana Dunes National Lakeshore ranks **seventh among** national parks in plant diversity. Dunes are also the **home of** many **endangered** animals and plants. The piping plover, a small shorebird, **nests** in the shoreline dunes.

The freshwater wetlands of the Great Lakes are ecologically **unique**. They **range from** small wetlands in bays **to extensive** wetlands along the shoreline. Wetlands are an important part of **duck** and **geese** migration. They **provide** food, **resting stops** and habitats. Wetlands also **improve water quality** by **slowing runoff**, and **processing organic waste** before it **reaches open** water. This process **protects aquatic life** and sources of **drinking** water.

The shorelines of The Great Lakes are threatened by human impacts, such as **housing developments**, tourism, and erosion. **We need** to **ensure** that we don't **destroy** this diverse and beautiful area that took nature **years to create**.

Protecting Our Environment

The **natural resources available** to people—for food and other production, **maintaining healthy lives**, and the **pleasure** of a beautiful **landscape**—can seem **boundless**. But **growing populations** are **placing increasing pressure** on the resources. Many of these resources, **once used**, are not **renewable**.

Fresh water **supplies** are essential for agricultural production, for **drinking**, and for **maintenance** of important habitats of animals. Fresh water supplies are **projected** to be inadequate to **meet the needs** of one-third of the world's population by 2025, unless better **use** is made of this precious resource. In many **coastal areas**, pollution has **reduced** the **quality** of the water, **affecting** the quality of water and **aquatic life.** **Forests** are being **cut down** faster than they are being **regenerated** or **planted**.

USAID takes an **integrated approach** to natural resources **management**. Land and water must be **managed skillfully** so that they are able to maintain our **basic ability** to **produce** food. Water supplies must be used more efficiently—and water quality must be maintained or even **improved**—if people are to **remain healthy**.

Forests must be **protected** by those who live in or **close** to them. New approaches to involving these people in the wise management of a resource important to everyone in the world are being developed and applied in many areas. **Sound methods** for **harvesting** trees for **timber** and management of forest trees are being **implemented**. These kinds of programs **promise to slow** the **rate** of deforestation. However, illegal and destructive **logging** remains a **threat** to biodiversity conservation. **Once lost**, it will be impossible for the world **to recover** that diversity of our natural resources.

USAID is an **outstanding** organization that works to protect the environment in more than 100 countries **worldwide**. The work they do provides a **better future** for all.

For more information visit: www.usaid.gov.

---

natural resources available: recursos naturales disponibles
maintaining/to maintain: manteniendo/mantener
healthy lives: vidas saludables
pleasure: placer
landscape: paisaje
boundless: sin límites
growing populations: crecientes poblaciones
placing/to place: poniendo/poner
increasing pressure: presión creciente
once used: una vez usadas
renewable: renovables
fresh: fresca *(aquí: dulce)*
supplies: suministros
drinking: tomar, beber
maintenance: mantenimiento
projected/to project: proyectan/ proyectar
meet the needs: satisfacer las necesidades
use: uso
coastal areas: áreas costeras
reduced/to reduce: reducido/reducir
quality: calidad
affecting/to affect: afectando/afectar
aquatic life: vida acuática
forests: bosques, selvas
cut down/to cut down: cortadas/cortar
regenerated/to regenerate: regeneradas/ regenerar
planted/to plant: plantadas/plantar
integrated approach: enfoque integrado
management: manejo
managed/to manage: manejados/ manejar
skillfully: hábilmente
basic ability: habilidad básica
produce: producir
improved/to improve: mejorada/mejorar
remain healthy: mantenerse saludable
protected/to protect: protegidos/ proteger
close: cerca
sound methods: métodos sensatos
harvesting: recoger
timber: madera
implemented/to implement: implementados/ implementar
promise/to promise: prometen/ prometer
to slow: frenar
rate: ritmo
logging: tala *(de árboles)*
threat: amenaza
once lost: una vez perdida
to recover: recobrar
outstanding: sobresaliente
worldwide: por todo el mundo
better future: mejor futuro

Land of Waterfalls

America's **outstanding waterfalls** can **be found hiking through forests**, **alongside rivers** or **even** in **scorching deserts**. Whether a **trickle**, a **stream** or a **cascade**, the **delight** and **serenity** of a waterfall is **enjoyed** by people of **all ages**.

NIAGARA FALLS, NEW YORK

Niagara Falls is a group of **massive** waterfalls **located** on the Niagara River on the **border between** the United States and Canada. The Falls are **comprised** of three separate waterfalls: Horseshoe Falls, American Falls, and the smaller, adjacent Bridal Veil Falls. Niagara Falls is very **wide**, and the most voluminous waterfall in North America. Niagara Falls is **not only renowned** for its **beauty**. The Falls are a **valuable source** of hydroelectric **power** for **both** Ontario and New York.

CALF CREEK FALLS, UTAH

The Calf Creek Recreation Area in **south central** Utah offers a **little-known treasure** in one of the American deserts, the Calf Creek Falls. **While** a **year-round creek** is **relatively rare** in the desert, a year-round 126-foot waterfall is rare and **stunning**. It is 5.5 miles **roundtrip** to hike into the falls. Most of the trail is **sandy** and the **walk** can **become** very **tiring**, especially in **warm weather**. **However, once** you **reach** the falls you will **find** a **cool**, **shady haven** well **worth the effort**.

YOSEMITE FALLS, CALIFORNIA

Yosemite Falls is the **highest** waterfall in North America. Located in Yosemite National Park in California, it's a major attraction in the park, especially in **late spring** when the water **flow** is at its **peak**. At 2425 feet, Yosemite Falls is the **sixth**-highest waterfall in the world.

---

outstanding: sobresalientes
waterfalls: cataratas
be found: ser encontradas
hiking/to hike: andando/andar
through: a través de
forests: bosques, selvas
alongside: a lo largo de
rivers: ríos
even: aún, incluso
scorching: abrasadores
deserts: desiertos
trickle: hilito *(de agua)*
stream: riachuelo, corriente
cascade: cascada
delight: delicia
serenity: serenidad
enjoyed/to enjoy: disfrutado/disfrutar
all ages: todas las edades
massive: masiva
located: ubicada
border: frontera
between: entre
comprised: compuesto
wide: ancha
not only: no sólo
renowned: renombrada
beauty: belleza
valuable source: fuente valiosa
power: energía
both: ambos
south central: sur central
little-known treasure: tesoro poco conocido
while: mientras que
year-round: todo el año
creek: arroyo
relatively rare: relativamente raro
stunning: impresionante
roundtrip: de ida y vuelta
sandy: arenoso
walk: caminata
become: volverse
tiring: cansadora
warm weather: clima cálido o caluroso
however: sin embargo
once: una vez
reach/to reach: alcanzas/alcanzar
find/to find: encontrar
cool: fresco
shady: sombreado
haven: refugio
worth the effort: vale la pena el esfuerzo
highest: *(la)* más alta
late spring: final de la primavera
flow: flujo, caudal
peak: pico
sixth: sexta

MULTNOMAH FALLS, OREGON

Multnomah Falls is the **tallest** waterfall in Oregon and also the second-highest year-round waterfall in the United States. The water of the falls **plummets** 620 feet from its origin on Larch Mountain. **Unusually cold** weather can **turn** this waterfall into a **frozen icicle**! The frozen falls are a **sight to behold**.

AMICALOLA FALLS, GEORGIA

Amicalola Falls is **derived** from a Cherokee **word meaning "tumbling waters."** The falls reach the **height** of 729 feet, which makes it the highest waterfall east of the Mississippi. **In addition,** the falls are just a hike away from Springer Mountain, famous for being the **southern end** of the Appalachian Trail.

NORTH CLEAR CREEK FALLS, COLORADO

The **unusual setting** for these waterfalls **sets them apart** from others and makes them even more spectacular. North Creek Falls are **surrounded** by **flat lands covered** with **prairie grasses**. Located **above** the Rio Grande, these falls **crash** more than 100 feet to the **canyon below** and are **believed** to be the most **photographed** waterfall in Colorado.

SHOSHONE FALLS, IDAHO

Shoshone Falls are the **most well known** falls in Idaho, and the most **powerful** falls in the Northwest. The falls are **controlled** by the Milner **Dam** and they are **turned off during** the **agricultural season** by **diverting** the water to the **farmlands**. They **let them flow freely** in the **winter** and spring, **completely covering** the **cliff**. These falls are 212 feet high and 1200 feet wide.

PUNCH BOWL FALLS, OREGON

Punch Bowl Falls is spectacular and is the most photographed waterfall in the Pacific Northwest. The falls **occur** where Eagle Creek **cuts through** a **narrow channel flanked** by cliffs, and **drops powerfully** into a large **bowl**. The falls' **name comes from** the **resemblance** of the area to an **actual punch** bowl.

Tropical Rain Forests

Hawaii is the only state with a **true tropical rain forest**. Hawaiian tropical forests are home to a large **diversity** of species. The **isolation** of the Hawaiian Islands from the rest of the world has **resulted** in an incredible diversity of **fungi**, **mosses**, **snails**, **birds**, and other **wildlife**. This diversity makes Hawaii's tropical forests some of the most spectacular **places** on Earth.

The world's **wettest** rain forest is found in Hawaii on Mount Waialeale. This forest **averages** 450 inches of **rainfall** per year.

An incredible variety of plants and animals **live** in the tropical forests of Hawaii. Birds native to the forest are hawks, crows, thrushes, and honeycreepers. The honeycreepers have **developed** diverse **bills formed** for **feeding** on the different plants in these **wet** forests. **Rare** carnivorous **caterpillars** are native to Hawaii. When **triggered** by **touch**, these caterpillars **snatch** their **prey**. The caterpillars **mimic twigs** and **grab** prey that **comes too close**.

The native plants in the Hawaiian islands are **found** nowhere else on Earth. **In turn**, most native plants are **defenseless against** introduced species such as **pigs**. Pigs were **brought** to Hawaii from Polynesia and Europe. **Over the years** the pigs have **escaped** and **turned feral**. These **wild** pigs are very destructive to the Hawaiian forests. They have destroyed vegetation, caused **soil erosion**, **spread weeds** and **diseases**, and **polluted** water **supplies**. Other introduced plants and animals are **crowding out** the native plants and animals. Hawaii has **lost two-thirds** of its original forests to agriculture, **clearing**, and **fire**, and **half** its native birds through **habitat loss** and **disease**. **Saving** Hawaii's **remaining** native species is now **a race against time**.

Temperate Rain Forests

Temperate rainforests are **much younger** than tropical rainforests. The **soil** in temperate forests **contains** more **nutrients** than that of the tropics. Temperate rainforests are **located** **along** the Pacific coast of the United States. Temperate rainforests are much more **scarce** than tropical rainforests. Some of the best forests are found in Olympic National Park, Mount Rainier National Park, Tongass National Forest, Mount St. Helens National Monument and Redwood National Park.

Olympic National Park is located on the Olympic Peninsula of Washington state. The **western side** of the park is **home to** a temperate rain forest and the **wettest** area in the continental United States. **Because** this is a temperate rainforest it contains **dense timber**, **including** spruce and fir.

The Tongass National Forest in southeastern Alaska is the **largest** national forest in the United States. It **spans** over 17 **million acres**. It is a **northern** temperate rain forest, home to rare flora and fauna that are **endangered elsewhere**. The Tongass National Forest is also home to about 70,000 people who **depend** on the national forest for their **livelihood**. Several Alaska Native **tribes live throughout** Southeast Alaska. 31 **communities** are located within the forest; the largest is Juneau, the state capital, with a **population** of 31,000. The forest is **named** for the Tongass group of the Tlingit people, who **inhabited** the Alaska **panhandle**.

---

temperate: templados
much younger: mucho más jóvenes
soil: suelo
contains/to contain: contiene/
  contener
nutrients: nutrientes
located/to locate: ubicados/ubicar
along: a lo largo de
scarce: escasos
western side: lado oeste
home to: hogar de
wettest: más mojadas
because: porque
dense timber: árboles densos
including: incluyendo
largest: más grande
spans/to span: abarca/abarcar,
  extenderse
million acres: millones de acres
northern: norteño
endangered: en peligro de extinción
elsewhere: en otro lugar
depend/to depend: dependen/
  depender
livelihood: sustento
tribes: tribus
live/to live: viven/vivir
throughout: por toda
communities: comunidades
population: población
named/to name: llamada/llamar
inhabited/to inhabit: habitaron/
  habitar
panhandle: faja estrecha de
  territorio

Volcanoes of the United States

all: todos
are found/to find: se encuentran/ encontrarse
including: incluyendo
designated/to designate: designados/ designar
high threat: amenaza grave
located/to locate: ubicados/ubicar
most: la mayoría
erupted/to erupt: hecho erupción/ hacer erupción
time: tiempo
far back: *(tiempo)* atrás
listed/to list: listados/listar
below: abajo
considered/to consider: considerado/ considerar
monarch: monarca
single: solo
any kind: cualquier clase, todo tipo
miles: millas
long: de largo
wide: de ancho
rises/to rise: se eleva/elevarse
base: base
sea floor: fondo del mar
last: última
eruption: erupción
ended/to end: terminó/terminar
period: período
silence: silencio
remains/to remain: continúa/ continuar
extremely: extremadamente
dangerous: peligroso
historically: históricamente
once: una vez
decade: década
recorded: registrada
slowed/to slow: frenado/frenar
pace: ritmo
scientists: científicos
constantly: constantemente
monitor/to monitor: controlan/ controlar, observar, seguir
anticipation: anticipación
next: próxima

All of the volcanoes in the United States **are found** in the western states, **including** Alaska and Hawaii. There are 169 volcanoes in the United States. Eighteen of them have been **designated** as "very **high threat**" volcanoes. These high-threat volcanoes are **located** in Hawaii, Oregon, Washington and Alaska. **Most** of them haven't **erupted** for a very long **time**, as **far back** as the 1700s.

Listed below are some of the most famous volcanoes in the United States.

Mauna Loa is **considered** the "**monarch** of mountains." It is the largest volcano and the largest **single** mountain of **any kind** in the world. It is 60 **miles long**, 30 miles **wide**, and **rises** 28,680 feet from its **base** on the **sea floor**. Mauna Loa's **last** major **eruption** was in 1984. It **ended** a 9-year **period** of **silence**. Mauna Loa **remains** an **extremely dangerous** volcano that can erupt in many different directions.

Historically, Mauna Loa has erupted at least **once** in every **decade** of **recorded** Hawaiian history. It has, however, **slowed** its **pace** with eruptions in 1950, 1975 and 1984. **Scientists** and residents of the Big Island **constantly monitor** Mauna Loa in **anticipation** of its **next** eruption.

Kilauea Volcano, on the **southeast side** of the Big Island, is one of the most active on earth. Its **current** eruption **started** in January 1983 and **continues** to this day. During this eruption over 500 acres have been **added** to the Big Island's **shoreline**. In the course of the eruption, lava flows have **destroyed** a famous 700 year-old Hawaiian **temple**, **overrun** many houses, and permanently **blocked highways**.

There are no indications that the current eruption **will come to an end anytime soon**. Visitors to Hawaii Volcanoes National Park have a **unique opportunity** to see lava in action. Near the southwestern **edge** of the caldera is the "**fire pit**," known as Halemaumau (House of **Everlasting Fire**), which has **at times contained** a **lake** of **boiling** lava.

Mount St. Helens is an active volcano in Skamania County, Washington. It is most famous for its **disastrous** eruption on May 18, 1980. This was the **deadliest** and most **economically** destructive volcanic **event** in the history of the United States. Fifty-seven people were **killed**, and 250 homes, 47 **bridges**, 15 miles of **railways** and 185 miles of highway were destroyed. The eruption caused a massive **debris avalanche, reducing** the **elevation** of the mountain's **summit** from 9,677 feet to 8,365 feet and **replacing** it with a mile-wide **horseshoe-shaped** crater. The debris avalanche was the largest in recorded history.

---

southeast: sureste
side: lado
current: actual
started/to start: empezó/empezar
continues/to continue: continúa/ continuar
added/to add: agregados/agregar, sumar
shoreline: costa
destroyed/to destroy: destruyeron/ destruir
temple: templo
overrun/to overrun: cubrieron enteramente/cubrir enteramente
blocked/to block: bloquearon/ bloquear, obstruir
highways: autopistas
will come to an end: terminará
anytime soon: pronto, en el futuro cercano
unique: única
opportunity: oportunidad
edge: borde
fire pit: foso de fuego
everlasting fire: fuego eterno
at times: a veces, en ocasiones
contained/to contain: contuvo/ contener
lake: lago
boiling: hirviente
disastrous: desastrosa
deadliest: más mortal
economically: económicamente
event: evento
killed/to kill: mató/matar
bridges: puentes
railways: vías de tren
debris avalanche: avalancha de escombros
reducing/to reduce: reduciendo/ reducir
elevation: elevación
summit: cima
replacing/to replace: reemplazando/ reemplazar
horseshoe-shaped: con forma de herradura de caballo

Test Your Comprehension

World Heritage Sites, page 166

1. ¿Cuál es el propósito de un Sitio de Patrimonio Histórico de la UNESCO?

2. ¿Dónde se encuentra la cueva más profunda del país?

3. ¿Qué animales raros y poco comunes se encuentran en el Parque Nacional de la Cueva del Mamut?

4. ¿Qué contiene el Parque Nacional Redwood?

Majestic Mountains, page 168

1. ¿Cuál es el pico de montaña más alto en América del Norte?

2. ¿Cuál es la atracción más popular en Georgia y por qué es famosa?

North American Deserts, page 170

1. ¿Qué es un desierto frío?

2. ¿Qué desierto se considera como el desierto biológicamente más rico del mundo?

3. ¿Cuál es el lugar más caliente en América del Norte?

4. ¿Por qué aúllan los coyotes en la noche?

The Great Lakes, page 172

1. ¿Cuál es el tipo de costa más común en la región de los Grandes Lagos?

2. ¿Por qué son importantes los humedales?

3. ¿Qué está amenazando a las costas de los Grandes Lagos?

Examina tu comprensión

Land of Waterfalls, page 174

1. Las Cataratas del Niágara son renombradas por su belleza y ¿qué otra cosa?

2. ¿Cuál es la catarata más alta de América del Norte?

3. ¿Dónde están las cataratas más poderosas del noroeste?

Temperate Rain Forests, page 177

1. ¿Qué hace que los bosques pluviales templados sean diferentes de los bosques pluviales tropicales?

2. ¿Qué bosque pluvial es el área más húmeda de los Estados Unidos continentales?

3. ¿Cuál es el bosque nacional más grande de los Estados Unidos?

Tropical Rain Forests, page 176

1. ¿En qué ha resultado el aislamiento de las Islas de Hawai del resto del mundo?

2. ¿Dónde está el bosque pluvial más húmedo del mundo?

3. ¿Qué cosas están destruyendo o dañando los bosques hawaianos?

Volcanoes of the U.S., page 178

1. ¿Cuántos volcanes de los Estados Unidos están designados como de muy alto riesgo?

2. ¿Cuál es el volcán y la montaña más grande de cualquier tipo en el mundo?

3. En el curso de la erupción del Volcán Kilauea, ¿qué fue destruido?

One cannot think well, love well, sleep well,
if one has not dined well.

Virginia Woolf

Gastronomy

American Apple Pie

You may have heard the expression, "as American as apple pie," in conversation. Apple pie has remained an iconic part of American culture through the years. Apple pie is considered a "comfort food" for many from coast to coast. The dessert has also been used in the phrase, "for mom and apple pie," said to be the popular answer that World War II American soldiers used when they were asked why they were going to war.

APPLE EXPRESSIONS

Apples have been a favorite fruit for generations of Americans and have become part of many common sayings.

1. The Big Apple: Nickname for New York City

2. Apple of my eye: Object of my affection or my darling.

3. The apple doesn't fall far from the tree: A child is displaying similar traits to his or her parents.

4. Bad Apple: troublemaker.

5. An apple a day keeps the doctor away: Eating fruits like apples will keep you healthy.

6. It's like apples and oranges: Comparing two things that are completely different and difficult to compare.

7. Apples for the teacher: Apples are associated with going back to school and children giving apples to the teacher as a present.

BASIC APPLE PIE RECIPE

8 servings

CRUST:
2½ cups **white flour**
2 tablespoons **sugar**
¼ teaspoon **salt**
½ cup cold **butter**
5 tablespoons cold **vegetable shortening**
8 tablespoons **ice water**

Measure flour, sugar and salt. **Stir** to combine. **Add** the **chilled** butter pieces and shortening to the **bowl**. **Cut them in** with a **pastry cutter** or **knife**. Do not **overmix**. Add ice water. Mix until the **dough** holds together. **Turn** dough onto a **lightly floured surface**, knead together, and then **divide in half**. **Flatten** each half into a **disk**, **wrap** in **plastic wrap** and chill for **at least** half an hour.

Roll out one of the disks on a floured surface until you have a **circle** that is 12 inches in **diameter**. Place the circle of dough into a 9" **pie plate**, **trimming** any extra dough from the edges with a sharp knife. **Return it to** the refrigerator **until** you are ready to make the pie. Add **filling** (**see below**). Roll out the **second ball** of dough and **cover**. **Pinch** the edges of the crust together. Cut two or three **slits** on top.

FILLING
⅓ to ⅔ cup sugar
¼ cup all-purpose flour
½ teaspoon **ground nutmeg**
½ teaspoon ground **cinnamon**
Pinch of salt
8 medium-sized apples (a medium apple = about 1 cup)
2 tablespoons margarine

Heat oven to 425 degrees. **Peel** and **slice** the apples. Mix sugar, flour, nutmeg, cinnamon, and salt in a bowl. Stir in apples. **Pour into pastry-lined pie plate** and **dot** with margarine. Cover with top crust and **seal the edges**. Cut slits in the top. **Bake** 40 to 50 minutes or until **crust is brown** and juice begins **to bubble** through slits in crust.

Serve warm with **ice cream** for "apple pie a la mode"!

---

white flour: harina blanca
sugar: azúcar
salt: sal
butter: mantequilla
vegetable shortening: margarina
ice water: agua helada
measure/to measure: mida/medir
stir/to stir: revuelva/revolver
add/to add: agregue/agregar
chilled: frios
bowl: cuenco
cut them in: córtelos
pastry cutter: cortador de masa
knife: cuchillo
overmix: mezcle demasiado
dough: masa
turn/to turn: dé vuelta/dar vuelta
lightly floured surface: superficie ligeramente enharinada
knead/to knead: amase/amasar
divide in half: divida a la mitad
flatten/to flatten: aplaste/aplastar
disk: disco
wrap/to wrap: envuelva/envolver
plastic wrap: envoltorio de plástico
at least: por lo menos
roll out/to roll out: extienda/extender
circle: círculo
diameter: diámetro
pie plate: molde para pasteles
trimming/to trim: recortando/recortar
return it to: devuélvala al
until: hasta
filling: relleno
see below: véase (la receta) más abajo
second ball: segunda pelota
cover/to cover: cubra/cubrir
pinch/to pinch: pellizque/pellizcar
slits: cortes, tajos
ground nutmeg: nuez moscada molida
cinnamon: canela
heat/to heat: caliente/calentar
oven: horno
peel/to peel: pele/pelar
slice/to slice: corte/cortar *(en rodajas)*
pour into/to pour: eche en/echar
pastry-lined pie plate: molde para pasteles cubierta con la masa
dot/to dot: salpique/salpicar
seal/to seal: selle/sellar
the edges: los bordes
bake/to bake: hornee/hornear
crust is brown: masa esté dorada
to bubble: burbujear
serve/to serve: sirva/servir
warm: templado
ice cream: helado

Taste of America

The United States is a **diverse** and multicultural nation. Diversity **is found** among people, **places** and **food**. America is **a land of** good eating. Delicious **regional cuisine** is found from **coast to coast**. **Neighborhoods**, cities and states **pride themselves** on their regional food and some locations **have been made famous** by the food they best prepare.

BOSTON BAKED BEANS

Beans slow-baked in **molasses** have been a favorite Boston **dish** since **colonial days**. The beans are so popular that Boston **was nicknamed** "Beantown." The **Pilgrims learned** how **to make** baked beans from the Native Americans. They **substituted** molasses and **pork fat** for the **maple syrup** and **bear fat** used by the Natives. The **navy bean** is the official vegetable of Massachusetts, and in 1993 the state **declared it** the original bean of Boston baked beans

FLORIDA KEY LIME PIE

Key West, Florida, is famous for its **key lime pie**, one of America's **best-loved** regional dishes. Every restaurant in the Florida Keys serves this **fabulous** pie. Key lime pie **is described as** "An American pie containing a **lime-flavored custard** topped with meringue." Key limes are very **sour**, and key lime juice is used to make a perfect custard filling. **Nestled in** a sweet **graham-cracker crust**, this official desert of the Florida Keys is **tart**, refreshing and delicious.

NEW ORLEANS GUMBO

Gumbo **has been called** Louisiana's **greatest contribution** to American **cuisine**. Gumbo is classic Cajun food and **can be found** throughout the South but is served **at its best** in Louisiana. When the first French **settlers** came to Louisiana, they brought their love for bouillabaisse, a **fish soup**. They substituted local ingredients because they were **missing** ingredients they **normally** used at home. The Spanish, Africans, and natives **of the area offered** their contributions of food and the **stew** was **no longer recognizable** as bouillabaisse. It became gumbo.

HOT DOGS

Hot dogs **are considered by some** the favorite American food. Charles Feltman, a German **butcher**, **opened** up the first Coney Island hot dog stand in Brooklyn, New York in 1867. Harry Magely **is credited for putting** the hot dog into a **bun** and **topping it** with condiments. He **reportedly instructed** his **vendors to shout**, "Red hots! Get your red hots!"

Some people say there is one place where a hot dog always **tastes best**—at a baseball game! The National Hot Dog and Sausage Council **reports that** baseball fans **will consume** over 27 million hot dogs at major-league parks just this year!

PHILLY CHEESE STEAK

Philadelphia **is home to** the cheese steak. The cheese steak is a **sandwich** prepared on a **long roll** and filled with **sliced pieces** of **steak** and **melted cheese**. The cheese steak is a **comfort food** for natives of Philadelphia. **It was invented** in the city in 1930 and is considered a city icon. According to Philadelphians, **you cannot make** an authentic Philadelphia cheese steak sandwich without an authentic Philadelphia roll. The rolls must be **long and thin**, **not fluffy** or soft, **but also not** too hard. They **also say** that if you are **more than** one hour from South Philly, you will not find an authentic **sandwich**!

TEXAS RED

Texans take chili **seriously**, and **as a result**, chili became the Texas State Dish in 1977. Chili **originated** in San Antonio in the 1880s. The **essential ingredients** are **ground beef**, **garlic**, **cumin**, and **chili peppers**. The **public environment** used **to celebrate** chili **is called** a "cook-off." At a cook-off, **thousands of people** gather **to create** their version of Texas Red. You can **attend** a cook-off **throughout** the year in Texas and **taste for yourself** some of the best chili in the United States.

are considered by some: son considerados por algunos
butcher: carnicero
opened/to open: abrió/abrir
is credited for: se le atribuye
putting/to put: poner/poner
bun: panecillo
topping it/to top: ponerle...por encima/poner
reportedly: según lo que se dice, según se informa
instructed/to instruct: ordenaba/ ordenar, mandar
vendors: vendedores
to shout: gritar
some people say: alguna gente dice
tastes best: sabe mejor
reports that/to report: informa que/ informar
will consume/to consume: consumirán/consumir
is home to: es el hogar de
sandwich: sandwich
long roll: panecillo largo
sliced pieces: rodajas cortadas
steak: bistec
melted cheese: queso fundido
comfort food: comida que genera una sensación de bienestar
it was invented/to invent: fue inventado/inventar
you cannot make: no puedes hacer
long and thin: largo y fino
not fluffy: no esponjosos
but also not: pero tampoco
also say: también dicen
more than: más de
seriously: en serio
as a result: como resultado
originated/to originate: se originó/ originarse
essential ingredients: ingredientes esenciales
ground beef: carne picada
garlic: ajo
cumin: comino
chili peppers: chiles
public environment: entorno público
to celebrate: para celebrar
is called/to call: se llama/llamar
thousands of people: miles de personas
to create: para crear
attend/to attend: asistir/asistir
throughout: a lo largo de
taste for yourself: probar tú mismo

Blue Plate Special

American diners are popular **neighborhood restaurants** that attract a **cross-section** of America, from **factory workers** to Wall Street **executives** and from **senior citizens** to **teenagers**. Americans of **all walks of life** and all ages love diners! The function of the diner **has always been to provide** a delicious and **inexpensive**, **home-style meal** in a **comfortable atmosphere**.

Diners **first evolved** from **mobile lunch wagons**. The first dining wagons with **seating** appeared in the late 19th century. The dining wagon **owners** were **able to serve** busy locations **without** buying expensive **real estate**. As the lunch wagons became more popular and more **customer** seating was needed, the diners were **converted** to buildings. The same **manufacturers** who had made the wagons **constructed** the **building**s. Like the lunch wagon, these diners allowed owners to set up a **food service** business quickly using the **preassembled equipment**.

By the early 1900s, the downtown centers of New England became so **crowded** with mobile lunch wagons that **city ordinances** began **limiting** their service to only **daylight hours**. However, owners **worked around** this **ruling**. They would find a busy location **by the side of the road**, take off the wheels, **hook up to** power, and **set up** business in a permanent location.

The term "diner" **originated** with Patrick J. Tierney, who called his prefabricated restaurants "dining cars." His salespersons later **shortened it** to "diners." A common **myth** was that diners were **converted railroad cars**. In reality, the **streamlined locomotives** of the 1930s inspired manufacturers **to copy** their **sleek** appearance.

By 1937, **one million** people **ate at least** one meal a day at a diner. In the 1940s, there were almost 10,000 diners across the U.S. **Today, fewer than** 3,000 **remain**.

"Blue plate special" refers to a special **low-priced** meal. This meal **usually** changes daily. It **typically** consists of **meat** and three vegetables on a **single** plate. **During** the Depression, a manufacturer started making plates with **separate sections** for each part of a meal. For a reason **that has never been determined**, the plates were **only available** in the color blue. Because they were inexpensive and **saved on dishwashing**, diners began using them for their low-priced daily specials.

The **term** "blue plate special" was **very common** from the 1920s through the 1950s. As of 2007 there are **still** a few restaurants and diners **that offer** blue-plate specials **under that name**. **Sometimes** they offer the special on blue plates, but it is a **vanishing tradition**. **The phrase itself** is still a common American expression.

Do you have a **craving** for American diner food? Check out Diner City web site: www.dinercity.com. Here you will find diners **throughout** the United States and an interesting photo collection. Also, visit The Roadside at www.roadsidemagazine.com. This site is **dedicated** to the **preservation** of the American diner.

People who **frequent** diners know diner **lingo**. **Employees use it to name** meals. It is **truly** a **language unto its own**!

- "One on the city" (a **glass** of water)
- "Make it moo" (coffee with milk)
- "Bird seed" (a **bowl** of cereal)
- "Cockleberries" (**eggs**)
- "Breath" (**onions**)
- "Frog sticks" (**french fries**)
- "Shivering Liz" (**Jello**)
- "Bossy in a bowl" (beef **stew**)
- "Sweep the kitchen" (a **plate** of **hash**)
- "Skid grease" (**butter**)

Chocolate Chip Cookies

It **may be hard** for **cookie aficionados to believe**, but **before** the 1930s, **no one had ever had** the **culinary pleasure** of **biting** into a chocolate chip cookie. Why? This chocolate delight **had not yet been** invented.

Ruth Wakefield is the woman **responsible for creating** the chocolate chip cookie. In 1930, Ruth and her husband Kenneth **purchased** a Cape Cod-style **tollhouse** located between Boston and New Bedford, Massachusetts. The house had originally **served as** a **haven** for travelers. **Tired passengers** stopped here **to pay tolls** and eat **home-cooked** meals.

The Wakefields decided **to revive** and continue the house's tradition. They **turned their home** into a hotel and called it the Toll House Inn. Ruth **cooked homemade** meals and **baked** for guests of the inn. Her incredible **desserts began attracting** people from all over New England.

Ruth's **favorite recipe** was Butter Drop Do cookies. As she prepared the batter one day **she realized** she **had run out of** baker's chocolate. She decided to use the chocolate she **had on hand**, a **semi-sweet** chocolate bar, **given to her** by Andrew Nestle. She cut it into **tiny bits** and **added them** to the dough. She **expected** the chocolate bits **to melt** as the cookies baked in the **oven**. However, the chocolate did not melt. **Instead**, it held its shape and softened to a **creamy texture**. **As you can imagine**, the cookies Ruth had created became very popular with guests at the inn. Her recipe **was published** in a Boston **newspaper, as well as** other papers in the New England area.

Meanwhile, Nestle saw **sales** of its Semi-Sweet Chocolate Bar **jump** dramatically because so many people were using the bits of chocolate in Ruth's recipe. Ruth and Nestle **agreed** that Nestle **would print** the "Toll House Cookie" recipe on its **packaging**. Part of this agreement included **supplying** Ruth with all of the chocolate she could use for the rest of her life.

Nestle began to package their chocolate bars with a **special chopper** designed to **easily cut** the chocolate into **small morsels**. **Eventually**, Nestle **came up with** a better idea, and began **offering** Nestlé Toll House Real Semi-Sweet Chocolate Morsels.

The rest is "chocolate-chip" **history**. Ruth continued to cook and published a series of **cookbooks.** In 1966, she sold the Toll House Inn to a family that tried to **turn it into** a nightclub. The Saccone family, who restored its original form, bought it in 1970. **Sadly**, fourteen years later, the Toll House **burned down** on New Years Eve.

Ruth Wakefield **passed away** in 1977 but her **legacy** lives on, enjoyed by millions of people nationwide. **Still**, **to this day**, you can find her Toll House recipe **on the back of** Nestlé's chocolate chip cookie packages.

---

meanwhile: mientras tanto
sales: ventas
jump/to jump: se dispararon/ dispararse
agreed/to agree: acordaron/acordar
would print/to print: imprimiría/ imprimir
packaging: embalaje, paquete
supplying/to supply: suplir/suplir
special chopper: aparato para cortar especial
easily: fácilmente
cut: cortar
small morsels: pedacitos pequeños
eventually: finalmente
came up with/to come up with: sugirió/sugerir
offering: a ofrecer
the rest is...history: el resto es...historia
cookbooks: libros de cocina
turn it into: lo convirtió en
sadly: lamentablemente
burned down/to burn down: se quemó/quemarse
passed away/to pass away: falleció/ fallecer
legacy: legado
still, to this day: aún, hasta el día de hoy
on the back of: en el reverso de

COOKING VOCABULARY

aluminum foil: papel de aluminio
bake: hornear
barbeque: barbacoa/parrillada
basil: albahaca
basting: rociando
batter: masa
bay leaf: hoja de laurel
blanch: escaldar, blanquear
boiling point: punto de ebullición
bread crumbs: migas de pan
broom: escoba
broth: caldo
curdle: cuajar
dash: chorrito

diced: cortado en cuadritos
dining room: comedor
dishwasher: lavaplatos
drain: escurrir
freezer: congelador
frozen: congelado
garnish: guarnición
ginger: jengibre
glaze: glasear
grated: rallado
ground: molido, pulverizado
herb garden: herbario
herb: hierba
juicy: jugoso

kitchen sink: fregadero
ladles: cucharones
mash: hacer puré
measuring cup: taza para medir
nutmeg: nuez moscada
quartered: cortado en cuatro
rosemary: romero
sauté: saltear
scald: escaldar
season with salt: sazonar con sal
stew: estofado
turn off: apagar
wedge: pedazo grande
whisk: batir

Buffalo Wings

Buffalo wings are **chicken wings deep-fried** and **coated** in a **spicy sauce**. Buffalo wings are **named after** the city of Buffalo, New York where they **originated**.

This **tasty** and popular **side dish** was created on October 3, 1964 and **first prepared** at the Anchor Bar in Buffalo, New York. Teressa Bellissimo, **owner** of the Anchor Bar with her husband Frank, had the **brilliant idea** of deep-frying chicken wings and **combining them** with her  husband's spicy **red-hot** sauce. **Typically**, chicken wings were **thrown away** or used only for making **stock**.

Teressa created this deep-fried and **sauced** creation, **served it** to her **son** and his friends, and they were an **instant hit**.

In the Southern United States, wings **are often called** "hot wings" and come with many different sauces. There are **local variations** all over the United States in how they are prepared and served and they **are most often found** on **bar menus** as bar food.

Buffalo wings are **usually** served with **celery** sticks, **carrot** sticks and **blue cheese** dip. Some restaurants serve their wings with ranch dressing as an **alternative** to blue cheese.

For a **truly authentic experience**, **order** the original sauce **directly from** the Anchor Bar that made Buffalo chicken wings famous!

---

chicken: pollo
wings: alas
deep-fried: fritas
coated: cubiertas
spicy sauce: salsa picante
named after: llevan el nombre de
originated/to originate: se originó/ originarse
tasty: sabroso
side dish: *(plato de)* acompañamiento
first prepared: preparado por primera vez
owner: dueña
brilliant idea: idea brillante
combining them/to combine: combinarlos/combinar
red-hot: muy caliente *(literalmente: al rojo vivo)*
typically: típicamente
thrown away/to throw away: tirados/ tirar
stock: caldo
sauced: con salsa
served it/to serve: la sirvió/servir
son: hijo
instant hit: éxito instantáneo
are often called: son llamadas a menudo
local variations: variaciones locales
are most often found: se encuentran más a menudo
bar menus: menús de bares
usually: normalmente
celery: apio
carrot: zanahoria
blue cheese: queso bleu
alternative: alternativa
truly authentic experience: experiencia verdaderamente auténtica
order/to order: pide/pedir, ordenar
directly from: directamente de

Saltwater Taffy

Taffy has been an American **beachside** tradition **for more than** 100 years. The exact history of how taffy **came to be** is still a mystery. Some **candy companies state** that David Bradley, a **shopkeeper** in Atlantic City, was the **first seller** of the candy. In 1883, a **huge** storm **hit the beaches**. Bradley's store **was filled with** the ocean water and his **entire stock** of taffy **was soaked**. A young girl asked if the store **still had** taffy **for sale**. **As a joke**, Bradley told the girl **to grab some** "saltwater taffy." **This is believed to be** the first reference to "saltwater taffy."

Joseph Fralinger is recognized **as the person who** made saltwater taffy popular. Fralinger observed **sunbathers** and **visitors** and **came up with the idea to package** saltwater taffy as a **treat** for **beachgoers** to take home with them. He thought tourists would want a reminder or **souvenir** of their vacation in Atlantic City. As an experiment, Fralinger **boxed the candy** and sold it one weekend. It was a huge **success**!

As Fralinger's success grew, competition **was sure to follow**. Shops **would compete** with new and different recipes **to entice** the visitors and **boost** their sales.

By the 1920s, everyone **was buying** and **enjoying** saltwater taffy after a day at the beach. Just as Fralinger **had predicted**, it was the perfect beach souvenir **to bring home** to family and friends.

Saltwater taffy **can be found** at boardwalks and in beach communities and is still a popular treat for people to bring home after visiting the beach. Traditional **flavors** include **peppermint**, **cinnamon** and chocolate. More adventurous **taste buds** can enjoy flavors like **rhubarb**, banana and marshmallow.

beachside: al lado de la playa, playera
for more than: por más de
came to be: se originó
candy companies: empresas de dulces
state/to state: declaran/declarar
shopkeeper: tendero
first seller: primer vendedor
huge: enorme
hit/to hit: azotó/azotar
the beaches: las playas
was filled with/to fill: estaba lleno de/ llenar
entire stock: todas (sus) existencias
was soaked/to soak: estaban empapadas/empapar
still had: todavía tenía
for sale: en venta
as a joke: de broma, en chiste
to grab: tomar, agarrar
some: algunas
this is believed to be: se cree que esto es
as the person who: como la persona que
sunbathers: personas que toman sol
visitors: visitantes
came up with the idea: se le ocurrió la idea
to package: embalar
treat: delicia
beachgoers: personas que van a la playa
souvenir: souvenir, recuerdo
boxed the candy: puso el dulce en cajas
success: éxito
was sure to follow: era seguro que vendría a continuación
would compete/to compete: competirían/competir
to entice: para atraer
boost: aumentar
was buying/to buy: estaba comprando/comprar
enjoying/to enjoy: disfrutando/ disfrutar
had predicted/to predict: había predicho/predecir
to bring home: traer a casa
can be found: pueden encontrarse
flavors: sabores
peppermint: menta
cinnamon: canela
taste buds: papilas gustativas
rhubarb: ruibarbo

Waldorf Salad

Waldorf salad **was created** at New York's Waldorf-Astoria Hotel in 1896 **not by** a chef, **but by** the maître d'hôtel, Oscar Tschirky. **After serving** the Waldorf Salad to **patrons** and **guests**, the Waldorf salad became an **instant success**.

The **original version** of this salad contained **only apples**, **celery** and **mayonnaise**. **Chopped walnuts later became** a **common part** of the **dish**. Waldorf salad **is usually** served **on top of** a **bed of lettuce**.

CLASSIC WALDORF SALAD

Ingredients:

1 **cup** apples, chopped (Granny Smith or a **sweet tart** apple or a **combination** of different tart apples)

1 **tablespoon lemon juice**

1 cup celery, chopped

¼ cup mayonnaise

¼ cup **raisins** (optional)

¼ cup walnuts (optional)

Sprinkle apples with lemon juice **after** they are **cut**.
Add all other ingredients.

Toss to **coat** all pieces with mayonnaise.

Another option for a modern Waldorf salad is to add **meat** to the recipe. Some **popular choices** include **strips of chicken breast**, **turkey**, **cubed smoked pork loin**, or **grilled salmon**. **Layer** the meat on top of the Waldorf salad, or **lightly toss** to make a delicious **entree**.

Clam Chowder

Clam Chowder is a popular **soup containing clams** and **broth**. **In addition to** the clams, the chowder may contain **potato** chunks or **onions**. Small **carrot** strips **might occasionally be added** for color.

Chowder **has its roots** in the **Latin word** "calderia," which **originally meant** a **place** for **warming** things, and **later came to mean cooking pot**.

New England clam chowder is white and contains milk or cream. **Some people say that** New England clam chowder has become creamier **over the years as a result of** tourism. **Allegedly,** tourists visiting New England, **squeamish** of clams and seafood, prefer the creamier chowder. **At one time**, some restaurants served **clear** chowder, and let customers add cream to taste.

Manhattan clam chowder has clear broth and lots of fresh tomato for red color and flavor. This **tomato-based** clam chowder **started with** the **increased popularity** of the tomato in the mid-1800s and the large population of Italians in New York. **Originally**, this chowder was called "Coney Island clam chowder," **most likely** because of the many restaurants on Coney Island that served it. By the 1930s the popular **name became** "Manhattan clam chowder."

Clam chowder **is usually** served with saltine or oyster **crackers**. Throughout the United States, creamy New England-style clam chowder is served in **sourdough bread bowls**. **You will find** warm chowder in **fresh** sourdough bread bowls all over San Francisco, where sourdough is popular with tourists and has been considered a **signature dish** since 1849.

---

soup: sopa
containing/to contain: conteniendo/contener
clams: almejas
broth: caldo
in addition to: además de
potato: papa
onions: cebollas
carrot: zanahoria
might occasionally be added: de vez en cuando se puede agregar
has its roots: tiene sus raíces
Latin word: palabra latina
originally: originalmente
meant/to mean: significaba/significar
place: lugar
warming: calentar
later came to mean: luego pasó a significar
cooking pot: olla
some people say that: algunas personas dicen que
over the years: con el pasar de los años
as a result of: como resultado de
allegedly: presuntamente, supuestamente
squeamish: les da aprensión comer
at one time: en un momento, en una época
clear: claro
tomato-based: a base de tomate
started with/to start with: empezó con/empezar con
increased popularity: popularidad creciente
originally: originalmente
most likely: seguramente, probablemente
name: nombre
became/to become: se convirtió/convertirse
is usually: se suele
crackers: galletas
sourdough bread bowls: cuenco hecho de pan de masa fermentada
you will find: tú encontrarás/usted encontrará
fresh: fresco
signature dish: plato que lo caracteriza

Farmers' Markets

America's first **farmers' markets** were **modeled after** similar markets in Europe. Wagons filled with produce from local farms **rolled into town** ready to sell their **goods** to the **city folk**. Most markets **took place** in **empty lots** on a **major street**. This is where the **term** "market streets" came from.

The first market in the history of the United States was in Boston in 1634. Twenty-eight years later, **the city built** a **wooden building** for the market to create a more permanent presence.

Philadelphia had the **best-designed** and regulated markets. William Penn's **city plan** included a market along the **main artery**, High Street, later named Market Street. The market **opened twice a week** with the **ringing of bells**.

One of the most famous **daily** markets today is the Pike Place Market in Seattle, Washington. The market opened August 17, 1907 and is the **third-oldest** farmers' market in the country. The market's **major attraction** is the Pike Place Fish Market, where employees **throw fish to each other** rather than passing them by hand. The "flying fish" are **famous worldwide**.

Farmers' markets are good for **consumers**, farmers, and for the community. Markets create **gathering places to bring** customers downtown, where they **shop** at local businesses **as well as** at the market. Farmers **can provide** the community with food and produce that **may not be available** at other stores in the area. Farmers' markets can also provide extra **income** for **community workers** and possible **employment** for local **youth**.

There are 4500 markets in the U.S. today, **nearly twice as many as** a decade ago. People visit the farmers' markets **for many reasons**: for the wonderful produce they **cannot find** anywhere else; for the benefits of **eating seasonally**; for the beauty and **smells** of the **fresh herbs** and produce and **flowers**; and of course, **to support** their local farmers and to **come together** with their community.

Soul Food

Soul food is a **term associated with** food **created by** African-Americans of the Southern United States. In the mid-1960s, "soul" was a **familiar adjective** used **to describe** African-American culture.

African-Americans **working as slaves** would **make the most of** what ingredients they had **at hand**. The fresh vegetables they had used in Africa **were replaced** by the **throwaway** foods from the **plantation house**. Their vegetables were the **tops of turnips** and **beets** and **dandelions**. They were cooking with **greens** they had never tasted before: collards, kale, cress, mustard and pokeweed. African-American slaves developed **recipes** that used **discarded meat**, such as **pigs' feet** and **ears**, **beef tongue** or **tail**, tripe and **skin**. Cooks added onions and garden herbs such as garlic, thyme, and bay leaf **to enhance** the **flavors**.

The slave diet **began to change** when slaves started working in the plantation houses as cooks. They **had access to** a **wider variety** of food and started **to share** their favorite meals with the families they were cooking for. Fried chicken began **to appear** on the tables; sweet potatoes **accompanied** the white potato. Local foods like apples, peaches and berries **were transformed** into delicious puddings and pies.

Nothing was ever **wasted** in the African-American kitchen. Bread pudding was created out of **stale bread**, and each part of the pig had its own special **dish**. Even the liquid from the **boiled** vegetables was **made into gravy** or turned into a drink.

The slaves' cuisine **became known as** "good times" food. The evening meal was a time for families to come together **after long days and hours** of hard work. **Songs** and **stories** were shared and dinnertime became a meal for **both body and soul**.

Soul food originated in the South, but this cooking tradition **has since spread** all throughout the United States. Today, soul food restaurants exist in **nearly every** African-American community in the U.S.

---

term: término
associated with/to associate with: asociado con/asociar con
created by/to create: creado por/crear
familiar adjective: adjetivo familiar
to describe: para describir
working/to work: trabajando/trabajar
as slaves: como esclavos
make the most of: aprovechar al máximo
at hand: a mano
were replaced/to replace: fueron reemplazados/reemplazar
throwaway: para tirar
plantation house: casa de la plantación
tops of: hojas de
turnips: nabos
beets: remolachas
dandelions: diente de león
greens: verduras de hoja verde
recipes: recetas
discarded meat: carne desechada
pigs' feet: manos de cerdo
ears: orejas
beef tongue: lengua de vaca
tail: cola
skin: piel
to enhance: para mejorar
flavors: sabores
began/to begin: empezó/empezar
to change: a cambiar
had access to: tenían acceso a
wider variety: variedad más amplia
to share: a compartir
to appear: a aparecer
accompanied/to accompany: acompañaban/acompañar
were transformed/to transform: eran transformados/transformar
wasted/to waste: desperdiciado/desperdiciar
stale bread: pan duro
dish: plato
boiled/to boil: hervidos/hervir
made into gravy: convertido en salsa
became known as: llegó a conocerse como
after long days and hours: luego de largos días y horas
songs: canciones
stories: relatos, cuentos
both body and soul: el cuerpo y el alma
has since spread: desde entonces se ha extendido
nearly every: casi toda

great: gran
pastime: pasatiempo
barbecue festivals: festivales de la barbacoa
are popping up/to pop up: están apareciendo/aparecer
statewide: en todo el estado
cook-offs: competencias de cocina
turning it into: volviéndola
sport: deporte
to gather with: reunirse
friends: amigos
back yard: jardín trasero
to enjoy: para disfrutar
hot grill: parrilla caliente
state/to state: afirman/afirmar
began/to begin: empezó/empezar
in the south: en el sur
however: sin embargo
taste: gusto, sabor
sometimes: a veces
method: método
may vary: puede variar
from state to state: de estado a estado
argue/to argue: sostiene/sostener
unknown: desconocido
primary meat: carne principal
the way it is cut: la forma en la que es cortada
pulled/to pull: desmenuzar/desmenuzado
rather than: en vez de
chopped/to chop: picada/picar
covered with/to cover with: cubierta con/cubrir con
ribs: costillas
coated/to coat: cubiertas/cubrir
a mix: una mezla
sharp spices: especias fuertes
pit cooking: cocinar en hoyo
hint: ligerísimo sabor a
pepper: pimienta
molasses: melaza
gets preference: se prefiere
pork: carne de cerdo

American Barbecue

Barbecue is a **great** American tradition and **pastime**. It has become so popular that **barbecue festivals are popping up** all across the nation and **statewide cook-offs** are **turning it into** a **sport**!

The popular tradition of "barbecuing" is **to gather with** your **friends** in the **back yard to enjoy** food prepared over a **hot grill**.

Barbecue experts **state** that the tradition of barbecue **began in the south**. **However**, the **taste**, ingredients used, and **sometimes** even the **method** of cooking **may vary from state to state**; so some people **argue** that its history is **unknown**.

In the central South, the **primary meat** used in barbeque is pork and ribs, but **the way it is cut** differs. It is **pulled rather than chopped**. The meat is slow cooked, shredded by hand and **covered with** large amounts of sauce. The **ribs** are **coated** with sauce or covered with **a mix of sharp spices** before **pit cooking**.

The sauce is a sweet tomato sauce with a **hint** of **pepper** and **molasses**. It is traditionally served with coleslaw, French fries, baked beans and cornbread. In the western United States, beef **gets preference** over **pork**.

The East Coast **is true to its original beginnings** and uses pork and vinegar sauces. Common **side dishes** are **coleslaw** and hushpuppies. The **main variations** are tasted in the vinegar sauces, such as **rich** tomato or **tangy** yellow **mustard-based** sauce.

The history and origin of how barbecue **came to** the United States is **under dispute**. The Barbecue Association states that barbecue first came to California with **Franciscan friars** who **brought** it from the Caribbean.

Another **theory** is that barbecue **originated** in the late 1800s during the **western cattle drives**. The cowboys would **slowly cook** the **tough meat** over a **fire**. This was a way **to tenderize** the meat and make it tastier. Some say **German butchers** brought barbecue to Texas in the mid-1800s. **What is certain** is that barbecuing has been an American pastime for hundreds of years. **Today** almost everyone barbecues **at one time or another**, whether it's a small grill on an **urban patio** or a **complete pig roast** in your own **backyard**. **As time marches on**, Americans **continue to perfect** this **culinary delight** and tradition.

is true to its original beginnings: conserva sus comienzos originales, es fiel a sus orígenes
side dishes: platos de acompañamiento
coleslaw: ensalada de col
main variations: variaciones principales
rich: concentrado, rico
tangy: ácido
mustard-based: a base de mostaza
came to/to come to: llegaron a/llegar a
under dispute: no se ha llegado a un acuerdo *(literalmente: bajo disputa)*
Franciscan friars: frailes franciscanos
brought/to bring: trajeron/traer
theory: teoría
originated/to originate: se originó/ originarse
western cattle drives: conducción de ganado del oeste
slowly cook: cocinar lentamente
tough meat: carne dura
fire: fuego
to tenderize: para ablandar
German butchers: carniceros alemanes
what is certain: lo que es seguro
today: hoy
at one time or another: en uno u otro momento
urban patio: patio urbano
complete pig roast: cerdo asado completo
backyard: patio trasero
as time marches on: a medida que el tiempo pasa
continue/to continue: continúan/ continuar
to perfect/to perfect: perfeccionando/ perfeccionar
culinary delight: delicia culinaria

Test Your Comprehension

American Apple Pie, page 184

1. ¿La tarta de manzana es considerada como qué para muchas personas?

2. ¿La Gran Manzana es el apodo de qué ciudad estadounidense?

Taste of America, page 186

1. ¿Cuál es la verdura oficial de Massachussets?

2. ¿Dónde tienen mejor sabor los perros calientes, según la opinión de alguna gente?

3. ¿Cuáles son los ingredientes esenciales para el chili texano?

Blue Plate Special, page 188

1. ¿Cuál es la función de un restaurante económico?

2. ¿A qué se refiere el "blue plate special"?

3. Si alguien en un restaurante económico pide "frog sticks" (bastones de rana), ¿qué está pidiendo?

Chocolate Chip Cookies, page 190

1. ¿Quién creó la galleta con pedacitos de chocolate?

2. Cuando a Ruth se le acabó el chocolate para hornear, ¿qué hizo?

Examina tu comprensión

Buffalo Wings, page 192

1. ¿Qué son las "buffalo wings" (alas de búfalo)?

2. ¿Por qué se llaman "buffalo wings"?

Saltwater Taffy, page 193

1. ¿Quién popularizó el "saltwater taffy"?

2. ¿Por qué pensó que sería popular?

Clam Chowder, page 195

1. Describe la sopa de almeja estadounidense.

2. ¿Por qué la sopa de almejas de New England se ha vuelto más cremosa con el pasar de los años?

Farmers' Markets, page 196

1. ¿Cuándo y dónde fue el primer mercado de agricultores en los Estados Unidos?

2. ¿Qué es famoso a nivel mundial en el mercado de Pike Place?

American Barbecue, page 198

1. ¿Dónde afirman los expertos en barbacoas que empezó la tradición de la barbacoa?

2. ¿Qué carne se usa principalmente en el sur central y cómo se cocina?

3. ¿Cuáles son las tres teorías sobre cómo la barbacoa llegó a los Estados Unidos?

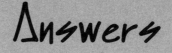

Answers

Culture

The American Dream page 4 1. Inmigración – el sueño de prosperidad y libertad. 2. Creó miles de trabajos y mejoró el estándar de vida. 3. Vivir una vida satisfactoria. **A Melting Pot page 5** 1.Gente de diferentes culturas y razas viviendo juntos. 2. la región oeste 3. los nativos y los españoles **The American Cowboy page 6** 1. New Orleans, Louisiana 2. En los años 1880 los afroamericanos desarrollaron nuevas formas de música. **Early American Literature page 14** 1. Mark Twain nació en Missouri. 2. John Steinbeck escribió *The Grapes of Wrath* (*Las uvas de la ira*) **Artistic Expression page 15** 1. Estar libre de necesidad, libertad de expresión, libertad de credo, y estar libre de temor. 2. pop art **The Birthplace of Broadway 16** 1. En la ciudad de Nueva York. 2. La comunidad de Broadway fue especialmente activa apoyando la guerra. 3. chapines **Cultural Values 18** 1. libertad individual 2. educación

Travel

Camping Trips page 24 1. Campamento con autos, campamentos con servicios completos, y campamento en la naturaleza salvaje. 2. Investigar y hacer preguntas sobre alojamiento. 3. Responsabilidad al acampar para preservar la belleza de la naturaleza. **Rafting the Grand Canyon page 25** 1. El Río Colorado 2. visitas guiadas sobre historia, geología y fotografía **Down by the Boardwalk page 26** 1. En los 1800s en New Jersey. 2. Atlantic City en New Jersey 3. un pabellón de mariposas **Treasure Islands page 28** 1. Oahu, la ciudad es Honolulu 2. Kauai 3. selvas tropicales, inhóspitos macizos de lava, playas, y montañas altas con pendientes para esquiar **The First National Park page 30** 1. El parque nacional Yosemite en California 2. Abraham Lincoln 3. Half Dome y El Capitán **A Walking Tour of D.C. page 32** 1. 555 pies 2. El segundo discurso inaugural de Lincoln, y el discurso de Gettysburg 3. unidad, sacrificio, victoria y libertad **Made in the USA page 36** 1. palomitas de maíz con mantequilla y jalapeño 2. El Departamento del Tesoro de los Estados Unidos en Washington DC o en Fort Worth, Texas **San Juan Orcas page 38** 1. el estado de Washington 2. desde la primavera hasta el otoño 3. kayak

Tradition

Choices in Education page 44 1. 16-18 2. Elementary, Junior High y Senior High 3. 4 o más **Traditions for the New Year page 46** 1. 31 de diciembre 2. La ciudad de Nueva York 3. el Rose Bowl **April Fool's! page 49** 1. Primero de abril 2. en Francia en los 1500 3. es tiempo de bromas **An American Christmas page 50** 1. Inglaterra, Alemania, los Países Bajos 2. eggnog **Giving Thanks page 52** 1. el cuarto jueves en noviembre 2. Los nativos americanos y los colonos, quienes fueron los primeros inmigrantes a los Estados Unidos. **America's Favorite Sport page 54** 1.el partido del Rose Bowl 2. Canton, Ohio 3. las animadoras de los Dallas Cowboys **The National Pastime page 56** 1. comer frankfurters y Cracker Jacks; cánticos y ovaciones en los estadios, coleccionar autógrafos, hacerse miembro de clubes de fanáticos. 2. Babe Ruth **The American Flag page 58** 1. libertad y orgullo 2. Francis Bellamy **Remembrance and Honor page 61** 1. Día de la Decoración 2. Para honrar a aquellos que dieron sus vidas por nuestro país.

Respuestas

Celebration

Luck of the Irish page 66 1. 1737 en Boston, Massachusetts 2. son pellizcados **Powwows page 68** 1. gente reuniéndose para bailar, cantar y alternar 2. falso **Seasonal Celebrations page 70** 1. dar la bienvenida a la llegada del otoño y el cambio de color de las hojas 2. la mejor escultura esculpida en hielo 3. atrapando serpientes en el Rattlesnake Roundup **Flavor of America page 72** 1. Se lo monta en un marco para la posteridad. 2. Las Cruces, New Mexico 3. dos mil millones de libras, o el 25% del queso del país, por año **Parents Appreciation Day page 75** 1. clavel rojo 2. No está claro. Algunos dicen que empezó en un oficio religioso en Virginia Oeste o en Vancouver, Washington. **Celebrating the Worker page 79** 1. la ciudad de Nueva York en 1882, 1894 2. de la temporada de verano **Shakespeare Festivals page 80** 1.un poeta y dramaturgo inglés 2. un festival gratis celebrado en San Francisco 3. por donaciones de quienes apoyan la belleza de la obra de William Shakespeare

People

Trail of Discovery page 88 1. para explorar el oeste americano 2. Sacagawea 3. Al ser una mujer ella ayudó a disipar la noción de que el grupo era una banda de guerreros **Mother of Civil Rights page 89** 1. Dar su asiento a una persona blanca en un autobús urbano. 2. 1956 **The Founding Fathers page 90** 1. Los líderes políticos que firmaron la Declaración de la Independencia o la Constitución de los Estados Unidos, y que fueron activos en la Revolución Americana. 2. George Washington 3. Thomas Jefferson 4. Su experimento con la cometa, el cual verificó la naturaleza de la electricidad. **Frank Lloyd Wright page 94** 1. casas de la pradera 2. techos inclinados, perfiles limpios, líneas que se extienden y se confunden con el paisaje **Rags to Riches page 95** 1. Las personas ricas estaban obligadas moralmente a devolver su dinero a otras personas en la sociedad. 2. Cuando Carnegie era un hombre joven, el coronel James Anderson, un hombre rico, le permitió usar su biblioteca personal de forma gratuita. 3. más de $350 millones **America Takes Flight page 96** 1. Las ganancias de su negocio de bicicletas pagaron sus operaciones construyendo aviones. 2. Era un área que tenía vientos constantes. Podían planear y aterrizar de forma segura en las dunas de arena del área. 3. En 1928 fue la primera mujer en volar sobre el Océano Atlántico como pasajera. En 1932 se convirtió en la primera mujer en volar sola sobre el Océano Atlántico. **Dr. Jonas Salk page 99** 1. la vacuna contra la polio 2. Que la vacuna fuera distribuida tan ampliamente como fuera posible, para tantas personas como fuera posible. **Angel of the Battlefield page 100** 1. Por su trabajo compasivo durante la guerra civil, ayudó a muchos soldados heridos en el campo de batalla. 2. Ayudó al gobierno a buscar información sobre soldados desaparecidos.

Business

Introduction to Taxes page 108 1. El Servicio de Impuestos Internos 2. A la Tesorería de los Estados Unidos, que paga varios gastos gubernamentales. 3. El gobierno te cobrará intereses y penalizaciones. **Entrepreneurship page 110** 1. lenguaje, habilidades en los negocios, y dinero para comenzar 2. bancos 3. Montar un negocio que no necesita mucho dinero para montarse. **Banking in America page 112** 1. Falta de identificación para abrir una cuenta bancaria, diferencias culturales. 2. Los oficiales que hacen cumplir la ley dicen que los criminales ven a los hispánicos como blanco fácil porque se los conoce por llevar dinero al contado a menudo. 3. La finalidad de la tarjeta es introducir a los clientes al sector bancario y ayudar a crear una historia de credito. **Negotiating Your Salary 114** 1. 20 por ciento más 2. quédate callado 3. obtenlo por escrito **Retirement Plans page 116** 1. Un plan de jubilación calificado patrocinado por una empresa para empleados. 2. Impuestos federales a la renta y la mayoría de los impuestos estatales a la renta. 3. 401k **Mastering the Interview page 118** 1. falso 2. confianza 3. Hace que te veas y suenes comprometido o interesado en la entrevista. 4. usted 5. están prohibidas

Answers

Empowerment

Citizenship page 124 1. Gente que ha dejado un país extranjero para vivir en los Estados Unidos. Tienen algunas de las mismas libertades y derechos legales de los ciudadanos de Estados Unidos, pero no pueden votar en las elecciones. 2. Nativos de las posesiones territoriales de los Estados Unidos. Tienen todas las protecciones legales que tienen los ciudadanos, pero no tienen todos los derechos políticos de los ciudadanos de los Estados Unidos. **Empowerment with Education page 126** 1. Latinos 2. Elegir algunas escuelas y ponerte en contacto con sus oficinas de ayuda financiera 3. más de 78.000 **Community Colleges page 128** 1. más de 1200 2. un certificado de dos años 3. enfermería registrada, cumplimiento de la ley, enfermería práctica registrada, radiología, y tecnologías en computación **Helping Children Succeed page 130** 1. verdadero 2. Los niños aprenden más y padres y maestros se sienten más apoyados. 3. pasa tiempo en la escuela, busca a alguien que hable tu idioma, pregunta acerca de clases de idiomas, trabaja como voluntario desde tu hogar **Bilingual Resources page 132** 1. industrias de servicio al consumidor, venta, comunicaciones, y la banca 2. Muchos de quienes reclutan ponen a prueba a los candidatos durante el proceso de entrevista. 3. Hablar inglés, tener experiencia previa de trabajo. **Legal Resources page 134** 1. Un abogado que ha estudiado las leyes de inmigración de los Estados Unidos y se ha graduado de una escuela de abogacía. 2. Pueden ayudarte a obtener estadus legal del Departamento de Seguridad Nacional o representarte ante la Corte de Inmigración. **Owning Your Own Home page 136** 1. 46% 2. Lograr seguridad económica y ayudar a las comunidades a lograr mayor estabilidad. **You and Your Community page 138** 1. conocer a tus vecinos, integrarte a tus alrededores cercanos, ayudarte a identificar y utilizar los recursos disponibles 2. Programas para adultos y niños, cuidado para niños, programas de verano, conciertos y festivales locales. 3. trabajar como voluntario/a

History

Independence Day page 146 1. 50 estados 2. el día de la independencia **Stars and Stripes page 147** 1. rojo, blanco y azul 2. una por cada estado 3. 50 estrellas 4. 13 barras, rojas y blancas 5. los primeros 13 estados **Electoral College page 148** 1. el colegio electoral 2. el vicepresidente **Supreme Law of the Land 149** 1. la ley suprema del país 2. enmiendas **Divisions of Power page 150** 1. ejecutivo, judicial y legislativo 2. el Congreso 3. el Congreso 4. Hay 100 senadores en el Congreso, 2 de cada estado. **Bill of Rights page 153** 1. del Bill of Rights 2. Las primeras 10 enmiendas a la Constitución de los Estados Unidos. 3. Todas las personas que viven en los Estados Unidos. **United States Presidency page 154** 1. George Washington 2. cuatro años 3. haber nacido en los Estados Unidos, no ser un ciudadano naturalizado, tener por lo menos 35 años de edad, y haber vivido en los Estados Unidos durante 14 años por lo menos 4. dos mandatos completos

Respuestas

Geography

World Heritage Sites age 166 1. Conservar los lugares de importancia cultural o natural y preservar cada sitio para las generaciones futuras. 2. en el Parque Nacional de las Cavernas de Carlsbad 3. peces ciegos y arañas sin color 4. Los seres vivos más altos del planeta, árboles de hoja perenne que crecen hasta 350 pies. **Majestic Mountains page 168** 1. el Monte McKinley o Denali en Alaska 2. El Parque de la Montaña de Piedra, es el pedazo de granito expuesto suelto que se conoce más grande del mundo **North American Deserts page 170** 1. Un desierto con temperaturas diurnas bajo cero durante parte del año. 2. el desierto de Sonora 3. el Valle de la Muerte 4. Para mantenerse en contacto con otros coyotes en el área. **The Great Lakes page 172** 1. la playa de arena 2 . son parte de la migración de patos y gansos y proveen comida, paradas de descanso y hábitats 3. impactos humanos, tales como construcción de viviendas, turismo, y erosión **Land of Waterfalls page 174** 1. Una fuente valiosa de energía hidroeléctrica para Ontario y Nueva York. 2. las Cataratas Shoshone en Idaho **Tropical Rain Forests page 176** 1. una diversidad increíble de hongos, musgos, caracoles, pájaros, y otra vida silvestre 2. en Hawai, en el Monte Waialeale 3. los cerdos salvajes, plantas y animales introducidos, agricultura, corte, fuegos **Temperate Rain Forests page 177** 1. Los bosques pluviales templados son más jóvenes, el suelo de los bosques templados contiene más nutrientes, los bosques templados son más escasos. 2. el Parque Nacional Olympic 3. el Bosque Nacional Tongass en el sureste de Alaska **Volcanoes in the United States page 178** 1. 18 2. Mauna Loa 3. un famoso templo hawaiano de 700 años, casas, autopistas

Gastronomy

American Apple Pie page 184 1. na comida que te hace sentir bien 2. la ciudad de Nueva York **Taste of America page 186** 1. el frijol o poroto blanco 2. un juego de béisbol 3. carne molida, ajo, comino, y chiles **Blue Plate Special page 188** 1. Proveer una comida deliciosa y barata, de estilo casero en un ambiente cómodo. 2. un plato especialmente rebajado 3. papas fritas **Chocolate Chip Cookies page 190** 1. Ruth Wakefield 2. Usó el chocolate que tenía a mano – una barra de chocolate semi-dulce, que Andrew Nestle le había dado. **Buffalo Wings page 192** 1. alitas de pollos fritas y cubiertas con una salsa picante 2. Se les llama así por la ciudad de Buffalo, Nueva York, donde se originaron. **Saltwater Taffy page 193** 1. Joseph Fralinger 2. Pensó que los turistas querrían algo delicioso como recuerdo de sus vacaciones en Atlantic City. **Clam Chowder page 194** 1. Una sopa popular que contiene almejas y caldo y a veces pedazos de papa, cebollas y palitos de zanahorias. 2. A los turistas les daba aprensión comer mariscos y preferían una sopa más cremosa. **Farmers' Markets page 196** 1. Boston en 1634. 2. El "pescado volador" donde los empleados se tiran los pescados unos a otros en vez de pasarlos de mano en mano. **American Barbecue page 198** 1. en el sur 2. cerdo y costillas - la carne se desmenuza en vez de picarla, la carne se cocina lentamente, se desmenuza a mano y se cubre con grandes cantidades de salsa 3. Frailes franciscanos la trajeron del Caribe, se originó durante las conducciones de ganado cuando los vaqueros cocinaban la carne sobre el fuego, carniceros alemanes trajeron la barbacoa a Texas a mediados del 1800.